Understanding International Conflicts

An Introduction to Theory and History

Second Edition

Joseph S. Nye, Jr.

Harvard University

 LONGMAN

An imprint of Addison Wesley Longman, Inc.

New York • Reading, Massachusetts • Menlo Park, California • Harlow, England
Don Mills, Ontario • Sydney • Mexico City • Madrid • Amsterdam

To MHN, as always

Acquisitions Editor: Peter Glovin
Text Design and Project Management: Interactive Composition Corporation
Art Studio: Interactive Composition Corporation
Photo Researcher: Mira Schachne
Full Service Production Manager: Eric Jorgensen
Manufacturing Manager: Hilda Koparanian
Electronic Page Makeup: Interactive Composition Corporation
Printer and Binder: RR Donnelley & Sons Company
Cover Printer: Phoenix Color Corp.

For permission to use copyrighted material, grateful acknowledgment is made to the copyright holders on pp 197–198, which are hereby made part of this copyright page.

Library of Congress Cataloging-in-Publication Data
Nye, Joseph S.
    Understanding international conflicts : an introduction to theory
and history / Joseph S. Nye, Jr.—2nd ed.
        p.   cm.
    Includes bibliographical references and index.
    ISBN 0-321-01101-5
    1. International relations.   2. War (International law)   3. World
politics—20th century.   I. Title.
JX1391.N93   1997
327.1'09'04--dc21   97-33683
                                                            CIP

ISBN 0-321-01101-5

1 2 3 4 5 6 7 8 9 10—DOC— 00 99 98 97

Contents

PREFACE   IX

1   IS THERE AN ENDURING LOGIC OF CONFLICT
    IN WORLD POLITICS?   1

Two Theoretical Traditions: Realism and Liberalism   1
    What Is International Politics?   2
    Two Views of Anarchic Politics   4
    Building Blocks   6

The Peloponnesian War   9
    A Short Version of a Long Story   9
    Causes and Theories   12
    Inevitability and the Shadow of the Future   14

Ethical Questions and International Politics   16
    Limits on Ethics in International Relations   18
    Three Views of the Role of Morality   19

Notes   24
Selected Readings   24
Further Readings   25
Study Questions   25

2   ORIGINS OF THE GREAT TWENTIETH-CENTURY
    CONFLICTS   27

International Systems and Levels of Causation   27
    Levels of Analysis   29
    Systems: Structure and Process   30
    Revolutionary and Moderate Goals and Instruments   32
    The Structure and Process of the Nineteenth-Century System   33
    A Modern Sequel   35
    Domestic Politics and Foreign Policy   36

Neoliberalism   37
Liberal Democracy and War   40
Definition of National Interests   41
Variations in Foreign Policies   42

Counterfactuals   42
Plausibility   43
Proximity in Time   44
Relation to Theory   44
Fact   45

Notes   45
Selected Readings   46
Further Readings   46
Study Questions   47
Chronologies: Europe   47

3   BALANCE OF POWER AND WORLD WAR I   50

Balance of Power   50
Power   51
Balances as Distributions of Power   54
Balance of Power as Policy   54
Balance of Power as Multipolar Systems   57
Alliances   58

The Origins of World War I   59
Three Levels of Analysis   60
Was War Inevitable?   65
What Kind of War?   68
The Funnel of Choices   69
Lessons of History Again   70

Notes   71
Selected Readings   71
Further Readings   72
Study Questions   72
Chronology: The Road to World War I   73

4   THE FAILURE OF COLLECTIVE SECURITY
     AND WORLD WAR II   74

The Rise and Fall of Collective Security   74

The League of Nations   75
The United States and the League of Nations   76
The Early Days of the League   77
The Manchurian Failure   80
The Ethiopian Debacle   81

The Origins of World War II   82
Hitler's War?   83
Hitler's Strategy   83
The Role of the Individual   86
Systemic and Domestic Causes   88
Was War Inevitable?   89
The Pacific War   90
Appeasement and Two Types of War   94

Notes   95
Selected Readings   95
Further Readings   96
Study Questions   96
Chronology: Between the World Wars   97

5   **THE COLD WAR   98**

Deterrence and Containment   99

Three Approaches to the Cold War   99

Roosevelt's Policies   102

Stalin's Policies   103

Phases of the Conflict   103

Inevitability?   108

Levels of Analysis   110

U.S. and Soviet Goals in the Cold War   112

Containment   113

The Rest of the Cold War   114

The End of the Cold War   116

The Role of Nuclear Weapons   120
Physics and Politics   120
Balance of Terror   123

Problems of Nuclear Deterrence   124
The Cuban Missile Crisis   125
Moral Issues   127

Notes   129
Selected Readings   129
Further Readings   129
Study Questions   130
Chronology: The Deep Cold War Years   131

6   INTERVENTION, INSTITUTIONS, AND REGIONAL
CONFLICTS   133

Sovereignty and Intervention   133
Defining Intervention   134
Sovereignty   135
Judging Intervention   135
Exceptions to the Rule   136
Self-Determination   137
Motives, Means, and Consequences   139

International Law and Organization   140
Domestic Analogies   141
Predictability and Legitimacy   142
The Suez Canal   143
UN Peacekeeping and Collective Security   146

Conflicts in the Middle East   148
The Questions of Nationalism   149
The Arab-Israeli Conflicts   151
The 1991 Gulf War and Its Aftermath   155

Notes   157
Selected Readings   157
Further Readings   157
Study Questions   158
Chronology: The Arab-Israeli Conflict   159

7   INTERDEPENDENCE AND POWER   161

The Concept of Interdependence   162
Sources of Interdependence   162
Benefits of Interdependence   163

Costs of Interdependence   165
Symmetry of Interdependence   166
Leadership in the World Economy   168
Realism and Complex Interdependence   170

The Transnational Politics of Oil   171
Oil as a Power Resource   174

Transnational Actors   175

Notes   178
Selected Readings   178
Further Readings   179
Study Questions   179

8   A NEW WORLD ORDER?   181

Alternative Designs for the Future: The Nation-State and the Future
of International Conflicts   181

Nationalism and Transnationalism   183
The End of History?   183
Transnationalism   185
Proliferation   186

A New World Order?   188
Different Concepts of Order   188
Future Configurations of Power   189
The Prison of Old Concepts   191
The Evolution of a Hybrid World Order   192

Thinking About the Future   193

Selected Readings   194
Further Readings   195
Study Questions   195

CREDITS   197

INDEX   199

PREFACE

This text grows out of the course on international conflicts in the modern world that I have taught as part of the Harvard core curriculum for more than a decade. Its aim is to introduce college freshmen to the complexities of international politics by giving them a good grounding in the traditional realist approach before turning to liberal theories of interdependence and institutions that are becoming more prominent after the Cold War.

Twice in the first half of this century the great powers engaged in devastating world wars that cost nearly 50 million lives. The second half of the century was wracked by a cold war, regional wars, and the threat of nuclear weapons. Why did those conflicts happen? Could they happen again? Or will rising economic and ecological interdependence, the growth of transnational and international institutions, and the spread of democratic values bring about a new world order? No good teacher can honestly answer such questions with certainty, but we can provide our students with conceptual tools that will help them shape their own answers as the future unfolds. That is the purpose of this book.

This is not a soup-to-nuts textbook with all the concepts or history a student will need. Instead, it is an example of how to think about the complex and confusing domain of international politics. It should be read not for a complete factual account, but for the way it approaches the interplay of theory and history. Neither theory nor history alone is sufficient. Those historians who believe that understanding comes from simply recounting the facts fail to make explicit the hidden principles by which they select some facts rather than others. Equally mistaken are the political scientists who become so isolated and entangled in a maze of abstract theory that they mistake their mental constructs for reality. It is only by going back and forth between history and theory that we can avoid such mistakes. This text is an example of such a dialogue between theory and history. When combined with the suggested reading, it can provide a central thread for an introductory course. Alternatively, it can be used in a supplementary role as an example of one approach to the subject.

Over the years, I have sometimes taught this course with junior colleagues: Stephan Haggard, Yuen Khong, Michael Mandelbaum, and M. J. Peterson. I have learned from all of them, and, I am sure, unconsciously stolen a number of their ideas. The same is true of Stanley Hoffmann, who has taught me since graduate days. I am grateful to him and to David Dessler, Robert Keohane, Charles Maier, and Ernest May for commenting on the manuscript. Others who reviewed the manuscript and offered constructive comments include June Teufel Dreyer, University of Miami; Kathie Stromile Golden, University of Colorado—Colorado Springs; and Richard A. Melanson, Brown University. I have also learned from my excellent students and teaching fellows. I want, in particular, to thank my most recent head course assistants: Vin Auger, Peter Feaver, Meryl Kessler, Sean Lynn-Jones, Pam Metz, John Owen, Gideon Rose, and Gordon Silverstein. Veronica McClure has been a wonderful colleague in transcribing and correcting my prose. In many ways, this is her book as well as mine. Richard Wood and Dan Philpott helped check facts and notes. In preparing the second edition, Zachary Karabell provided invaluable assistance on everything from words to pictures. I am fortunate to have had his help. To all, I am deeply grateful.

Joseph S. Nye, Jr.

Is There an Enduring Logic of Conflict in World Politics?

War scene on Greek vase

TWO THEORETICAL TRADITIONS: REALISM AND LIBERALISM

The world is shrinking. The *Mayflower* took 3 months to cross the Atlantic. In 1924, Charles Lindbergh's flight took 24 hours. Today's Concorde can do it in 3 hours; ballistic missiles, in 30 minutes. In the 1990s, a transatlantic flight costs one-third of what it did in 1950, and a call from New York to London costs only 6 percent of what it did at mid-century. Internet communications are nearly instantaneous. On a more somber note, nuclear weapons have added a new dimension to war which one writer calls "double death," meaning that not only could individuals die, but under some circumstances the whole human species could be threatened.

Yet, some things about international politics have remained the same over the ages. Thucydides's account of Sparta and Athens fighting the Peloponnesian War 2500 years ago reveals eerie resemblances to the Arab-Israeli conflict after 1947. The world at the end of the twentieth century is a strange cocktail of continuity and change. Some aspects of international politics have not changed since Thucydides. There is a certain logic of hostility, a dilemma about security that goes with inter-state politics. Alliances, balances of power, and choices in policy between war and appeasement have remained similar over the millennia.

On the other hand, Thucydides never had to worry about nuclear weapons or the ozone layer. The task for students of international politics is to build on the past, but not be trapped by it, to understand the continuities as well as the changes. We must learn the traditional theories and then adapt them to current circumstances.

International politics would be transformed if separate states were abolished, but world government is not around the corner. The peoples who live in the 180-odd states on this globe want their independence, separate cultures, different languages. In fact, rather than vanishing, nationalism and the demand for separate states have increased. Rather than fewer states, the end of the twentieth century will see more. Nor would world government automatically solve the problem of war. Most wars today are civil wars. In fact, the bloodiest war of the nineteenth century was not among the quarreling states of Europe. It was the American Civil War. We will continue to live in a world of separate states, and it is important to understand what that means for our prospects.

WHAT IS INTERNATIONAL POLITICS?

Over the centuries, there have been three basic forms of world politics. In a *world imperial system,* one government is dominant over most of the world with which it has contact. The greatest example in the Western world was the Roman Empire. Spain in the sixteenth century and France in the late seventeenth century tried to gain similar supremacy, but they failed. In the nineteenth century, the British Empire spanned the globe, but even the British had to share the world with other strong states. Ancient world empires—the Sumerian, the Persian, the Chinese—were actually regional empires. They thought they ruled the world, but they were protected from conflict with other empires by the lack of communication. Their fights with barbarians on the peripheries of the empire were not the same as wars among roughly equal states.

A second basic form of international politics is a *feudal system,* in which human loyalties and political obligations are not fixed primarily by territorial boundaries. Feudalism was common in the West after the collapse of the Roman Empire. An individual had obligations to a local lord, but might also owe duties to some distant noble or bishop as well as to the pope in Rome. Political obligations were determined in large extent by what happened to one's superiors. If a ruler married, an area and its people might find their obligations rearranged as part of a wedding dowry. Townspeople born French might suddenly find themselves made Flemish or even British. Cities and leagues of cities sometimes had a special semi-independent status. The crazy quilt of wars that accompanied the feudal situation were not what we think of as modern territorial wars. They could occur within as well as across territories and were related to these crosscutting, nonterritorial loyalties and conflicts.

A third form of world politics is an *anarchic system of states,* composed of states that are relatively cohesive but with no higher government above them. Examples include the city-states of ancient Greece or Machiavelli's fifteenth-century Italy. Another example of an anarchic state system is the dynastic territorial state whose coherence comes from control by a ruling family. Examples can be found in India or China in the fifth century B.C. Large territorial dynasties reemerged in Europe about 1500, and other forms of international polities such as city-states or loose leagues of territories began to vanish. In 1648, the Peace of Westphalia ended the Thirty Years' War, sometimes called the last of the great wars of religion and the first of the wars of modern states. In retrospect, that treaty enshrined the sovereign territorial state as the dominant form of international organization.

Thus today when we speak of international politics, we usually mean this territorial state system, and we define *international politics* as politics in the absence of a common sovereign, politics among entities with no ruler above them. International politics is often called anarchic. As monarchy means one ruler, *anarchy*—"an-archy"—means the absence of any ruler. International politics is a self-help system. Thomas Hobbes, the seventeenth-century British philosopher, called such anarchic systems a "state of nature." For some, the words *state of nature* may conjure up a herd of cows grazing peacefully in Vermont, but that is not what Hobbes meant. Think of a Texas town without a sheriff in the days of the Old West, or Lebanon after its government broke down in the 1970s. Hobbes's state of nature is not benign; it is a war of all against all because there is no higher ruler to enforce order. As Hobbes said, life in such a world tends to be nasty, brutish, and short.

The result is that there are legal, political, and social differences between domestic and international politics. Domestic law is generally obeyed and if not, the police and courts enforce sanctions against lawbreakers. International law, on the other hand, rests on competing legal systems, and there is no common enforcement. There is no international police to enforce the law.

Force plays a different role in domestic and international politics. In a well-ordered domestic political system, the government has a monopoly on the legitimate use of force. In international politics, no one has a monopoly on the use of force. Since international politics is the realm of self-help, and some states are stronger than others, there is always a danger that they may resort to force. When force cannot be ruled out, the result is mistrust and suspicion.

Domestic and international politics also differ in their underlying sense of community. In a well-ordered domestic society, there is a widespread sense of community that gives rise to common loyalties, standards of justice, and views of what is legitimate authority. In international politics, divided peoples do not share the same loyalties. Any sense of global community is weak. People often disagree about what seems just and legitimate. The result is a great gap between two basic political values: order and justice. In such a world, most people place national before international justice. Law and ethics play a role in international politics, but in the absence of a sense of community, they are not as binding as they are in domestic politics.

Of the three basic systems—*world imperial, feudal,* and *anarchic system of states*—the last is most relevant to international politics in the contemporary world.

Two Views of Anarchic Politics

International politics is anarchic in the sense that there is no higher government, but even in political philosophy there were two different views of how harsh a state of nature need be. Hobbes, who wrote in a seventeenth-century Britain wracked by civil war, stressed insecurity, force, and survival. He summarized it as a state of war. A half century later, John Locke, writing in a less tormented Britain, argued that although a state of nature lacked a common sovereign, people could develop ties and make contracts, and therefore anarchy was less threatening. Those two views of a state of nature are the philosophical precursors of two current views of international politics, one more pessimistic and one more optimistic: the *realist* and *liberal* approaches to international politics.

Realism has been the dominant tradition in thinking about international politics. For the realist, the central problem of international politics is war and the use of force, and the central actors are states. Among modern Americans, realism is exemplified by the writings and policies of President Richard Nixon and his secretary of state, Henry Kissinger. The realist starts from the assumption of the anarchic system of states. Kissinger and Nixon, for example, sought to maximize the power of the United States and minimize the ability of other states to jeopardize U.S. security. According to the realist, the beginning and the end of international politics is the individual state in interaction with other states.

The other tradition is called *liberalism,* not because of American domestic politics, but because it can be traced back in Western political philosophy to Baron de Montesquieu and Immanuel Kant in eighteenth-century France and Germany respectively and the nineteenth-century British philosopher John Stuart Mill. A modern American example can be found in the writings and policies of the political scientist and president Woodrow Wilson.

Liberals see a global society that functions alongside the states and sets part of the context for states. Trade crosses borders, people have contacts with each other (such as students studying in foreign countries), and international institutions such as the United Nations create a context in which the realist view of pure anarchy is insufficient. Liberals complain that realists portray states as hard billiard balls careening off one another in the attempt to balance power, but that is not enough because people do have contacts across borders and there is an international society. Realists overstate the difference between domestic and international politics. Because the realist picture of anarchy as a Hobbesian "state of war" focuses only on extreme situations, it misses the growth of economic interdependence and the evolution of a transnational global society.

Realists respond by quoting Hobbes: "Just as stormy weather does not mean perpetual rain, so a state of war does not mean constant war."[1] Just as Londoners carry umbrellas on sunny April days, the prospect of war in an anarchic system makes states keep armies even in times of peace. Realists point to previous liberal predictions that went awry. For example, in 1910 the president of Stanford University said future war was impossible because the nations could not afford it. Books proclaimed war to be obsolete; civilization had gone beyond war. Economic interdependence, ties between labor unions and intellectuals, the flow of capital, all made war impossible. Of course, these predictions failed catastrophically in 1914, and the realists felt vindicated.

1910: THE "UNSEEN VAMPIRE" OF WAR

If there were no other reason for making an end of war, the financial ruin it involves must sooner or later bring the civilized nations of the world to their senses. As President David Starr Jordan of Leland Stanford University said at Tufts College, "Future war is impossible because the nations cannot afford it." In Europe, he says, the war debt is $26 billion, "all owed to the unseen vampire, and which the nations will never pay and which taxes poor people $95 million a year." The burdens of militarism in time of peace are exhausting the strength of the leading nations, already overloaded with debts. The certain result of a great war would be overwhelming bankruptcy.

—The New York World[2]

Neither history nor the argument stopped in 1914. The 1970s saw a resurgence of liberal claims that rising economic and social interdependence was changing the nature of international politics. In the 1980s, Richard Rosecrance, a California professor, wrote that states can increase their power in two ways, either by territorial conquest or peacefully through trade. He used the experience of Japan as an example: In the 1930s, Japan tried territorial conquest and suffered the disaster of World War II. But since then, Japan has been a trading state, becoming the second largest economy in the world and a significant power in East Asia. Japan succeeded without a major military force. Thus Rosecrance and modern liberals argue that there is a change occurring in the nature of international politics.

Some new liberals look even further to the future and believe that dramatic growth in ecological interdependence will so blur the differences between domestic and international politics that humanity will evolve toward a world without borders. For example, everyone will be affected without regard to boundaries if the depletion of ozone in the upper atmosphere causes skin cancer. If CO_2 accumulation warms the climate and causes the polar icecaps to melt, rising seas will affect all coastal states. Some problems like AIDS and drugs cross borders with such ease that we may be on our way to a different world. Professor Richard Falk of Princeton argues that these transnational problems and values will produce new nonterritorial loyalties which will change the state system that has been dominant for the last 400 years. Transnational forces are undoing the Peace of Westphalia, and humanity is evolving toward a new form of international politics.

In 1990, realists replied, "Tell that to Saddam Hussein!" Iraq showed that force and war are ever present dangers. The liberal comeback was that politics in the Middle East is the exception. Over time, they say, the world is moving beyond the anarchy of the sovereign state system. These divergent views on the nature of international politics and how it is changing will not soon be reconciled. The realists stress continuity; the liberals stress change. Both claim the high ground of realism with a small *r*. Liberals tend to see realists as cynics whose fascination with the past blinds them to change. Realists, in turn, call the liberals utopian dreamers and label their thought "globaloney."

Who's right? Both are; and both wrong. A clear-cut answer might be nice, but it would also be less accurate and less interesting. The mix of continuity and change that characterizes the world entering the twenty-first century makes it impossible to arrive at one, easy, synthetic explanation. There will always be uncertainties and qualifications in the theories. Because it involves changeable human behaviors, international politics will never be like physics: It has no strong determinist theory.

Building Blocks

Actors, *goals*, and *instruments* are three concepts that are basic to theorizing about international politics, but each is changing. In the traditional realist view of international politics, the only significant "actors" are the states, and only the big states really matter. But this is changing. The number of states has grown enormously in the postwar period: In 1945 there were about 50 states in the world; by 1992 there were 178 members of the United Nations, with more to come. More important than the number of states is the rise of nonstate actors. For example, large multinational corporations straddle international borders and sometimes command more economic resources than some nation-states do. At least 12 transnational corporations have annual sales that are larger than the GNP of more than half of the states in the world. The sales of a company such as Shell, IBM, or General Motors are larger than the GDP of countries such as Hungary, Ecuador, or Zaire. While these multinational corporations lack some types of power such as military force, they are very relevant to a country's economic goals. In terms of the economy, IBM is more important to Belgium than Burundi, a former Belgian colony.

A picture of the Middle East without the warring states and the outside powers would be downright silly, but it would also be woefully inadequate if it did not include a variety of nonstate actors. Multinational oil companies like Shell, British-Petroleum, and Mobil are one type of nonstate actors, but there are others. There are large intergovernmental institutions such as the United Nations, and smaller ones such as the Organization of American States (OAS), the Arab League, and the Organization of Petroleum Exporting Countries (OPEC). There are nongovernmental organizations (NGOs) like the Red Cross and Amnesty International. There are also a variety of transnational ethnic groups, such as the Kurds who live in Turkey, Syria, Iran, and Iraq, or the Armenians scattered throughout the Middle East and the Caucasus. Guerrilla movements, drug cartels, mafia organizations transcend national borders and often divide their resources among several states. International religious movements, particularly political Islam in the Middle East and North Africa, add a further dimension to the range of possible nonstate actors.

The question is not whether the state or the nonstate groups are more important—usually the states are—but how new complex coalitions affect the politics of a region in a way that the traditional view fails to disclose. States are the major actors in current international politics, but they do not have the stage to themselves.

What about goals? Traditionally the dominant goal of states in an anarchic system is military security. Countries today obviously care about their military security, but they often care as much or more about their economic wealth, about social issues such as drug traffic or the spread of AIDS, or ecological changes. Moreover, as threats change, the definition of security changes; military security is not the only

ESTIMATED GDP OF SELECT COUNTRIES (IN US $)

United States	6.74 trillion
China	2.98 trillion
Japan	2.53 trillion
Germany	1.34 trillion
India	1.25 trillion
Russia	721.2 billion
Vietnam	83.5 billion
Syria	74.4 billion
Guatemala	33.0 billion
Zaire	18.8 billion
Jamaica	7.8 billion
Albania	3.8 billion

Source: CIA World Factbook, 1995

SELECT SALES OF MULTINATIONAL CORPORATIONS (IN US $)

General Motors (US)	154.9 billion
Mitsubishi (Japan)	154.3 billion
Toyota Motor Corp. (Japan)	95.0 billion
Royal Dutch Shell (UK/Neth.)	92.5 billion
Philip Morris (US)	65.1 billion
IBM (US)	64.1 billion
Daimler-Benz (Ger.)	56.2 billion
Siemens AG (Ger.)	46.9 billion
Unilever (UK/Neth.)	41.9 billion
Nestlé Ltd. (Switz.)	38.6 billion
Elf Aquitaine (Fr.)	35.5 billion
PepsiCo (US)	28.5 billion

Source: Hoover's Handbook of World Business 1995–96 & Hoover's Handbook of American Business 1996

goal that states pursue. Looking at the relationship between the United States and Canada where the prospects of war are rather slim, a Canadian diplomat once said his fear was not that the United States would march into Canada and capture Toronto again as it did in 1813, but that Toronto would be programmed out of relevance by a computer in Texas—a rather different dilemma than the traditional one of states in an anarchic system. Economic goals have not replaced the goal of military security (as Kuwait discovered when Iraq invaded in August 1990), but the agenda of international politics has become more complex as states pursue a wider range of goals.

Third, the instruments of international politics are changing. The traditional view is that military force is the instrument that really matters. Describing the world before 1914, the British historian A. J. P. Taylor defined a great power as one able to prevail in war. States obviously use military force today, but over the past half century, there have been changes in its role. Many states, particularly large ones, find it more costly to use military force to achieve their goals than was true in earlier times. As Professor Stanley Hoffmann of Harvard University has put it, the link between military strength and positive achievement has been loosened.

What are the reasons? One is that the ultimate means of military force, nuclear weapons, are muscle-bound. Although they have numbered over 50,000, nuclear weapons have not been used in war since 1945. The disproportion between the devastation that nuclear weapons can create and any reasonable political goals has made leaders very loath to use them. So the ultimate form of military force tends to be too costly to use in war.

Even conventional force has become more costly when it is used to rule nationalistically awakened populations. In the nineteenth century, European countries conquered other parts of the globe with a handful of soldiers armed with modern weapons and administered them with relatively modest garrisons. But in an age of socially mobilized populations, it is difficult to rule an occupied country whose people have become nationalistically aware. Americans found this out in Vietnam in the 1970s; the Soviets discovered it in Afghanistan in the 1980s. Vietnam and Afghanistan had not become more powerful than the nuclear superpowers, but trying to rule those nationalistically awakened populations was too expensive for either the United States or the Soviet Union.

A third change in the role of force relates to internal constraints. Over time there has been a growing ethic of antimilitarism, particularly in democracies. Such views do not prevent the use of force, but they make it a more costly choice for leaders, particularly when its use is large or prolonged. Force is not obsolete, but it is more costly and more difficult to use than in the past.

Finally, a number of issues do not lend themselves to forceful solutions. Take, for example, economic relations between the United States and Japan. In 1853, Commodore Perry sailed into a Japanese port and threatened bombardment unless Japan opened its ports to trade. This would not be a very useful way to solve current United States–Japan trade disputes. Thus, while force remains a critical instrument in international politics, it is not the only instrument. The use of economic interdependence, communication, international institutions, and transnational actors sometimes plays a larger role than force. Military force is not obsolete as an instrument, but changes in its cost and effectiveness make today's international politics more complex.

Nonetheless, the basic game of security goes on. Five years before the Gulf War, a Stockholm International Peace Research Institute study showed there were 36 wars that killed between 3 and 5 million people. Some political scientists argue that the balance of power is usually determined by a leading, or hegemonic state—such as Spain in the sixteenth century, France under Louis XIV, Britain in most of the nineteenth century, and the United States in most of the twentieth century. Eventually the top country will be challenged, and this challenge will lead to the kind of vast conflagrations we call hegemonic, or world wars. After world wars, a new treaty sets the new framework of order: the Treaty of Utrecht in 1713, the Congress of Vienna in 1815, the United Nations system after 1945. If nothing basic has changed in international politics since the struggle for supremacy between Athens and Sparta, will there be a new challenge leading to another world war or is the cycle of hegemonic war over? Has nuclear technology made war too devastating? Has economic interdependence made it too costly? Has global society made it socially and morally unthinkable? We have to hope so because the next hegemonic war would probably be the last. But first, it is important to understand the case for continuity.

THE PELOPONNESIAN WAR

Thucydides is the father of realism, the theory most people use when thinking about international politics even when they do not know they are using a theory. Theories are the indispensable tools we use to organize facts. The economist John Maynard Keynes said that practical men of affairs who think they do not have any use for theory are probably prisoners of some unknown scribbler whose name they have long forgotten. Many of today's statesmen and editorial writers use realist theories even if they have not heard of Thucydides. Robert Gilpin, a realist, says, "In honesty, one must inquire whether or not twentieth-century students of international relations know anything that Thucydides and his fifth-century B.C. compatriots did not know about the behavior of states." He answers his own question: "Ultimately international politics can still be characterized as it was by Thucydides."[3] That is a debatable proposition, but to debate it, we must know Thucydides's argument. And what better introduction to realist theory is there than one of history's great stories? However, like many great stories, it has its limits. One of the things we learn from the Peloponnesian War is how to avoid too simplistic a reading of history.

A Short Version of a Long Story

Early in the fifth century, Athens and Sparta were allies who had cooperated to defeat the Persian Empire (480 B.C.). Sparta was a conservative land-oriented state that turned inward after the victory over Persia; Athens was a commercial and sea-oriented state that turned outward. In the middle of the century, Athens had 50 years of growth that led to the development of an Athenian empire. Athens formed the Delian League, an alliance of states around the Aegean Sea, for mutual protection against the Persians. Sparta, in turn, organized its neighbors on the Peloponnesian peninsula into a defensive alliance. States that had joined Athens freely for protection against the Persians soon had to pay taxes to the Athenians. Because of the growing strength of Athens and the resistance of some to its growing empire, a war broke out in 461 B.C., about 20 years after the Greek defeat of the Persians. By 445 B.C., the first Peloponnesian War ended and was followed by a treaty that promised peace for 30 years. Thus Greece enjoyed a period of stable peace before the second, or big, Peloponnesian War.

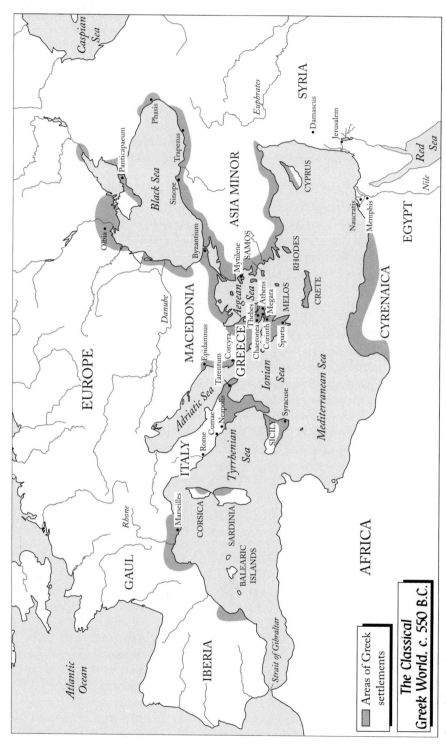

The Classical Greek World. c. 550 B.C.

Areas of Greek settlements

Figure 1.1

In 434 B.C., a civil war broke out in the small peripheral city-state of Epidamnus. Like a pebble that begins an avalanche, this event triggered a series of reactions that led ultimately to the Peloponnesian War. Large conflicts are often precipitated by relatively insignificant crises in out of the way places, as we shall see when we turn to World War I.

In Epidamnus, the democrats fought with oligarchs over how the country would be ruled. The democrats appealed to the city-state of Corcyra, which had helped to establish Epidamnus, but were turned down. They then turned to another city-state, Corinth, and the Corinthians decided to help. This angered the Corcyraeans who sent a fleet to recapture Epidamnus, their onetime colony. In the process, the Corcyraeans defeated the Corinthian fleet. Corinth was outraged and declared war on Corcyra. Corcyra, fearing the attack from Corinth, turned to Athens for help. Both Corcyra and Corinth sent representatives to Athens.

The Athenians, after listening to both sides, were in a dilemma. They did not want to break the truce that had lasted for a decade, but if the Corinthians (who were close to the Peloponnesians) conquered Corcyra and took control of its large navy, the balance of power among the Greek states would be tipped against Athens. The Athenians felt they could not risk letting the Corcyraean navy fall into the hands of the Corinthians, so they decided to become "a little bit involved." They launched a small endeavor to scare the Corinthians, sending ten ships with instructions not to fight unless attacked. But deterrence failed; Corinth attacked, and when the Corcyraeans began to lose the battle, the Athenian ships were drawn into the fray more than intended. The Athenian involvement infuriated Corinth, which in turn worried the Athenians. In particular, Athens worried that Corinth would stir up problems in Potidaea, which, although an Athenian ally, had historic ties to Corinth. Sparta promised to help Corinth if Athens attacked Potidaea. When a revolt did occur in Potidaea, Athens sent forces to put it down.

At that point there was a great debate in Sparta. The Athenians appealed to the Spartans to stay neutral. The Corinthians urged the Spartans to go to war and warned them against failing to check the rising power of Athens. Megara, another important city, agreed with Corinth because contrary to treaty, the Athenians had banned Megara's trade. Sparta was torn, but the Spartans voted in favor of war because they were afraid that if Athenian power was not checked, Athens might control the whole of Greece. Sparta went to war to maintain the balance of power among the Greek city-states.

Athens rejected Sparta's ultimatum, and Sparta attacked in 431 B.C. The Athenian mood was one of imperial greatness, with pride and patriotism about their city and their social system, and optimism about how they would prevail in the war. The early phase of the war came to a stalemate. A truce was declared after ten years (421 B.C.), but the truce was fragile and war broke out again. In 413, Athens undertook a very risky venture. It sent two fleets and infantry to conquer Sicily, the great island off the south of Italy, which had a number of Greek colonies allied to Sparta. The result was a terrible defeat. At the same time Sparta received additional money from the Persians, who were only too happy to see the Athenians defeated. After the defeat in Sicily, Athens was internally divided. In 411, the oligarchs overthrew the democrats, and 400 oligarchs tried to rule Athens. These events were not the end, but Athens never really recovered. An Athenian naval victory in 410 was followed five years later by a Spartan naval victory, and by 404 Athens was compelled to sue for peace. Sparta demanded that Athens pull down the long walls that protected it from attack by land-based powers. Athens's power was broken.

Causes and Theories

This is a dramatic and powerful story. What caused the war? Thucydides is very clear. After recounting the various events in Epidamnus, Corcyra, and so forth, he said that those were not the real causes. What made the war inevitable was the growth of Athenian power and the fear this caused in Sparta.

Did Athens have a choice? With better foresight, could Athens have avoided this disaster? Pericles, the Athenian leader in the early days of the war, had an interesting answer for his fellow citizens. "It is right and proper for you to support the imperial dignity of Athens. Your empire is now like a tyranny: it may have been wrong to take it, but it is certainly dangerous to let it go."[4] In other words, Pericles told his fellow citizens they had no choice. Perhaps they should not be where they were, but once they had an empire, there was not much they could do about it without even larger risks. Thus Pericles favored war. But there were other Athenian voices such as those of the Athenian delegates to the debate in Sparta in 432 who said to the Spartans, "Think, too, of the great part that is played by the unpredictable in war: think of it now before you are actually committed to war. The longer a war lasts, the more things tend to depend on accidents."[5] That turned out to be good advice; why didn't the Athenians take their own advice? Perhaps the Athenians were carried away by emotional patriotism or anger that clouded their reason. But there is a more interesting possibility: Perhaps the Athenians acted rationally but were caught in a security dilemma.

Security dilemmas are related to the essential characteristic of international politics: *anarchic organization,* the absence of a higher government. Under anarchy, independent action taken by one state to increase its security may make all states more insecure. If one state builds its strength to make sure that another cannot hurt it, the other, seeing the first getting stronger, may build its strength to protect itself against the first. The result is that the independent efforts of each to build its own strength and security makes both more insecure. It is an ironic result, yet neither has acted irrationally. Neither acted from anger or pride, but from fear caused by the threat perceived in the growth of the other. After all, building defenses is a rational response to a perceived threat.

States could cooperate to avoid this security dilemma; that is, they could agree that neither should build up its defenses and all would be better off. If it seems obvious that states should cooperate, why then don't they? An answer can be found in the game called "Prisoner's Dilemma." (Security dilemmas are a specific type of Prisoner's Dilemma.) The Prisoner's Dilemma scenario goes like this: Imagine that somewhere the police arrest two men who have small amounts of drugs in their possession, which would probably result in one-year jail sentences. The police have good reason to believe that these two are really drug dealers, but they do not have enough evidence for a conviction. As dealers, the two could easily get 25-year jail sentences. The police know that the testimony of one against the other would be sufficient to convict the other to a full sentence. The police offer to let each of them off if he will testify that the other is a drug dealer. They tell them that if both testify, both will receive 10-year sentences. The police figure that this way these dealers will be out of commission for 10 years; otherwise they are both in jail for only a year and soon will be out selling drugs again.

The suspects are put in separate cells and are not allowed to communicate with each other. Each prisoner has the same dilemma: He can squeal on the other, sending him to jail for 25 years, and go free himself, or he can stay silent and spend a year in jail. But if each squeals, they both get 10 years in jail. Each of them thinks, "I'm better off if I squeal. If he stays quiet and if I don't talk, I'll spend a year in jail. What if the other guy does talk? If I squeal too, I get 10 years, but if I'm quiet, I'll spend 25 years in jail and he'll be free; I'll be a sucker. If I help him by staying quiet, how can I be sure that he won't squeal on me?" That is the basic structural dilemma of independent rational action. The best outcome for the individual is to cheat on the other and get to go free. The second best outcome is both stay silent and spend a year in jail. A worse outcome is for both to squeal and spend 10 years behind bars. Worst of all is to be played for a sucker by staying quiet while the other talks and spend 25 years in jail. If each of them does what's best for himself, they both wind up with a bad outcome. Choosing the best outcome, freedom, is the expression of a rational preference, but if both independently seek their own best outcome, they both get a bad result. Cooperation is difficult in the absence of communication. If the two could talk to each other, they might agree to make a deal to stay silent and both spend one year in jail.

But even if communication were possible, there is another problem: trust and credibility. Continuing with the metaphor in Prisoner's Dilemma, each suspect could say to himself, "We are both drug dealers. I have seen the way the other acts. How do I know that after we've made this deal, he won't say, 'Great! I've convinced him to stay quiet. Now I can get my best outcome, without risk of getting stuck.'" Similarly, in international politics, the absence of communication and trust encourages states to provide for their own security even though doing so may reduce all states to mutual insecurity. In other words, one state could say to another, "Don't build up your armaments and I will not build up my armaments, and we will both live happily ever after," but the second state may wonder whether it can afford to trust the first state.

During the debate at Sparta, the Spartans told the Athenians that the way to solve the problem was to pull down the walls surrounding Athens. Reduce those defenses and we would not feel so worried about you and then we could both have a sense of trust. But when the Athenians returned to Athens after the debate in Sparta, they did not pull down the walls. Instead, they built them higher because they did not trust the Spartans. The Athenians' position in 432 B.C. looks very much like Prisoner's Dilemma. In the middle of the century, the Athenians and Spartans agreed they were both better off to have a truce. Even after the events in Epidamnus and the dispute between Corcyra and Corinth, the Athenians were reluctant to break the truce. The Corcyraeans finally convinced the Athenians with the following argument: "There are three considerable naval powers in Hellas: Athens, Corcyra, and Corinth. If Corinth gets control of us first, and you allow our navy to be united with hers, you will have to fight against the combined fleets of Corcyra and the

Peloponnese. But if you receive us into your alliance, you will enter upon the war with our ships as well as your own."[6]

Should Athens have cooperated with the Peloponnesians by keeping the treaty and turned Corcyra down? If they did, what would have happened if the Peloponnesians had cheated and captured the Corcyraean fleet? Then the naval balance would have been two to one against Athens. Should Athens have trusted the Peloponnesians to keep their promises? The Athenians decided to break the treaty, the equivalent of squealing on the other prisoner. Thucydides tells why: "The general belief was that whatever happened, war with the Peloponnese was bound to come."[7] If so, Athens could not risk letting the strong navy of Corcyra pass into the hands of Corinth.

Inevitability and the Shadow of the Future

Ironically, the belief that war was inevitable played a major role in causing it. Athens felt that if the war was going to come, it was better to have a two-to-one naval superiority rather than one-to-two naval inferiority. The belief that war was imminent and inevitable was critical to the decision. Why should that be so? Look again at Prisoner's Dilemma. At first glance, it is best for each prisoner to cheat and let the other fellow be a sucker, but since each knows the situation, they also know that if they can trust each other, both should go for second best and cooperate by keeping silent. Cooperation is difficult to develop when playing the game only once. Playing a game time after time, people can learn to cooperate, but if it is a onetime game, whoever cheats can get the reward and whoever trusts is a sucker. Political scientist Robert Axelrod played Prisoner's Dilemma on a computer with different strategies. He found that after many games, on average the best results were obtained with a strategy he calls *tit for tat*, "I will do to you what you did to me." If on the first move you cheat, I should cheat. If you cheat again, I should cheat again. If you cooperate, I should cooperate. If you cooperate again, I cooperate again. Eventually, players find that the total benefit from the game is higher by learning to cooperate. But Axelrod warns that tit for tat is a good strategy only when you have a chance to continue the game for a long period, when there is a "long shadow of the future." When you know you are going to be playing with the same people for a long time, you can learn to cooperate.

That is why the belief war is inevitable is so corrosive in international politics. When you believe war is inevitable, you are very close to the last move. When you get to the last move (which may involve your survival, in other words, whether you will ever play in this game again), then you may worry about whether you can still trust your opponent. If you suspect your opponent will cheat, better rely on yourself and take the risk of defecting rather than cooperating. That is what the Athenians did. Faced with the belief war would occur, they decided they could not afford to trust the Corinthians or the Spartans. Better to have the Corcyraean navy on their side than against them when it looked like the last move in the game and inevitable war.

Was the Peloponnesian War really inevitable? Thucydides had a pessimistic view of human nature; he said, "My work is not a piece of writing designed to meet the taste of an immediate public, but was done to last forever."[8] His history shows human nature caught in the situation of Prisoner's Dilemma then and for all time. Thucydides was not deliberately misleading, but like all historians, he had to emphasize certain things and not others. Thucydides concluded the cause of the war was the growth of the power of Athens and the fear that caused in Sparta. But the classicist Donald Kagan argues that Athenian power was *not* growing just before the war broke out in 432—things had begun to stabilize a bit. Furthermore, says Kagan, Sparta was not as afraid of Athens as of war. Both Athens and Sparta were slave states and both feared that going to war might provide an opportunity for the slaves to revolt. The difference was that the slaves, or Helots, in Sparta were 90 percent of the population, and the Spartans had recently experienced a Helot revolt in 464. According to Kagan, the Spartans worried about the rise of Athenian power and that caused fear, but Sparta had an even greater fear of a slave revolt.

Thus the immediate or precipitating causes of the war, according to Kagan, were more important than Thucydides's theory of inevitability admits. Corinth, for example, thought Athens would not fight; it misjudged the Athenian response, partly because it was so angry at Corcyra. Pericles overreacted; he made mistakes in giving an ultimatum to Potidaea and in punishing Megara by cutting off its trade. Those policy mistakes made the Spartans think that war might be worth the risk after all. Kagan argues that Athenian growth caused the first Peloponnesian War but the Thirty-Year Truce poured water on that flame. So to start the second Peloponnesian War, "the spark of the Epidamnian trouble needed to land on one of the rare bits of flammable stuff that had not been thoroughly drenched. Thereafter it needed to be continually and vigorously fanned by the Corinthians, soon assisted by the Megarians, Potidaeans, Aeginetans, and the Spartan War Party. Even then the spark might have been extinguished had not the Athenians provided some additional fuel at the crucial moment."[9] In other words, the war was not caused by impersonal forces but by bad decisions in difficult circumstances.

It is hard to question Thucydides, the father figure of historians, but nothing is ever inevitable in history. Human behavior is voluntary, but only within limits. Karl Marx observed that men make history, but not in conditions of their own choosing. The ancient Greeks made flawed choices because they were caught in the situation well described by Thucydides and by Prisoner's Dilemma. The security dilemma made war highly probable, but highly probable is not the same as inevitable. The 30-year unlimited war that devastated Athens was not inevitable. Human decisions mattered. Accidents and personalities make a difference even if they work within limits set by the larger structure, the situation of insecurity that resembles Prisoner's Dilemma.

What modern lessons can we learn from this ancient history? We need to be aware of both the regularities and the changes. Some structural features of international politics predispose events in one direction rather than another. That is why it is necessary to understand security dilemmas and Prisoner's Dilemma. On the other hand, such situations do not prove that war is inevitable. There are degrees of freedom, and human decisions can sometimes prevent the worst outcomes. Cooperation does occur in international affairs, even though the general structure of anarchy tends to discourage it.

It is also necessary to beware of patently shallow historical analogies. During the Cold War, it was often popular to say that because the United States was a democracy and a sea-based power while the Soviet Union was a land-based power and a slave state, America was Athens and the Soviet Union was Sparta locked into replaying a great historical conflict. But such shallow analogies ignored the fact that ancient Athens was a slave-holding state, wracked with internal turmoil, and democrats were not always in control. Moreover, unlike the Cold War, Sparta won.

Another lesson is to be aware of the selectivity of historians. No one can tell the whole story of anything. Imagine trying to tell everything that happened in the last hour, much less the entire story of your life or a whole war. Too many things happened. A second-by-second account in which everything was replicated would take as long to tell as it took for the events to happen in the first place. Thus historians always abstract. To write history, even the history of the last hour or the last day, we must simplify. We must select. What we select is obviously affected by the values, inclinations, and theories on our minds, whether choate or inchoate.

Historians are affected by their contemporary concerns. Thucydides was concerned about how Athenians were learning the lessons of the war, blaming Pericles and the democrats for miscalculating. He therefore stressed those aspects of the situation that we have described as the Prisoner's Dilemma. Yet while these aspects of the war were important, they are not the whole story. Thucydides did not write much about the decree that cut off Megara's trade, or about Athens raising the amount of tribute that others in the Delian League had to pay. Thucydides's history was not deliberately misleading or biased, but it is an example of how each age tends to rewrite history because the questions brought to the vast panoply of facts tend to change over time.

The need to select does not mean that everything is relative or that history is bunk. Such a conclusion is unwarranted. Good historians and social scientists do their best to ask questions honestly, objectively bringing facts to bear on their topic. But they and their students should be aware that what is selected is by necessity only part of the story. Always ask what questions the writer was asking as well as whether he or she carefully and objectively ascertained the facts. Beware of biases. Choice is a very important part of history and of writing history. The cure to misunderstanding history is to read more, not less.

ETHICAL QUESTIONS AND INTERNATIONAL POLITICS

Given the nature of the security dilemma, some realists believe that moral concerns play no role in international conflicts. However, ethics do play a role in international relations, although not the same role as in domestic politics. Moral arguments have been used since the days of Thucydides. When Corcyra went to Athens to plead for help against Corinth, it used the language of ethics: "First of all, you will not be helping aggressors, but people who are the victims of aggression. Secondly, you will win our undying gratitude."[10] Substitute "Bosnia" for "Corcyra" and "Serbia" for "Corinth," and those words could be uttered in modern times.

Moral arguments move and constrain people. In that sense morality is a power reality. However, moral arguments can also be used as propaganda to disguise less elevated motives, and those with more power are often able to ignore moral consid-erations. During the Peloponnesian War, the Athenians sailed to the island of Melos to suppress a revolt. The Athenian spokesmen told the Melians that they could fight and die or they could surrender. When the Melians protested that they were fighting for their freedom, the Athenians responded that "the strong do what they have the power to do and the weak accept what they have to accept." In essence, the Athenians stated that in a realist world, morality has little place. When Iraq invades Kuwait, the United States invades Grenada, the Russians suppress a revolt in Chechnya, they all to some degree employ similar logic. But, in the modern world, it is increasingly less acceptable to state one's motives as plainly as Thucydides suggests the Athenians did in Melos. Does this mean that morality has come to occupy a more prominent place in international relations? Or simply that states have become more adept at propaganda? Has international politics changed dramatically, with states more attuned to ethical concerns, or is there a clear continuity between the actions of the Athenians two-and-a-half thousand years ago and the actions of the Iraqis or Serbians in the late twentieth century?

Moral arguments are not all the same. Some are more compelling than others. We ask whether they are logical and consistent. For instance, when Phyllis Schlafly argued that nuclear weapons are a good thing because God gave them to the free world, we should wonder why God also gave them to Stalin's Soviet Union and Mao's China. Moral arguments are not all equal.

The basic touchstone for moral arguments is impartiality—the view that all interests are judged by the same criteria. Your interests deserve the same attention as mine. Within this framework of impartiality, however, there are two different tradi-tions in Western political culture about how to judge moral arguments. One descends from Immanuel Kant, the eighteenth-century German philosopher, the other from British utilitarians of the early nineteenth century such as Jeremy Bentham. As an illustration of the two approaches, imagine walking into a Central American village and finding that a military officer is about to shoot three people lined up against the wall. You ask, "Why are you shooting these peasants? They look quite harmless." The officer says, "Last night somebody in this village shot one of my men. I know that somebody in this village is guilty, so I am going to shoot these three to set an example." You say, "You can't do that! You're going to kill an innocent person. If only one shot was fired, then at least two of these people are innocent, perhaps all three. You just can't do that." The officer takes a rifle from one of his men and hands it to you saying, "You shoot one of them for me and I'll let the other two go. You can save two lives if you will shoot one of them. I'm going to teach you that in civil war you can't have these holier-than-thou attitudes." What are you going to do?

You could try to mow down all the troops in a Rambo-like move, but the officer has a soldier aiming his gun at you. So your choice is killing one innocent person in order to save two or dropping the gun and having clean hands. The Kantian tradi-tion that you do things only when they are right would require that you refuse to perpetrate the evil deed. The utilitarian tradition might suggest that if you can save two lives, you should do it. If you choose the Kantian solution, imagine the numbers were increased. Suppose there were 100 people against the wall, or imagine you could save a city full of people. Should you refuse to save a million people in order to keep your hands and conscience clean? At some point, consequences matter. Moral arguments can be judged in three ways: by the motives or intentions involved, by the means used, and by their consequences or net effects. Although these dimensions are not always easily reconciled, good moral argument does try to take all three into account.

Limits on Ethics in International Relations

Ethics plays less of a role in international politics than in domestic politics for four reasons. One is the weak international consensus on values. There are cultural and religious differences over the justice of some acts. Second, states are not like individuals. States are abstraction, and although their leaders are individuals, statesmen are judged differently than when they act as individuals. For instance, when picking a roommate, most people want a person who believes "thou shalt not kill." But the same people might vote against a presidential candidate who said, "Under no circumstances will I ever take an action that will lead to a death." A president is entrusted by citizens to protect their interests, and under some circumstances this may require the use of force. Presidents who saved their own souls but failed to protect their people would not be good trustees.

In private morality, sacrifice may be the highest proof of a moral action, but should leaders sacrifice their whole people? During the Peloponnesian War, the Athenians told the leaders of the island of Melos that if they resisted, Athens would kill everyone. The Melian leaders resisted and their people were slaughtered. Should they have come to terms? In 1962, should President Kennedy have run a risk of nuclear war to force the Soviets to remove missiles from Cuba when the United States had similar missiles in Turkey? Different people may answer these questions differently. The point is that when individuals act as leaders of states, their actions are judged somewhat differently.

A third reason ethics plays a lesser role in international politics is the complexity of causation. It is hard enough to know the consequences of actions in domestic affairs, but in international relations there is another layer of complexity: the interaction of states. That extra dimension makes it harder to make accurate predictions of consequences. A famous example is the 1933 debate among students at the Oxford Union, the debating society of Oxford University. Mindful of the 20 million people killed in World War I, the majority of students voted for a resolution that they would never again fight for king and country. But someone else was listening: Adolf Hitler. He concluded the democracies were soft and he could press them as hard as he wanted because they would not fight back. In the end, he pressed too far and the result was World War II, a consequence not desired or expected by those students who voted never to fight for king and country. Many later did, and many died.

A more trivial example is the "hamburger argument" of the early 1970s when people were worried about shortages of food in the world. A number of students in American colleges said, "When we go to the dining hall, refuse to eat meat because a pound of beef equals eight pounds of grain that could be used to feed poor people around the world." Many students stopped eating hamburger and felt good about themselves, but they did not help starving people in India or Bangladesh one bit.

Why not? The grain freed up by not eating hamburgers in America did not reach the starving people in Bangladesh because they had no money to buy the grain. The grain freed up was simply a surplus on the American market, which meant American prices went down and farmers produced less. To help peasants in Bangladesh required getting money to them so that they could buy some of the grain freed up by not eating hamburgers. By launching a campaign against eating hamburger and failing to look at the complexity of the causal chain that would relate their well-intended act to its consequences, the students failed.

Finally, there is the argument that the institutions of international society are particularly weak and that the disjunction between order and justice is greater in international than in domestic politics. Order and justice are both important. In a domestic polity, we tend to take order for granted. In fact, sometimes protesters purposefully disrupt order for the sake of promoting their view of justice. But if there is total disorder, it is very hard to have any justice; witness the bombing, kidnapping, and killing by all sides in Lebanon in the 1980s. Some degree of order is a prior condition for justice. In international politics, the absence of a common legislature, central executive, or strong judiciary makes it much harder to preserve the order that precedes justice.

Three Views of the Role of Morality

There are at least three different views of ethics in international relations: the *skeptics,* the *state moralists,* and the *cosmopolitans.* Although there is no logical connection, people who are realists in their descriptive analysis of world politics often tend to be skeptics or state moralists in their evaluative approach, whereas those who emphasize a liberal analysis tend toward the state moralist or cosmopolitan moral viewpoints.

The *skeptic* says that moral categories have no meaning in international relations because there are no institutions to provide order. In addition, there is no sense of community, and therefore there can be no moral rights and duties. For the skeptics, the classic statement about ethics in international politics was the Athenians' response to the Melians' plea for mercy: "The strong do what they have the power to do and the weak accept what they have to accept."[11] Might makes right. And that, for the skeptics, is all there is to say.

Philosophers often say that "ought" (moral obligation) implies "can" (the capacity to do something). Morality requires choice. If something is impossible, we cannot have an obligation to do it. If international relations is simply the realm of kill or be killed, then presumably there is no choice, and that would justify the skeptics' position. But there is more to international politics than mere survival. If there are choices in international relations, pretending there is not a choice is merely a disguised form of choice. To think only in terms of narrow national interests is simply smuggling in values without admitting it. The French diplomat who once told me "what is moral is whatever is good for France" was ducking hard choices about why only French interests should be considered. The statesman who says "I had no choice" often did have a choice, albeit not a pleasant one. If there is some degree of order and of community in international relations—if it is not constantly "kill or be killed"—then there is room for choices. "An-archy" means without government, but it does not necessarily mean chaos or total disorder. There are rudimentary practices and institutions that provide enough order to allow some important choices: balance of power, international law, and international organizations. Each is critical to understanding why the skeptical argument is not sufficient.

Thomas Hobbes argued that to escape from "the state of nature" where anyone might kill anyone else, individuals give up their freedom to a leviathan, or government, for protection because life in the state of nature is nasty, brutish, and short. Why then don't governments form a superleviathan? Why isn't there a world government? The reason, Hobbes said, is that insecurity is not so great at the international level as at the individual level. Governments provide some degree of protection against the brutality of the biggest individuals taking whatever they want, and the balance of power among states provides some degree of order. Even though states are in a hostile posture of potential war, "they still uphold the daily industry of their subjects." The international state of nature does not create the day-to-day misery that would accompany a state of nature among individuals. In other words, Hobbes believed that the existence of states in a balance of power alleviates the condition of international anarchy enough to allow some degree of order.

Liberals point further to the existence of international law and customs. Even if rudimentary, such rules put a burden of proof on those who break them. Consider the Persian Gulf crisis in 1990. Saddam Hussein claimed that he annexed Kuwait to recover a province stolen from Iraq in colonial times. But because international law forbids crossing borders for such reasons, an overwhelming majority of states viewed his action as a violation of the UN charter. The 12 resolutions passed by the UN Security Council showed clearly that Saddam's view of the situation ran against international norms. Law and norms did not stop Saddam from invading Kuwait, but they did make it more difficult for him to recruit support, and they contributed to the creation of the coalition that expelled him from Kuwait.

International institutions, even if rudimentary, provide a degree of order by facilitating and encouraging communication and some degree of reciprocity in bargaining. Given this situation of nearly constant communication, international politics is not always, as the skeptics claim, kill or be killed. The energies and attention of leaders are not focused on security and survival all the time. There are large areas of economic, social, and military interaction where cooperation (as well as conflict) occurs. And even though there are cultural differences about the notion of justice, moral arguments take place in international politics and principles are enshrined in international law.

Even in the extreme circumstances of war, law and morality may sometimes play a role. The *just war doctrine*, which originated in the early Christian church and became secularized after the seventeenth century, prohibits the killing of innocent civilians. The prohibition on killing innocents starts from the premise "thou shalt not kill." But if that is a basic moral premise, how is any killing ever justified? Absolute pacifists say that no one should kill anyone else for any reason. However, the just war tradition has argued that if someone is about to kill you and you refuse to act in self-defense, the result is that evil will prevail. By refusing to defend themselves, the good die. If one is in imminent peril of being killed, it can be moral to kill in self-defense. But we must distinguish between those who can be killed and those who cannot be killed. For example, if a soldier rushes at someone with a rifle, he can be killed in self-defense, but the minute the soldier drops the rifle, puts up his hands, and says, "I surrender," no one has any right to take his life. In fact, this is enshrined in international law, and also in the U.S. military code. An American soldier who shoots an enemy soldier after he surrenders can be tried for murder in an American court. Some American officers in the Vietnam War were sent to prison for violating such laws. Even though often violated, there are certain norms that exist even under the most harsh international circumstances. The fact there is a rudimentary sense of justice enshrined in an imperfectly obeyed international law belies the skeptics' argument that there are no choices in a situation of war.

We can reject complete skepticism because there is some room for morality in international politics. Morality is about choice, and meaningful choice varies with the conditions of survival. The greater the threats to survival, the less room for moral choice. At the start of the Peloponnesian War, the Athenians argued, "Those who really deserve praise are the people who, while human enough to enjoy power, nevertheless pay more attention to justice than they are compelled to do by their situation."[12] Unfortunately, the Athenians lost sight of that wisdom later in their war, but it reminds us that situations with absolutely no choice are rare and that national security and degrees of threat are often ambiguous. Skeptics duck hard moral choices by pretending to the contrary. To sum up in an aphorism: Humans may not live wholly by the word, but neither do they live solely by the sword.

Many writers and leaders who are realists in their descriptive analysis are also skeptics in their views about values in world politics. But not all realists are complete skeptics. Some accept there are some moral obligations, but say that order has to come first. Peace is a moral priority, even if it is an unjust peace. The disorder of war makes justice difficult, especially in the nuclear age. The best way to preserve order is to preserve a balance of power among states. Moral crusades disrupt balances of power. For example, if the United States becomes too concerned about spreading democracy or human rights throughout the world, it may create disorder that will actually do more damage than good in the long run.

The realists have a valid argument, up to a point. International order is important, but it is a matter of degrees, and there are trade-offs between justice and order. How much order is necessary before we start worrying about justice? For example, after the 1990 Soviet crackdown in the Baltic republics when a number of people were killed, some Americans urged a break in relations with the Soviet Union. In their view, Americans should express their values of democracy and human rights in foreign policy, even if that meant instability and the end of arms control talks. Others argued that while concerns for peace and for human rights were important, it was more important to control nuclear weapons and negotiate an arms reduction treaty. In the end, the American government went ahead with the arms negotiations, but linked the provision of economic aid to respect for human rights. Over and over in international politics, the question is not absolute order versus justice, but how to trade off choices in particular situations. The realists have a valid point of view, but they overstate it when they assume it has to be all order before any justice.

State moralists argue that international politics rests on a society of states with certain rules, although those rules are not always perfectly obeyed. The most

---

INTERVENTION

Imagine the following scene in Afghanistan in December 1979:

> An Afghan communist leader came to power trying to become more independent of the Soviet Union. This worried the Soviet leaders because an independent regime on their border might foment trouble throughout Central Asia (including Soviet Central Asia) and would create a dangerous precedent of a small communist neighbor escaping the Soviet empire. Imagine the Russian general in charge of the Soviet invasion force confronting the renegade Afghan leader, whom he is about to kill, explaining why he is doing these things against the international rules of sovereignty and nonintervention. "So far as right and wrong are concerned, China and others think that there is no difference between the two and if we fail to attack you, it is because we are afraid. So by conquering you, we shall increase not only the size but the security of our empire. We rule the Central Asian landmass and you are a border state, and weaker than the others. It is therefore particularly important that you should not escape."

Those words are Thucydides's Melian dialogue with the words "China" added and "Central Asia" substituted for "sea" and "border state" for "islands." Intervention is not a new problem!

---

important rule is state sovereignty, which prohibits states from intervening across borders into each others' jurisdiction. The political scientist Michael Walzer, for example, argues that national boundaries have a moral significance because states represent the pooled rights of individuals who have come together for a common life. Thus respect for the sovereignty and territorial integrity of states is related to respect for individuals. Others argue more simply that respect for sovereignty is the best way to preserve order. Good fences make good neighbors.

In practice, these rules of state behavior are violated very frequently. In the last two decades, Vietnam invaded Cambodia, China invaded Vietnam, Tanzania invaded Uganda, Israel invaded Lebanon, the Soviet Union invaded Afghanistan, the United States invaded Grenada and Panama, Iraq invaded Iran and Kuwait, just to name a few. Intervention is a long-standing problem. In 1979, Americans condemned the Soviet invasion of Afghanistan in strong moral terms. The Soviets pointed to the Dominican Republic, where, in 1965, the United States sent 25,000 troops to prevent the formation of a communist government. The intention behind the American intervention in the Dominican Republic, preventing a hostile regime from coming to power in the Caribbean, and the intention of the Soviet intervention in Afghanistan, preventing the formation of a hostile government on their border, were quite similar.

To find differences, we have to look further than intentions. In terms of the means used, very few people were killed by the American intervention in the Dominican Republic, and the Americans soon withdrew. In the Afghan case, a large number of people were killed, and the Soviet forces remained for nearly a decade. More recently, critics compared the Iraqi invasion of Kuwait with the American invasion of Panama. In December 1989, the United States sent troops to overthrow the Panamanian dictator, Manuel Noriega, and in August 1990, Iraq sent troops into Kuwait to overthrow the emir. Both the United States and Iraq violated the rule of nonintervention. But again there were differences in means and consequences. In Panama, the Americans put into office a government that had been duly elected but which Noriega had not permitted to take office. The Americans did not try to annex Panama. In Kuwait, the Iraqi government tried to annex the country and caused much bloodshed in the process. Such considerations do not mean that the Panama case was all right or all wrong, but as we see in Chapter 6, there are often problems when applying simple rules of nonintervention and sovereignty.

Cosmopolitans see international politics not just as a society of states, but as a society of individuals. When we speak about justice, say the cosmopolitans, we should speak about justice for individuals. Realists focus too much on issues of war and peace. If they focused on issues of distributive justice, that is, who gets what, they would notice the economic interdependence of the world. Constant economic intervention across borders can sometimes have life or death effects. For example, it is a life and death matter if you are a peasant in the Philippines and your child dies of a curable disease because the local boy who went to medical school is now working in the United States for a much higher salary.

Cosmopolitans argue that national boundaries have no moral standing; they simply defend an inequality that should be abolished if we think in terms of distributive justice. Realists reply the danger in the cosmopolitan's approach is it may lead to enormous disorder. Taken literally, efforts at radical redistribution are likely to lead to violent conflict because people do not give up their wealth easily. A more limited cosmopolitan argument rests on the fact that people often have multiple loyalties—to families, friends, neighborhoods, nations, perhaps to some transnational religious groups, and to the concept of common humanity. Most people are moved by pictures of starving Ethiopian children, for there is some common community beyond the national level, albeit a weaker one. We are all humans. Cosmopolitans remind us there are distributive dimensions to international relations where morality matters as much in peace as in war. Policies can be designed to assist basic human needs and basic human rights without destroying order.

Of the approaches to international morality, the realist makes a valid point about order being necessary for justice but misses the trade-offs between order and justice. The state moralist who sees a society of states with rules against intervention illustrates an institutional approach to order but does not provide enough answers about when some interventions may be justified. Finally, the cosmopolitan who focuses on a society of individuals has a profound insight about common humanity but runs the risk of fomenting enormous disorder. Most people develop a hybrid position; labels are less important than the central point that there are trade-offs among these approaches.

Because of the differences between domestic and international politics, morality is harder to apply in international politics. But just because there is a plurality of principles, it does not follow there are no principles at all. How far should we go in applying morality to international politics? The answer is to be careful, for when moral judgments determine everything, morality can lead to a sense of outrage, and outrage can lead to heightened risk. After all, there are no moral questions among the incinerated. But we cannot honestly ignore morality in international politics. Each person must study events and make his or her own decisions about judgments and trade-offs. The enduring logic of international conflict does not remove the responsibility for moral choices, although it does require an understanding of the special setting that makes those choices difficult.

While the specific moral and security dilemmas of the Peloponnesian War are unique, many of the issues recur over history. As we trace the evolution of international relations, we will see again and again the tension between realism and liberalism, between skeptics and cosmopolitans, between an anarchic system of states and international organizations. We will revisit the Prisoner's Dilemma and continue to grapple with the ethical conundrums of war. We will see how different actors on the world stage have approached the crises of their time and how their goals and instruments vary. As mentioned at the outset, certain variables that characterize international politics today simply did not exist in Thucydides's day. Not only were there no nuclear weapons, there were no United Nations, no transnational corporations, no cartels. The study of international conflict is an inexact science combining history and theory. In weaving our way through the theories and their examples, we try to keep in mind both what has changed and what has remained constant so that we may better understand our past and our present and better navigate the unknown shoals of the future.

NOTES

1. Thomas Hobbes, *Leviathan,* ed. C. B. MacPherson (London: Penguin, 1968, 1981), p. 186.
2. "From Our Dec. 13 Pages, 75 Years Ago," *International Herald Tribune,* December 13, 1985.
3. Robert Gilpin, *War and Change in World Politics* (Cambridge, England: Cambridge University Press, 1981), pp. 227–228.
4. Thucydides, *History of the Peloponnesian War,* trans. Rex Weiner, ed. M. K. Finley (London: Penguin, 1972), p. 161.
5. Ibid., pp. 82–83.
6. Ibid., p. 57.
7. Ibid., p. 62.
8. Ibid., p. 48.
9. Donald Kagan, *The Outbreak of the Peloponnesian War* (Ithaca, NY: Cornell University Press, 1969), p. 354.
10. Thucydides, *History of the Peloponnesian War,* p. 55.
11. Ibid., p. 402.
12. Ibid., p. 80.

SELECTED READINGS

1. Morgenthau, Hans, *Politics Among Nations* (New York: Knopf, 1955), Chapter 1.
2. Waltz, Kenneth, *Man, the State, and War* (New York: Columbia University Press, 1959), pp. 1–15.

3. Thucydides, *History of the Peloponnesian War,* trans. Rex Weiner, ed. M. K. Finley (London: Penguin, 1972), pp. 35–87, 400–408.

4. Kagan, Donald, *The Outbreak of the Peloponnesian War* (Ithaca, NY: Cornell University Press, 1969), pp. 31–56, 345–356.

FURTHER READINGS

Axelrod, Robert M., *The Evolution of Cooperation* (New York: Basic, 1984).

Beitz, Charles R., *Political Theory and International Relations* (Princeton, NJ: Princeton University Press, 1979).

Bull, Hedley, *The Anarchical Society: A Study of Order in World Politics* (New York: Columbia University Press, 1977).

Gilpin, Robert, *War and Change in World Politics* (Cambridge, England: Cambridge University Press, 1981).

Hinsley, F. H., *Power and the Pursuit of Peace* (Cambridge, England: Cambridge University Press, 1963).

Hoffmann, Stanley, *Duties Beyond Borders: On the Limits and Possibilities of Ethical International Politics* (Syracuse, NY: Syracuse University Press, 1981).

Holsti, K. J., *The Dividing Discipline: Hegemony and Diversity in International Theory* (Boston: Allen & Unwin, 1985).

Jervis, Robert, "Realism, Game Theory, and Cooperation," *World Politics,* Vol. 40, No. 3 (April 1988), pp. 317–349.

Keohane, Robert O., ed., *Neo-Realism and Its Critics* (New York: Columbia University Press, 1986).

Khong, Yuen Foong, *Analogies at War: Korea, Munich, Dien Bien Phu, and the Vietnam Decisions of 1965* (Princeton: Princeton University Press, 1992).

Kissinger, Henry, *Diplomacy* (New York: Simon & Schuster, 1994).

Levy, Jack S., *War in the Modern Great Power System, 1495–1975* (Lexington: University Press of Kentucky, 1983).

Rosecrance, Richard N., *The Rise of the Trading State: Commerce and Conquest in the Modern World* (New York: Basic, 1986).

Rosenau, James N., *Turbulence in World Politics: A Theory of Change and Continuity* (Princeton, NJ: Princeton University Press, 1990).

Waltz, Kenneth N., *Theory of International Relations* (Reading, MA: Addison-Wesley, 1979).

STUDY QUESTIONS

1. What role should ethical considerations play in the conduct of international relations? What role *do* they play? Can we speak meaningfully about moral duties to other nations or their populations?

2. Is there a difference between moral obligations in the realms of domestic politics and international politics? On the basis of the Melian dialogue, did the Athenians act ethically? Did the Melian elders?

3. What is *realism?* How does it differ from the liberal view of world politics?

4. What does Thucydides pinpoint as the main causes of the Peloponnesian war? Which were immediate? Which were underlying?

5. What sort of theory of international relations is implicit in Thucydides's account of the war?

6. Was the Peloponnesian War inevitable? If so, why and when? If not, how and when might it have been prevented?

CHRONOLOGY: PELOPONNESIAN WARS

490 B.C.	First Persian War
480 B.C.	Second Persian War
478 B.C.	Spartans abdicate leadership
476 B.C.	Formation of Delian League and Athenian Empire
464 B.C.	Helot revolt in Sparta
461 B.C.	Outbreak of first Peloponnesian War
445 B.C.	Thirty-Year Truce
445–434 B.C.	Ten years of peace
434 B.C.	Epidamnus and Corcyra conflicts
433 B.C.	Athens intervenes in Potidaea
432 B.C.	Spartan Assembly debates war
431 B.C.	Outbreak of second Peloponnesian War
430 B.C.	Pericles's Funeral Oration
416 B.C.	Melian dialogue
413 B.C.	Athens's defeat in Sicily
411 B.C.	Oligarchs revolt in Athens
404 B.C.	Athens defeated, forced to pull down walls

ORIGINS OF THE GREAT TWENTIETH-CENTURY CONFLICTS

The Berlin Wall coming down

INTERNATIONAL SYSTEMS AND LEVELS OF CAUSATION

War is often explained in terms of international systems, but what is an "international system"? According to the dictionary, a *system* is a set of interrelated units. Many domestic political systems are easy to identify because of clear institutional referents: the presidency, Congress, Parliament, and so forth. International political systems are less centralized and less tangible. Even without the United Nations, there would still be an international system. The international system is not just the states. The international political system is the *pattern of relationships* among the states.

Do not be misled, however, by the institutional concreteness of domestic political systems. They also include intangible aspects such as public attitudes or the role of the press or some of the unwritten conventions of the Constitution. The important point about any system, however, is that the whole pattern is greater than the sum of the parts. Systems can create consequences not intended by any of their constituent actors. For example, think of the market system in economics. Every business firm in a perfect market tries to maximize its profits, but the market system produces competition that reduces profits to the break-even point, thereby benefiting the consumer. The businessperson does not set out to benefit the consumer, but the pattern of behavior in a perfect market leads to that effect. In other words, the system produces the consequences, which may be quite different from the intention of the actors in the system.

The international political system can similarly lead to effects that the actors did not originally intend. For example, in 1917 when the Bolsheviks came to power in Russia, they regarded the whole system of interstate diplomacy that had preceded World War I as bourgeois nonsense. They intended to sweep away the interstate system. Revolutions would unite all the workers of the world and abolish borders. Transnational proletarian solidarity would replace the interstate system. Indeed, when Leon Trotsky took charge of the Russian Foreign Ministry, he said that his intent was to issue some revolutionary proclamations to the peoples and then "close up the joint." But the Bolsheviks found themselves part of an interstate system, and that began to affect their behavior. In 1922, the new communist state signed the Treaty of Rapallo with Germany. It was an alliance of the outcasts, the countries that were not accepted in the post–World War I diplomatic world. And in 1939, Josef Stalin entered a pact with his ideological arch enemy, Adolf Hitler, in order to turn Hitler westward. Soviet behavior, despite the initial proclamations and Trotsky's illusions, soon became similar to that of other actors in the international system.

The distribution of power among states in an international system helps us make predictions about certain aspects of states' behavior. The tradition of geopolitics holds that location and proximity will tell a great deal about how states will behave. If a state feels threatened by its neighbor, it is likely to act in accord with the old adage that "the enemy of my enemy is my friend." This pattern has always been found in anarchic systems. For example, three centuries before Christ's birth, the Indian writer Kautilya pointed out that the states of the Indian subcontinent tended to ally with distant states to protect themselves against their neighbors, thus producing a checkerboard pattern of alliances. Machiavelli noted the same behavior among the city-states in fifteenth-century Italy. In the early 1960s, as West African states emerged from colonial rule, there was a great deal of talk about African solidarity, but the new states soon began to produce a checkerboard pattern of alliances similar to what Kautilya described in ancient India. Ghana, Guinea, and Mali were ideologically radical while Senegal, Ivory Coast, and Nigeria were relatively conservative, but they were also balancing against the strength of their neighbors. Another example was the pattern that developed in East Asia after the Vietnam War. If the Soviet Union were colored black, China would be red, Vietnam black, and Cambodia red. A perfect checkerboard pattern developed. Ironically, the United States got into the Vietnam War because of a domino theory in which one state would fall to communism, leading another state to fall, and so forth. With more foresight, the United States should have realized that the game in East Asia was more like checkers than dominoes, and the United States might have stayed out. The checkerboard pattern based on "the enemy of my enemy is my friend" is an old tradition of geopolitics that helps us to make useful predictions in an anarchic situation.

SYSTEMS AND WAR

After the last war, the international system developed two rigid camps. This bipolarity led to a loss of flexibility and heightened insecurity. One of the new alliances developed around an authoritarian land-based power, the other around a democratic power with an expansive commerce and culture that held naval supremacy. Each side feared the other would achieve a decisive advantage in the conflict that both expected. Ironically, it was civil conflict in a small, weak state threatening a marginal change in the alliances that heightened the sense of threat in both alliances and actually triggered the war.

Which war does this describe: the Peloponnesian War, World War I, or the Cold War?

Levels of Analysis

Systems are not the only way of explaining what happens in international politics. Kenneth Waltz distinguishes three levels of causation, which he calls "images": the *individual,* the *state,* and the *international system.*

Explanations at the level of the individual are rarely sufficient because the very nature of international politics implies *states* rather than individuals. Too much emphasis on an individual's intentions may blind us to the unintended consequences of individual acts caused by the larger systems in which the individuals operate. Taking the African example, if we focused primarily on the sincerity of African leaders' desire for pan-African unity, that is, their intentions, we would miss the importance of the effect of the anarchic structure on those new African states.

This is not to say that individuals never matter. Quite the contrary. Pericles made a difference in the Peloponnesian War. In 1991, Iraq's Saddam Hussein was a critical factor in the Gulf War. In the 1962 Cuban missile crisis, John F. Kennedy and Nikita Khrushchev faced the possibility of nuclear war and the ultimate decision was in their hands. But why they found themselves in that incredible position cannot be explained at the level of individuals. Something in the structure of the situation brought them to that point. Similarly, knowing something about the personality of the kaiser or Hitler is necessary to an understanding of the causes of World War I and World War II, but it is not a sufficient explanation. As we see later, it made a difference that the kaiser fired his chancellor, Otto von Bismarck, in 1890, but that does not mean World War I was brought about primarily by the kaiser.

Another version of the first image looks for explanations not in the particularities of individuals, but in their common characteristics, the "human nature" common to all individuals. For example, we could take a Calvinist view of international politics and assign the ultimate cause of war to the evil that lies within each of us. That would explain war as the result of an imperfection in human nature. But such an explanation does not tell us why some evil leaders go to war and others do not, or why some good leaders go to war and others do not. Explanation at the level of human nature cannot give the answer. Such a theory overpredicts, meaning that it accounts for some things, but it also accounts for too much. By not discriminating, it is not explaining. The hands of a stopped clock tell the correct time twice a day, but most of the time they mislead us.

Overpredicting also plagues some efforts to explain international politics at the second level of analysis, the nature of the state or society. There is a similar question— if certain types of societies cause war, then why do some bad societies or bad states not go to war? And why do some good societies or good states go to war? Insert your favorite description for "good" and "bad"—"democratic," "communist," "capitalist," or whatever. For example, after World War I there was a great deal of enthusiasm for the belief that the victory of the democracies would mean less chance of war. But clearly democracies can go to war, and often do. After all, Athens was a democracy. Marxist theorists argued that war would be abolished when all states were communist, but obviously there have been military clashes among communist countries—witness China and the Soviet Union or Vietnam and Cambodia. Thus the nature of the society, democratic or capitalist or communist, is not a sufficient predictor of how likely it is to go to war.

There is a proposition (which we discuss later) that if *all* countries were democratic, there would be less war. In fact, it is difficult to find cases in which liberal democracies have fought against other liberal democracies, although there are many situations in which democracies have fought against authoritarian states. The cause of this empirical finding and whether it will continue to hold in the future is not clear, but it suggests there may be something interesting to investigate at this second level of analysis.

Interesting explanations often involve an interplay between the second (the state or society) and third (the international system) levels of analysis. But which is more important, the system or the nature of the states in the system? A system-level analysis is explanation from the outside in—looking at the way the overall system constrains the states. The second level is explanation from the inside out—explaining outcomes by what is happening inside the states.

Since we often need information about both levels of analysis, where should we start? A good rule of thumb is to start with the simplest approach, for if a simple explanation is adequate, it is preferable. This is called "the rule of parsimony," or "Occam's razor" after the fourteenth-century philosopher William of Occam, who argued that good explanations shave away unnecessary detail. Parsimony—the ability to explain a lot with a little—is only one of the criteria by which we judge the adequacy of theories. We are also interested in the range of a theory (how much behavior does it cover?) and its explanatory fit (how many loose ends or anomalies it accounts for). Nonetheless, parsimony suggests a place to start. Since systemic explanations tend to be the simplest, they provide a good starting point. If they prove to be inadequate, then we can look at the units of the system and add complexity until a reasonable fit is obtained.

Systems: Structure and Process

How simple or complicated should a systemic explanation be? Some, like Kenneth Waltz, argue for extreme parsimony and focus only on structure. Others, like Stanley Hoffmann, argue that Waltz's concept of system is so spare it explains very little. We can understand this dispute by distinguishing between two aspects of systems: structure and process. The *structure* of a system refers to its distribution of power, and the *process* refers to patterns and types of interaction among its units. Structure and process obviously affect each other, and may vary with the length of the period we examine, but structure is more basic and changes more slowly than process.

Economists characterize the structure of markets by the concentration of sellers' power. A monopoly has one big seller, a duopoly two big sellers, an oligopoly several big sellers, and in a perfect market selling power is widely dispersed. Similarly, political scientists describe as unipolar the structure of an international system where there is one preponderant power. In bipolar systems, two major centers of power, either two large countries or two tightly knit alliance systems, dominate politics. Multipolar structures have three or more centers of power, but where there is a large number of roughly equal countries, we speak of a dispersed distribution of power.

To return to the earlier economic example, the businesspersons who tried to maximize profits in a perfect market found themselves benefiting the consumer, but that result depended on the structure of the market system. If the market was a monopoly or oligopoly, the result would be quite different. The big seller could increase profits by restricting production in order to raise prices. Thus when the structure of the system is known, economists are better able to make a prediction about the behavior and who will benefit.

Similarly, political analysts look at the structure of the international system to predict behavior of states and their propensity toward war. Unipolar systems tend to erode as states try to preserve their independence by balancing against the hegemon, or a rising state eventually challenges the leader. In multipolar or dispersed power systems, states will form alliances to balance power, but alliances will be flexible. Wars may occur, but they will be relatively limited. In bipolar systems, alliances become more rigid, which in turn contributes to the probability of a large conflict, perhaps a global war. Some analysts say that "bipolar systems either erode or explode." This happened in the Peloponnesian War when Athens and Sparta tightened their grips on their respective alliances. It was also true before 1914 when the multipolar European balance of power gradually consolidated into two strong alliance systems that lost their flexibility. But predictions about war based on multipolarity versus bipolarity encounter a major anomaly after 1945. During the Cold War the world was bipolar with two big players, the United States and its allies and the Soviet Union and its allies, yet there was no overall central war. Some people say that nuclear weapons made the prospect of global war too awful. Thus, the structure of the international system offers a rough explanation, but it does not explain enough all by itself.

We learn more if we look beyond a system's structure and examine its process, the regular pattern of interactions between the states. The distinction between structure and process at any given time can be illustrated by the metaphor of a poker game. The *structure* of a poker game is in the distribution of power, that is, how many chips the players have and how many high cards they are dealt. The *process* is how the game is played (Is the player a good bluffer? Does she obey the rules? If she cheats, does she get caught?) and in the types of interactions between the players. The process of an international system is determined by three things:

(1) its structure (bipolar structures tend to produce less flexible processes), (2) the incentives and capabilities that states have for cooperation because of economic interdependence and international institutions, and (3) whether the states are revolutionary or moderate in their goals and instruments.

Revolutionary and Moderate Goals and Instruments

How do state goals affect international processes? Most systems have some basic rules or practices. States can challenge those rules and practices or they can accept them. An international system may have a stable or revolutionary process depending on the goals of the major states. In the eighteenth century, for example, the basic rule of the game was the legitimacy of the monarchical state—the divine right of rulers—and maintaining a balance of power among these monarchies. The 1713 Treaty of Utrecht referred explicitly to the importance of the balance of power. There were many small wars but few large ones disrupted the system. Consider Frederick the Great of Prussia and the way he treated his neighbor Maria Theresa of Austria. In 1740, Frederick decided he wanted Silesia, a province belonging to Maria Theresa. Frederick had no great revolutionary cause, only a simple goal of aggrandizement. He did not try to foment a popular revolution against Maria Theresa by appealing to the people in Silesia to overthrow the German-speaking autocrats of Vienna. After all, Frederick was a German-speaking autocrat in Berlin. He took Silesia because he wanted it and was careful not to do anything else that would damage Austria or the basic principle of monarchical legitimacy.

Compare that to the French Revolution 40 years later, when the prevailing view in France was that all monarchs should be sent to the gallows or the guillotine and that power should emanate from the people. Napoleon spread this revolutionary idea of popular sovereignty throughout Europe, and the Napoleonic Wars posed an enormous challenge to both the rules of the game and to the balance of power. The moderate process and stable balance of the middle of the century system changed to a revolutionary process and unstable balance at the end of the century.

In addition to changing their goals, states can also change their means. The process of a system is also affected by the nature of the instruments that states use. Different means can have stabilizing or destabilizing effects. Some instruments change because of technology. For example, the development of new weapons such as the machine gun made World War I a particularly bloody encounter. Means can also change because of new social organization. In the eighteenth century, Frederick the Great not only had limited goals, he was also limited by his means. He had a mercenary army with limited loyalties and poor logistics. Eighteenth-century armies generally campaigned in the summer, when food was readily available or when the treasury had accumulated enough gold to pay the soldiers who were often from the fringes of society. When the food or the gold ran out, the soldiers deserted. The French Revolution changed the social organization of war to what the French called the *levée en masse*, or what we call the draft. Citizens rallied to the motherland, and there was a feeling that all should participate. War was no longer a matter between a few thousand mercenaries who campaigned far away; war now involved everyone. This large-scale involvement and mass support overwhelmed the old mercenary

---

STRUCTURE AND PROCESS

Statesmen regularly judged the European balance to be satisfactory or unsatisfactory on the basis of factors that had little or nothing directly to do with power and its distribution—e.g., the rank and status a state enjoyed, its honor and prestige, whether it was considered worthy of alliance, whether it was allowed a voice in international questions, etc. It helps explain how crises could and did arise when the balance of power was not affected or threatened, but the balance of satisfactions was. It shows how devices other than power-political ones—international laws, Concert practices, alliances used as devices for restraining one's ally—were more common and more useful in promoting and preserving the European equilibrium than power-political ones such as rival alliances or blocking coalitions.

—Paul Schroeder, "The Nineteenth Century System"[1]

---

infantries. The change in the means available to states also helped to change the process of the eighteenth-century international system.

The Structure and Process of the Nineteenth-Century System

These distinctions help us understand the nineteenth-century origins of the great twentieth-century conflicts. By the rule of parsimony, we should first seek a simple structural explanation if we want to explain what happened over the course of the nineteenth century.

At the beginning of the century, Napoleon tried to create a French hegemony over Europe, but he failed. His efforts united the other countries in a coalition that eventually defeated France. Had he succeeded, he would have changed the system to a unipolar structure. But after Napoleon's defeat in 1815, the Congress of Vienna restored the old multipolar order with five major powers balancing each other. Revolutionary France changed the process of the system for 20 years and threatened to change its structure, but in the end, France failed to make the structure of the European interstate system unipolar.

For structuralists, the big change came with the unification of Germany in 1870. The nineteenth-century system remained multipolar, but there was a major change in the distribution of power in central Europe. Before that, Germany consisted of 37 states and had been an arena of international politics in which others intervened. After 1870, Germany became a united actor. Furthermore, it was located right in the center of Europe, which had tremendous geopolitical consequences. From a structuralist perspective, a united Germany was potentially either too strong or too weak. If Germany was strong enough to defend itself against both Russia and France at the same time, it was also strong enough to defeat either the Russians or the French alone. And if Germany was not strong enough to defeat Russia and France simultaneously, it might look weak enough to invite the Russians and the French to join together to invade it.

But the newly unified German state in the center of Europe did not produce instability because of its brilliant first chancellor, Otto von Bismarck. From 1870 to

1890, Bismarck was such an agile diplomat that he was able to allay the sense of threat on the part of his neighbors, thus delaying the effects of this major structural change on the system's political process. But Bismarck's successors were not so adept. From 1890 on, the alliance systems of Europe grew more rigid, with one alliance centered around Germany and another on Russia and France. The bipolarity of alliances gradually grew more and more rigid and finally exploded in 1914.

There is a strong core of truth in this structural explanation of nineteenth-century change, but it is not an adequate explanation by itself. It does not account for the role of an individual such as Bismarck, nor does it tell us why Germany was allowed by the other European states to unify in the first place. Why didn't Germany's neighbors try to prevent the unification? If Britain and France could see this challenger arising, why didn't they stop it at the time? Perceptions and domestic politics must be invoked to answer those questions. The structural explanation says little about why it took 30 years for the bipolarity of alliances to develop, and it does not allow for the possibly crucial role of leadership. If the kaiser had not fired Bismarck in 1890, or if Bismarck's successors had kept his treasured alliance with Russia (which appealed to shared ideological interests in monarchical autocracy), perhaps the evolving bipolarity could have been avoided. If Bismarck's successors had not challenged Britain by launching a naval arms race, perhaps Britain's role in the conflict could have been avoided. Although the structural explanation of changes in the nineteenth-century system has much to offer, it is too narrowly deterministic. It removes the role of human choice and makes World War I look inevitable in 1870. It provides a start, but it does not tell us enough.

We also need to take into account the changes in the process, or patterns of relations, in the nineteenth-century system. There we find a change in states' goals and instruments that altered the incentives for cooperation. The ideology of democratization and nationalism grew stronger over the course of the nineteenth century and had a major effect on states' goals. The state and the ruler were no longer the same. Louis XIV's famous saying "l'état c'est moi" (I am the state) no longer held. In the eighteenth century, Frederick behaved in Prussia much as he wanted. He was not constrained by elected ministers or parliamentarians. Democratization added broader domestic influences to the complexity of international politics. Napoleon carried the new ideas across Europe, challenging and fomenting nationalism in other countries. The Napoleonic Wars may have failed to change the *structure* of European politics, but they certainly caused profound changes in the *process*. The Austrian Prince Metternich and his counterparts succeeded in restoring the old order at the Congress of Vienna in 1815, but beneath a surface of stability were the volcanic forces of nationalism and democracy that erupted in the revolutions of 1848.

As the century progressed, the nationalist challenge to the legitimacy of dynastic rulers led to some strange alliances that defied the classical balance of power. For example, in 1866, France failed to support Austria when it was attacked by Prussia, a long-term error from the structural point of view. France was opposed to Austrian repression of nationalism in the part of Italy that Austria occupied. Bismarck played on the nationalistic views of other German states in unifying Germany under Prussian leadership, but nationalism became a restraint on what could be done later.

When Bismarck took Alsace-Lorraine from France in the war of 1870, he created nationalist resentment in France that prevented France and Germany from becoming potential alliance partners in the future. The new ideologies changed states' goals and made the process of international politics less moderate over the course of the nineteenth century.

There were also changes in the means. The application of new industrial technology to military purposes produced massive yet inflexible instruments of war. Railway mobilization schedules, the ability to get large numbers of troops in one place at one time, began to play a key role in war by the middle of the century. Near the end, machine guns and trenches made a mockery of the idea of short, sharp, limited wars of the type that Bismarck used so successfully in the 1860s. Both structure and process help to explain the changes in the nineteenth-century international system in Europe and the origins of World War I. We started with structure because it is simpler, but attention to process reminds us not to be blind to social change.

A Modern Sequel

The so-called German problem from the nineteenth century reemerged in debates when East and West Germany were reunified in 1990. At first, Foreign Minister Eduard Shevardnadze of the Soviet Union argued that the reunification of Germany would profoundly destabilize the balance of power in Europe. Statesmen once again asked, "How many German-speaking states are consistent with stability in Europe?" Over time, there have been different answers to that question. As we have seen, at the Congress of Vienna in 1815 there were 37 German-speaking states. Bismarck felt there should be two, not one. He did not want the Austrians included in his new German empire because he feared they would dilute Prussian control of the new state. Hitler had a different answer: one, and that the center of a world empire, thus leading to World War II. In 1945, the victorious Allies eventually decided on three: East, West, and Austria. And there is always the quip attributed to a Frenchman at the end of World War II: When asked how many Germanies there should be, he replied, "I love Germany so much that the more, the better."

The decline of Soviet power in Eastern Europe ended the bipolar structure of postwar politics and made possible Germany's reunification. But reunification created new anxieties about 80 million people with the largest economy located in the heart of Europe. Would Germans search for a new role? Would they again cast about, turn eastward, and then westward? Would they be drawn into the countries to their east where German influence had always been strong? John Mearsheimer, a University of Chicago political scientist, said the answer was "back to the future." He relied on structural realist analysis to reach pessimistic conclusions that the future will be like the past because the structure of the situation is similar to the past.

But things have changed in three ways. At the structural level, the United States is involved in Europe and the United States is nearly four times the size of the reunified Germany. Structuralists worry that the Americans will not stay involved. With the end of the Cold War, the Americans may turn isolationist and go home. But there are other changes as well. The process of international politics in Europe is enormously changed by the development of new institutions. The European Union unites Germany and other European states in a way they were never tied together before. A third change is not at the system level, but at the state level. Germany's domestic politics represent more than four decades of democracy. The Germany that caused trouble in the heart of Europe in 1870, 1914, and 1939 was not democratic. Which of these approaches, structural or process or domestic, will best predict the future of Europe?

Domestic Politics and Foreign Policy

Realism, which rests very heavily on the systemic level of analysis, says that states will act similarly because of the international system. A state's place in the system makes it act in a certain way, and states with similar places will act similarly. Big states will act in one way and small states in another. But this is not enough. Because a parsimonious system level of analysis is often inadequate, we must look at what happens inside the units in the system. Everybody agrees that domestic politics matter. After all, the Peloponnesian War began with a domestic conflict between the oligarchs and the democrats in Epidamnus. The blocked democracy in Germany and the domestic politics of the Austro-Hungarian Empire played significant roles in the onset of World War I. To understand the end of the Cold War, we must look inside the Soviet Union to the failure of its centrally planned economy. It is easy to find examples in which domestic politics mattered, but can we generalize about them? After we have said that domestic politics is important, is there anything else to say?

Two major theories, Marxism and liberalism, rest heavily on the second level of analysis and the proposition that states will act similarly if they have similar domestic societies. To predict foreign policy, look at the internal organization of the state. Marxists argue that the source of war is capitalism. In Lenin's view, monopoly capital requires war: "Inter-imperialist alliances are inevitably nothing more than a truce in the periods between wars."[2] War can be explained by the nature of capitalist society. As we see later, Marxism did not do a very good job explaining the onset of World War I. Nor did it fit very well with the experience of the second half of this century. Communist states, such as the Soviet Union, China, and Vietnam, were involved in military clashes with each other, while the major capitalist states in Europe, North America, and Japan had peaceful relations. The arguments that capitalism causes war do not stand up very well in historical experience.

Classical liberalism, the philosophy that dominated much of British and American thought in the nineteenth century, came to the opposite conclusion: Capitalist states tend to be peaceful because war is bad for business. It is better to trade and to prosper than go to war. If we are interested in getting richer and improving the welfare of citizens, peace is best. In 1840, the British liberal Richard Cobden gave a good expression of the classical view in saying, "We can keep the world from actual war, and I trust that the world will do that through trade."[3]

The liberal view was very powerful on the eve of World War I. A number of books, including a classic by Norman Angell, said that war was unlikely because it had become too expensive. To illustrate the mindset of classical liberalism on the eve of World War I, we can look at the philanthropists of that era. Andrew

Carnegie, the steel magnate, established the Carnegie Endowment for International Peace in 1910. Carnegie worried about what would happen to the money he had given to this foundation after peace broke out, so he put a provision in his will to cover this possibility. Edward Ginn, a Boston publisher, did not want Carnegie to get all the credit for the forthcoming peace, so he set up the World Peace Foundation devoted to the same cause. Ginn also worried about what to do with the rest of the money after peace was established, so he designated it for low-cost housing for young working women.

This liberal outlook was severely discredited by World War I. Even though bankers and aristocrats had frequent contact across borders, and labor also had transnational contacts, none of this helped to stop the European states from going to war with each other. Statistical analysis has found no strong correlation between states' involvement in war and whether they are capitalist or democratic. The classical Marxist and liberal views are opposites in their view of the relationship between war and capitalism, but they are similar in locating the causes of war in domestic politics, and especially in the nature of the economic system.

Neoliberalism

The two world wars and the failure of collective security in the interwar period discredited liberal theories. Most writing about international politics in the United States after World War II was strongly realist in flavor. However, as transnational economic interdependence increased, the late 1960s and 1970s saw a revival of interest in liberal theories. There are three strands of this neoliberal thinking: economic, social, and political, and the political strand has two parts, one relating to institutions and the other to democracy.

The economic strand focuses heavily on trade. Neoliberals argue that trade is important, not because it prevents states from going to war, but because it may lead states to define their interests in a way that makes war less important to them. Trade offers states a way to transform their position through economic growth rather than through military conquest. Richard Rosecrance points to the example of Japan. In the 1930s, Japan felt the only way to get access to markets was to create a "Greater East Asia Co-Prosperity Sphere," which in turn required conquering its neighbors and requiring them to trade. Already in 1939, Eugene Staley argued that part of Japan's behavior in the 1930s could be explained by the economic protectionism at the time. Staley believed that when economic walls are erected along political boundaries, possession of territory is made to coincide with economic opportunity. A better solution for avoiding war is to pursue economic growth in an open trading system without military conquest. In contrast to the 1930s, Japan today has successfully transformed its position in the world through trade. Japan's share of the world product went from about 5 percent in 1960 to about 15 percent in 1990, becoming the second largest economy in the world.

Realists reply that Japan was able to accomplish this amazing economic growth because somebody else was providing for its security. Specifically, Japan relied on the United States for security against its large nuclear neighbors, the Soviet Union and China. Some realists predict that, with the Soviet Union gone, the United States

---

A NEW LIBERAL VIEW

What is interesting and different about the world since 1945 is that a peaceful trading strategy is enjoying much more efficacy than ever before. Through mechanisms
of industrial-technological development and international trade, nations can transform their positions in international politics, and they can do so while other states
also benefit from the enhanced trade and growth that economic cooperation makes
possible.

—Richard Rosecrance, The Rise of the Trading State[4]

---

will withdraw its security presence in East Asia and raise barriers against Japanese
trade. Japan will remilitarize, and eventually there will be conflict between Japan and
the United States as predicted by theories of hegemonic transition.

On the other hand, liberals reply that Japan today has a very different domestic society from the Japan of the 1930s. It is a nonmilitarist society, partly because
of the economic opportunities. The most attractive career opportunities in Japan
are in business, not in the military. They argue that the realists are not paying
enough attention to domestic politics and the way Japan has changed as a result of
economic opportunities. Whatever the outcome, the neoliberal economic argument says that trade may not prevent war, but it does lead to changes in how states
see their opportunities, which in turn may lead to a social structure that is less
inclined to war.

The second form of neoliberalism is social. It argues that person-to-person contacts will reduce conflict by promoting understanding. Such transnational contacts
occur at many levels, including students, businesspeople, and tourists. Such contacts
make others seem less foreign and less hateful. That, in turn, leads to a lower likelihood of conflict. The evidence for this view is mixed. After all, bankers, aristocrats,
and labor union officials had broad contacts in 1914, but that did not stop them
from killing one another once they put on khaki uniforms. Obviously, the idea that
social contact breeds understanding and prevents war is far too simple. Nonetheless,
it may make a modest contribution to understanding. Western Europe today is very
different from 1914. There are constant contacts across international borders in
Europe, and textbook editors try to treat other nationalities fairly. The images of the
other peoples of Europe are very different from the images of 1914. Public opinion
polls show that a sense of European identity coexists with a sense of national identity. Transnational society affects what people in a democracy want from their foreign policy. It is worth noting how France responded to the reunification of
Germany in 1990. There was a residue of uncertainty and anxiety among the foreign
policy experts, but public opinion polls showed that most French people welcomed
German unification. Such attitudes were a sharp contrast to August 1914.

Social contacts alone are not sufficient. They are likely to have more impact
when embedded in institutions. The third form of neoliberalism stresses the role of
institutions. Why do international institutions matter? Because they provide a
framework that shapes expectations. They allow people to believe there is not going

to be a conflict. They lengthen the shadow of the future and reduce the acuteness of the security dilemma. Institutions reduce the effect of the anarchy that the realists assume. Hobbes saw international politics as a state of war. He was careful to say that a state of war does not mean constant fighting, but a propensity to war, just as cloudy weather means a likelihood of rain. In the same sense, a state of peace means there is a propensity toward peace, and that people can develop peaceful expectations when anarchy is limited and stabilized by international institutions.

Institutions stabilize expectations in four ways. First, they provide a sense of continuity; for example, most West Europeans expect the European Union to last. It is likely to be there tomorrow. Many East Europeans agree and hope to join the European Union some day. That affects their current behavior. Second, institutions provide an opportunity for reciprocity. If the French get a little bit more today, the Italians might get a little more tomorrow. There is less need to worry about each transaction because over time it will likely balance out. Third, institutions provide a flow of information. Who is doing what? Are the Italians actually obeying the rules passed by the European Union? Is the flow of trade roughly equal? The institutions of the Union provide information on how it is all working out. Finally, institutions provide ways to resolve conflicts. In the European Union, bargaining goes on within the Council of Ministers and in the European Commission, and there is also a European court of justice. Thus institutions create a climate in which expectations of stable peace develop.

Classical liberals expect "peace breaking out all over"; neoliberals look for *islands* of peace where institutions and stable expectations have developed. The political scientist Karl Deutsch called such areas "pluralistic security communities" in which war between countries became so unthinkable that stable expectations of peace developed. Institutions helped reinforce such expectations. The Scandinavian countries, for example, once fought each other bitterly, and the United States fought Britain, Canada, and Mexico. Today such actions are unthinkable. The advanced industrial countries seem to have a propensity for peace, and institutions such as the European Union, the North American Free Trade Agreement (NAFTA), and the Organization of American States create a culture in which peace is expected and provide forums for negotiation. Expectations of stability can provide a way to escape the Prisoner's Dilemma situations that realists assume.

Many realists expect the security dilemma to reemerge in Europe despite the liberal institutions of the European Union (EU). After the high hopes that greeted European integration in 1992, there was a period of pessimism that saw heated opposition to further unity, particularly in the battles over the Maastricht Treaty. Countries such as Great Britain fear that ceding further power to the government of the European Union would jeopardize the autonomy and prosperity of the individual nations. Yet, they feel the pressure to strengthen the power of the community and worry that if they opt out, countries such as Germany, France, or Italy that opt in will gain a competitive edge.

The security dilemmas are further aggravated by the newly independent countries of Eastern Europe and of the former Soviet Union, many of which wish to enter the European Union and which are cementing closer economic and political ties with the West. If these countries are not able to make the transition to prosperous, stable democracies, the resulting turmoil may well create a power vacuum into which Western European countries will be drawn. Domestic politics may play a part as internal groups appeal to outsiders to bolster their side. If the Eastern European states fall into chaos, one or another group will appeal to the Russians or to the Germans to help their side in the resulting civil war. As we have seen, John Mearsheimer predicts that this turmoil will disrupt the liberal institutional framework of Western Europe and tear Germany away from its position in the European Union. Russia will become embroiled in conflict with Germany, not because either of them seek to rush in, but because they will be pulled into the power vacuum. Then the security dilemma will reemerge. Germany will return to the situation on the eve of 1914, in the center of Europe, worrying about how to solve its security dilemma in that difficult position.

Liberal Democracy and War

Neoliberals respond that these realist fears pay insufficient attention to the fourth strand of neoliberalism: democratic values. Germany today is a different country than the Germany of 1870, 1914, or 1939. Germany has experienced nearly a half century of democracy, with parties and governments changing peacefully. Public opinion polls show that the German people do not seek an expansive international role. Thus, the neoliberals are skeptical of realist predictions that fail to account for the effects of democracy.

Is there a relationship between domestic democracy and a state's propensity to go to war? The issue is disputed. At a conference sponsored by the Institute of Peace in Washington in June 1990, two former officials of the Reagan administration gave diametrically opposed views. Carl Gershman, president of the National Endowment for Democracy, argued, "It should be self-evident that a society organized democratically will behave more peacefully in its foreign relations." Eugene Rostow, former director of the Arms Control and Disarmament Agency, replied, "The notion that liberal democratic states do not go to war is the latest in a long series of myths which idealistic people have sought to save them from war."[5]

Absolute rulers can easily commit their states to war, as did Frederick the Great when he wanted Silesia in 1740 or Saddam Hussein when he wanted Kuwait in 1990. As Immanuel Kant and other classical liberals pointed out, in a democracy the people can vote against war. But the fact that a country is democratic does not mean its people will always vote against war. As we have seen, statistically democracies seem to be involved in wars as often as other countries. Democratic electorates have often voted for war. In ancient Greece, Pericles roused the people of Athens to go to war; in 1898, the American electorate dragged a reluctant President McKinley into the Spanish-American War. In 1991, opinion polls and a congressional vote supported President Bush in the war against Iraq.

Michael Doyle has pointed to a more limited proposition that can be derived from Kant and classical liberalism, namely the idea that democracies do not fight *other democracies*. The fact that two democratic states do not fight each other is a correlation, and some correlations involve spurious causation. Fires and the presence of fire engines are highly correlated, but we do not suspect fire engines of causing fires. Is the causation real or spurious? One possible source of spurious causation is that democratic countries tend to be rich countries, rich countries tend to be involved with trade, and according to trade liberalism, they are not likely to fight each other. But that dismissal does not fit with the fact that rich countries have often fought each other—witness the two world wars. Neoliberals suggest that the cause behind the correlation is a question of legitimacy. Maybe people in democracies feel that it is wrong to fight other democracies because there is something wrong with solving disputes through killing when the other people have the right of consent. In addition, constitutional checks and balances on war making may work better when there is widespread public debate about the legitimacy of a battle. It is harder to rouse democratic peoples when there is no authoritarian despot like a Hitler or Saddam Hussein.

Although these liberal theories need exploration via detailed case studies to look at what actually happened in particular instances, they do have promise. Then, if the number of democracies in the world grows, there might be less propensity to war, at least among the democracies. But a word of caution is in order. Some of the new democracies may be plebiscitary democracies without a liberal domestic process of free press, checks on executive power, and regular elections. The warring governments of Croatia, Serbia, and Bosnia were elected, though they were far from liberal democracies. The same was true of Ecuador and Peru, which fought a border skirmish in 1995. The theorized relation is between liberal democracies, not all democracies.

Definition of National Interests

Whatever their form of government, "states act in their national interest." That statement is normally true, but it does not tell us much unless we know how the states define their national interest. Realists say that states have little choice in defining their national interest because of the international system. They must define their interest in terms of balance of power, or they will not survive, just as a company in a perfect market that wants to be altruistic rather than maximize profits will not survive. So for the realists, a state's position in the international system tells how its national interests are defined and predicts its foreign policies.

Liberals argue that national interests are defined by much more than the state's position in the international system, and liberalism has a richer account of how national interests are formed. The definition of the national interest depends in large part on the type of domestic society a state has. For example, a domestic society that values economic welfare and places heavy emphasis on trade, or that views wars against other democracies as illegitimate, defines its national interest very differently from a despotic state that is similarly positioned in the international system. Liberals argue that this is particularly true if the international system is moderate, that is, if it is not purely anarchic. If institutions and channels of communication provide stable expectations of continuing peace, the Prisoner's Dilemma may be escaped.

Since these nonpower incentives can help to shape how states define their interests, it is important to know how closely a particular situation approximates the abstract concept of anarchy. If an international situation is totally anarchic, if you may be killed by your neighbor tomorrow, then there are limited opportunities for democracy or trade preferences to influence foreign policy. Survival comes first. But if the system only partially approximates anarchy because there are institutions and stable expectations of peace, then some of these other factors related to domestic society are likely to play a larger role. Realist predictions are more likely to be accurate in the Middle East, for example, and liberal predictions in Western Europe.

Variations in Foreign Policies

Even states in similar situations sometimes define their interests and strategies differently—witness Bismarck's, the kaiser's, and Hitler's solutions to Germany's security dilemma. When systemic differences fail to explain different foreign policies, we tend to look at domestic causes. Some of these are idiosyncratic to each of the 180-odd states in the world, but some can be captured by generalizations.

There are a variety of factors in their domestic affairs that sometimes make states act similarly. We have looked at trade and democracy, but there are others. For example, is there a revolution? Revolutionary leaders often view their predecessors' foreign policies and even the whole international system as illegitimate. Revolutions often create instability in the entire region. Revolutionary leaders frequently seek to export their ideology while neighboring states seek to contain it, as happened with France and its neighbors in the 1790s, and with Iran and Iraq in 1980. Sometimes the revolutionary state invades; sometimes it is invaded. Another low-level generalization is that poorly integrated countries, such as Germany or Austria before 1914, are more likely to project internal problems outward. German leaders diverted attention away from social democracy at home to expansion abroad. However, this tendency to find external scapegoats does not always hold true; some countries with poor internal integration, like Myanmar (Burma) today, turn inward.

Other regularities are sought in the behavior of bureaucracies. Because bureaucracies have standard operating procedures and do not change quickly, some analysts believe that foreign policy can be predicted by looking at the inertia of foreign policy and military bureaucracies. Certainly the German military bureaucracy resisted changes in its military plans in 1914. But bureaucratic predictions can mislead. After its defeat by mobile, irregular guerrilla forces in Vietnam, the American military adopted a strategy of high mobility during the Gulf War and won. Bureaucracies may not change quickly, but they do change.

Many of the variations in foreign policy behavior will yield only low-level generalizations. They are at best hypotheses to test rather than perfect predictions. Domestic politics matter, and liberal theories help, but in different ways and at different times and different places.

COUNTERFACTUALS

In 1990, President Vaclav Havel of Czechoslovakia spoke before the U.S. Congress. Six months earlier he had been a political prisoner. "As a playwright," Havel said, "I'm used to the fantastic. I dream up all sorts of implausible things and put them in my plays. So this jolting experience of going from prison to standing before you today, I can adjust to this. But pity the poor political scientists who are trying to deal with what's probable."[6] Few people, including Soviets and East Europeans, predicted the collapse of the Soviet empire in Eastern Europe in 1989. Humans sometimes make surprising choices, and human history is full of uncertainties. How can we sort out the importance of different causes and different levels of analysis?

International politics is not like a laboratory science. Controlled experiments do not exist because it is impossible to hold other things constant while looking at the one thing that changes. Aristotle said that one should be as precise in any science as the subject matter allows. Do not try to be too precise if the precision will be spurious. In international politics, there are so many variables, so many changes occurring at the same time that events are overdetermined—there are too many causes. But as analysts, we still want to sort out causes to get some idea of which ones are stronger than others. One of the tools we can use is mental experiments called counterfactuals.

Conterfactuals are *contrary-to-fact conditionals*, but it is simpler to think of them as thought experiments to define causal claims. Since there is no actual, physical laboratory for international politics, we imagine situations in which one thing changes while other things are held constant and then construct a picture of how the world would look. Actually, like speaking prose, we use counterfactuals every day. Many students might say, "If I had not eaten so much dinner, I could concentrate better on this reading." A few might use fancier counterfactuals: "If I hadn't skipped dinner at the student union, I wouldn't have met her, and my life would be much simpler today."

Though often without admitting it, historians use a more elaborate version of the same procedure to weigh causes. For example, imagine the kaiser had not fired Bismarck in 1890. Would that have made World War I less likely? Would Bismarck's policies have continued to lower the sense of threat that other countries felt from Germany and thus headed off the growing rigidity of the two alliance systems? In this instance, the use of a counterfactual examines how important a particular personality was in comparison to structural factors. Here is another counterfactual related to World War I: Suppose Franz Ferdinand's driver in Sarajevo had turned left instead of right at the crucial intersection and the Austrian archduke had not been assassinated; would the war have started or not? This counterfactual illuminates the role of the accidental. How important was the assassination? Given the overall tensions inherent in the alliance structure, was it likely that some other spark would have ignited the flame if this one had not occurred?

Contrary-to-fact conditional statements provide a way to explore whether a cause is significant or not, but there are also pitfalls in such "iffy history." Poorly handled, counterfactuals may mislead by destroying the meaning of history; the fact that once something has happened, other things are not equal. Time is a crucial dimension. We say that historical events are "path dependent"; that is, once events start down a certain path, all possible futures are not equally probable. Some events are more likely than others. There are four criteria we can use to test whether our counterfactual thought experiments are good or useful: plausibility, proximity, theory, and facts.

Plausibility

A useful counterfactual has to be within the reasonable array of options. This is sometimes called cotenability. It must be plausible to imagine two conditions existing at the same time. Suppose someone said that if Napoleon had stealth bombers, he could have won the Battle of Waterloo. She may say such a counterfactual is designed to test the importance of military technology, but it makes little sense to imagine twentieth-century technology in a nineteenth-century setting. The two are not cotenable. Although it might be good for laughs, it is not a fruitful use of counterfactual thinking because of the anachronism involved. In real life, there never was a possibility of such a conjunction.

Proximity in Time

Each major event exists in a long chain of causation, and most events have multiple causes. The further back in time we go, the more causes that must be held constant. The closer in time the questioned event is to the subject event (did A cause B?), the more likely the answer is "yes." Consider Pascal's famous counterfactual statement that if Cleopatra's nose had been shorter, she would have been less attractive to Marc Antony, and the history of the Roman Empire would have been different. If the history of the Roman Empire had been different, the history of Western European civilization would have been different. Thus the length of Cleopatra's nose was one of the causes of World War I. In some trivial sense, that may be true, but millions of events and causes channeled down to August 1914. The contribution of Cleopatra's nose to the cause of World War I is so small and remote that the counterfactual is more amusing than interesting when we try to ascertain why the war broke out. Proximity in time means that the closeness of two events in the chain of causation allows us better to control other causes and thereby obtain a truer weighing of factors.

Relation to Theory

Good counterfactual reasoning should rely on an existing body of theory that represents a distillation of what we think we know about things that have happened before. We should ask whether a counterfactual is plausible considering what we know about all the cases that have given rise to these theories. Theories provide coherence and organization to our thoughts about the myriad of causes and help us to avoid random guessing. For example, there is no theory behind the counterfactual that if Napoleon had stealth aircraft, he would have won the Battle of Waterloo. The very randomness of the example helps to explain why it is amusing, but also limits what we can learn from the mental exercise.

But suppose we were considering the causes of the Cold War and asked what if the United States had been a socialist country in 1945; would there have been a Cold War? Or suppose the Soviet Union had come out of World War II with a capitalist government; would there have been a Cold War? These counterfactual questions explore the theory that the Cold War was caused primarily by ideology. An alternative hypothesis is that the bipolar international structure caused the Cold War. Given the distribution of power after World War II, we could expect some sort of tension even if the United States had been socialist. And the counterfactual reasoning can be bolstered by observing that countries with a similar communist ideology have fought each other. The counterfactual allows us to assess theories of balance of power versus theories of ideological causation. In general, counterfactuals related to theory are more interesting and useful because the mental exercise ties into a broader body of knowledge.

Fact

It is not enough to imagine fruitful hypotheses. They must be carefully examined in relation to the known facts. Counterfactuals require accurate facts and careful history. In examining the plausibility of a mental experiment, we must ask whether what is held constant is faithful to what actually happened. We must be wary of piling one counterfactual on top of another in the same thought experiment. Such multiple counterfactuals are confusing because too many things are being changed at once, and we are unable to judge the accuracy of the exercise by a careful examination of its real historical parts.

In summary, we frequently use counterfactuals in our everyday lives. They are especially useful in international politics because there is no laboratory setting such as in physical science. But we need to be careful in constructing counterfactuals, for some are better constructed and thus more fruitful than others. Counterfactuals help us to relate history to theory and make better judgments as we try to understand a world where there are no controlled experiments.

Some historians are purists who say that counterfactuals which ask what might have been are not real history. Real history is what actually happened. Imagining what might have happened is not important. But such purists miss the point that we try to understand not just what happened, but *why* it happened. To do that, we need to know what else might have happened, and that brings us back to counterfactuals. So while there are some historians who interpret history as simply the writing down of what happened, many historians believe that good counterfactual analysis is essential to the writing of history. The purists help warn us against poorly disciplined counterfactuals such as Napoleon's stealth bombers. But, as we see in the next chapter, there is a distinction between saying some counterfactual analysis is trivial and saying that good counterfactual analysis is essential to clear thinking about causation.

NOTES

1. Paul Schroeder, "The Nineteenth Century System: Balance of Power or Political Equilibrium?" *Swords and Ploughshares*, Vol. 4, No. 1 (October 1989), p. 4.
2. Lenin, V. I. *Imperialism: The Highest Stage of Capitalism* (New York: International Publishers, 1977), p. 119.
3. Richard Cobden, quoted in Kenneth N. Waltz, *Man, the State, and War: A Theoretical Analysis* (New York: Columbia University Press, 1959), p. 104.
4. Richard Rosecrance, *The Rise of the Trading State* (New York: Basic, 1986), p. ix.
5. U.S. Institute of Peace, *Journal*, Vol. 3, No. 2 (June 1990), pp. 6–7.
6. Vaclav Havel, "Address to U.S. Congress," *Congressional Record*, February 21, 1990, pp. S 1313–1315.

SELECTED READINGS

1. Waltz, Kenneth, *Man, the State, and War: A Theoretical Analysis* (New York: Columbia University Press, 1959), pp. 1–15, 224–238.

2. Levy, Jack S., "Domestic Politics and War," in Robert Rotberg and Theodore Rabb, eds., *The Origin and Prevention of Major Wars* (Cambridge, England: Cambridge University Press, 1989), pp. 79–99.

3. Detwiler, Donald, *Germany: A Short History* (Carbondale, IL: Southern Illinois University Press, 1989), pp. 104–148.

4. Ritter, Harry, "Counterfactual Analysis," in *Dictionary of Concepts in History* (New York: Greenwood Press, 1986), pp. 70–73.

FURTHER READINGS

Albrecht-Carrie, René, *A Diplomatic History of Europe Since the Congress of Vienna* (New York: Harper & Row, 1958).

Bartlett, C. J., *The Global Conflict: The International Rivalry of the Great Powers, 1880–1970* (London: Longman, 1984).

Bueno de Mesquita, Bruce, and David Lalman, "Empirical Support for Systemic and Dyadic Explanations of International Conflict," *World Politics*, Vol. 41, No. 1 (October 1988), pp. 1–20.

Craig, Gordon A., *Germany, 1866–1945* (New York: Oxford University Press, 1978).

Doyle, Michael, "Kant, Liberal Legacies, and Foreign Affairs," *Philosophy and Public Affairs*, Vol. 12, No. 3 (Summer 1983), pp. 205–235.

Fearon, James D., "Counterfactuals and Hypothesis Testing in Political Science," *World Politics*, Vol. 43, No. 2 (January 1991), pp. 169–195.

Hoffmann, Stanley, "Liberalism and International Affairs," in *Janus and Minerva: Essays in the Theory and Practice of International Politics* (Boulder, CO: Westview Press, 1987), pp. 394–417.

Hopf, Ted, "Polarity, the Offense-Defense Balance, and War," *American Political Science Review*, Vol. 85, No. 2 (June 1991), pp. 475–494.

Jervis, Robert, *Perception and Misperception in World Politics* (Princeton, NJ: Princeton University Press, 1976).

Kennedy, Paul M., *Strategy and Diplomacy, 1870–1945: Eight Studies* (London: Allen & Unwin, 1983).

Keohane, Robert O., *International Institutions and State Power: Essays in International Relations Theory* (Boulder, CO: Westview Press, 1989).

Keohane, Robert O., and Joseph S. Nye, Jr., *Power and Interdependence: World Politics in Transition* (Boston: Little, Brown, 1977).

Kissinger, Henry A., *A World Restored: Metternich, Castlereagh, and the Problems of Peace, 1812–22* (Boston: Houghton Mifflin, 1957).

Mearsheimer, John, "Back to the Future," *International Security*, Vol. 15, No. 3 (Summer 1990), pp. 5–55.

Nye, Jr., Joseph S. "Neorealism and Neoliberalism," *World Politics*, Vol. 40, No. 2 (January 1988), pp. 235–251.

Schroeder, Paul W., "The Nineteenth Century International System: Changes in the Structure of World Power," *World Politics*, Vol. 39, No. 1 (October 1986), pp. 1–26.

Taylor, A. J. P., *The Struggle for Mastery in Europe, 1848–1918* (Oxford, England: Clarendon Press, 1954).

Zelikow, Philip, and Condoleezza Rice. *Germany Unified and Europe Transformed.* (Cambridge: Harvard University Press, 1995).

STUDY QUESTIONS

1. What were the main goals of the Congress of Vienna? Did the Congress restore the antebellum European order or did it shape a new one?

2. What were the characteristics of the European system from 1815 to 1848? Did they differ from those of the eighteenth-century balance of power and from those of the late nineteenth-century international systems? What factors caused changes?

3. What was the effect of the rise of Germany on the European system? What was Bismarck's strategy in Europe? Was he concerned with maintaining the balance or over-turning it?

4. Why do liberals think that democracy can prevent war? What are the limits to their view?

5. What are Waltz's three images? How can they be combined?

6. What is counterfactual history? How would you use it?

CHRONOLOGIES: EUROPE

The Seventeenth Century

1618–1648	Thirty Years' War: conflict between Catholic and Protestant Europe; last of the great religious wars; Germany devastated
1643–1715	Louis XIV, King of France
1648	Peace of Westphalia; end of Thirty Years' War
1649–1660	English King Charles I beheaded; commonwealth under Oliver Cromwell
1652–1678	Series of Anglo-French and Anglo-Dutch wars for supremacy of the seas
1660	Stuart restoration in England; accession of Charles II
1682–1725	Peter the Great begins "Westernization" of Russia
1683	Turkish siege of Vienna repulsed
1685	Louis XIV revokes Edict of Nantes; persecution of French Protestants
1688/1689	Glorious Revolution in England
1688–1697	War of the League of Augsburg; general war against Louis XIV

The Eighteenth Century

1700–1721	Great Northern War: Russia, Poland, and Denmark oppose Swedish supremacy in the Baltic; Russia emerges as a European power
1701–1714	War of the Spanish Succession and the Treaty of Utrecht; resulted in permanent separation of French and Spanish thrones; further decline of French power
1707	Great Britain formed by union of England and Scotland
1740–1748	War of the Austrian Succession

1756–1763	Seven Years' War: Britain and France in colonial wars; France loses Canada and India; Britain emerges as world's major colonial power
1775–1783	War of the American Revolution
1789–1799	French Revolution
1799	Coup d'état by Napoleon Bonaparte in France
1799–1815	Napoleonic Wars make France preeminent power on European continent

The Nineteenth Century

1801	United Kingdom formed by union of Great Britain and Ireland
1804–1814	Napoleon I, emperor of France
1806	End of Holy Roman Empire; imperial title renounced by Francis II
1810	Kingdom of Holland incorporated in French empire
1812	French invasion of Russia; destruction of Napoleon's army
1814–1815	Congress of Vienna: monarchies reestablished in Europe
1815	Battle of Waterloo: Napoleon escapes from Elba but defeated by British and Prussian armies
1833–1871	Unification of Germany
1837–1901	Victoria, queen of England: period of great industrial expansion and prosperity
1848	Revolutions in France, Germany, Hungary, and Bohemia; publication of Karl Marx's *Communist Manifesto*
1848–1916	Franz Joseph, emperor of Austria; becomes ruler of the Austro-Hungarian Empire in 1867
1852–1870	Napoleon III, emperor of Second French Empire
1854–1856	Crimean War: Britain and France support Ottomans in war with Russia
1855–1881	Alexander II, czar of Russia
1859–1870	Italian political unification and cultural nationalism led by Garibaldi
1861	Emancipation of Russian serfs by Czar Alexander II
1862–1890	Otto von Bismarck, premier and chancellor of Germany, forges German Empire
1864–1905	Russian expansion in Poland, Balkans, and central Asia
1867	Austro-Hungarian Empire founded
1870–1871	Franco-Prussian War: German invasion of France; Third French Republic created
1870–1914	European imperialism at peak; industrial growth; rise of labor movements and Marxism
1871	The Paris Commune: Paris, a revolutionary center, establishes own government and wars with national government
1878	Congress of Berlin: division of much of Ottoman empire among Austria, Russia, and Britain
1881	Alexander II of Russia assassinated
1882	Triple Alliance of Germany, Austria-Hungary, and Italy
1899–1902	Boer War in South Africa

The First Decade of the Twentieth Century

1904	Dual Entente between Britain and France
1904–1905	Russo-Japanese War ends in Russian defeat; Japan emerges as world power
1907	Russia joins Britain and France in Triple Entente

3 BALANCE OF POWER AND WORLD WAR I

Otto von Bismarck

BALANCE OF POWER

World War I is often blamed on the *balance of power*, one of the most frequently used concepts in international politics. But it is also one of the most confusing. The term is loosely used to describe and justify all sorts of things. The eighteenth-century British philosopher David Hume described the balance of power as a constant rule of prudent politics; but the nineteenth-century British liberal Richard Cobden called it "a chimera—an undescribed, indescribable, incomprehensible nothing."[1] Woodrow Wilson, the American president during World War I, felt that the balance of power was an evil principle because it encouraged statesmen to treat nations like cheeses to be cut up for political convenience regardless of the concerns of their peoples.

Wilson also disliked the balance of power because he believed it caused wars. Defenders of balance of power policies argue that they produce stability. However, peace and stability are not the same thing. Over the five centuries of the European state system, the great powers were involved in 119 wars. Peace was rare; during three-quarters of the time there was war involving at least one of the great powers. Nine of those wars were large general wars with many of the great powers involved—what we call hegemonic, or world wars. Thus if we ask whether the balance of power preserved peace very well over the five centuries of the modern state system, the answer is no.

That is not surprising, because states balance power not to preserve peace, but to preserve their independence. The balance of power helps to preserve the anarchic system of separate states. Not every state is preserved. For example, at the end of the eighteenth century, Poland was, indeed, cut up like a cheese, with Poland's neighbors—Austria, Prussia, and Russia—each helping itself to a large slice. More recently, in 1939 Stalin and Hitler made a deal in which they carved up Poland again and gave the Baltic states to the Soviet Union. So Lithuania, Latvia, and Estonia spent half a century as Soviet republics until 1991. The balance of power has not preserved peace, and has not always preserved the independence of each state, but it has preserved the anarchic state system.

Power

To understand the balance, we have to start with power. Power, like love, is easier to experience than to define or measure. Power is the ability to achieve one's purposes or goals. The dictionary tells us that it is the ability to do things and to control others. Robert Dahl, a Yale political scientist, defines power as the ability to get others to do what they otherwise would not do. But when we measure power in terms of the changed behavior of others, we have to know their preferences. Otherwise, we may be as mistaken about our power as the fox who thought he was hurting Brer Rabbit when he threw him into the briar patch. Knowing in advance how other people or nations would behave in the absence of our efforts is often difficult.

The behavioral definition of power can be useful to analysts and historians who devote considerable time to reconstructing the past, but to practical politicians and leaders it often seems too ephemeral. Because the ability to control others is often associated with the possession of certain resources, political leaders commonly define power this way. These resources include population, territory, natural resources, economic size, military forces, and political stability among others. The virtue of this definition is that it makes power appear more concrete, measurable, and predictable than the behavioral definition. Power in this sense means holding the high cards in the international poker game. A basic rule of poker is that if your opponent is showing cards that can beat anything you hold, fold your hand. If you know you will lose a war, don't start it.

Some wars, however, have been started by the eventual losers, which suggests that political leaders sometimes take risks or make mistakes. Japan in 1941 or Iraq in 1990 are examples. Often the opponent's cards are not all showing in the game of international politics. As in poker, playing skills such as bluff and deception can make a big difference. Even when there is no deception, mistakes can be made about which power resources are most relevant in particular situations. For example, France and Britain had more tanks than Hitler in 1940, but Hitler had greater maneuverability and a better military strategy.

Power conversion is a basic problem that arises when we think of power in terms of resources. Some countries are better than others at converting their resources into effective influence, just as some skilled card players win despite being dealt weak hands. Power conversion is the capacity to convert potential power, as measured by resources, to realized power, as measured by the changed behavior of others. Thus we have to know about a country's skill at power conversion as well as its possession of power resources to predict outcomes correctly.

Another problem is determining which resources provide the best basis for power in any particular context. In earlier periods, power resources were easier to judge. For example, in the agrarian economies of eighteenth-century Europe, population was a critical power resource because it provided a base for taxes and recruitment of infantry. In population, France dominated Western Europe. Thus, at the end of the Napoleonic Wars, Prussia presented its fellow victors at the Congress of Vienna with a precise plan for its own reconstruction in order to maintain the balance of power. Its plan listed the territories and populations it had lost since 1805 and the territories and populations it would need to regain equivalent numbers. In the prenationalist period, it did not much matter that many of the people in those provinces did not speak German or feel themselves to be German. However, within half a century, nationalist sentiments mattered very much. Another change that occurred during the nineteenth century was the growing importance of industry and rail systems that made rapid mobilization possible. In the 1860s, Bismarck's Germany pioneered the use of railways to transport armies for quick victories. Although Russia had always had greater population resources than the rest of Europe, they were difficult to mobilize. The growth of the rail system in western Russia at the beginning of the twentieth century was one of the reasons the Germans feared rising Russian power in 1914. Further, the spread of rail systems on the Continent helped deprive Britain of the luxury of concentrating on naval power. There was no longer time, should it prove necessary, to insert an army to prevent another great power from dominating the Continent.

The application of industrial technology to warfare has long had a powerful impact. Advanced science and technology have been particularly critical power resources since the beginning of the nuclear age in 1945. But the power derived from nuclear weapons has proven to be so awesome and destructive that its actual application is muscle-bound. Nuclear war is simply too costly. More generally, there are many situations where any use of force may be inappropriate or too costly.

Even if the direct use of force was banned among a group of countries, military force would still play an important background role. For example, the American military role in deterring threats to allies, or of assuring access to a crucial resource such as oil in the Persian Gulf, means that the provision of protective force can be used in bargaining situations. Sometimes the linkage may be direct; more often it is a factor not mentioned openly but present in the back of statesmen's minds.

In addition, there is the consideration sometimes called "the second face of power." Getting other states to change might be called the direct or commanding method of exercising power. Such "hard" power can rest on inducements ("carrots") or threats ("sticks"). But there is also a soft or indirect way to exercise power. A country may achieve the outcomes it prefers in world politics because other countries want to follow it or have agreed to a system that produces such effects. In this sense,

LEADING STATES AND MAJOR POWER RESOURCES

Period	Leading State	Major Resources
Sixteenth century	Spain	Gold bullion, colonial trade, mercenary armies, dynastic ties
Seventeenth century	Netherlands	Trade, capital markets, navy
Eighteenth century	France	Population, rural industry, public administration, army
Nineteenth century	Britain	Industry, political cohesion, finance and credit, navy, liberal norms, island location (easy to defend)
Twentieth century	United States	Economic scale, scientific and technical leadership, universalistic culture, military forces and alliances, liberal international regimes, hub of transnational communication and information technology

it is just as important to set the agenda and structure the situations in world politics as it is to get others to change in particular situations. This aspect of power—that is, getting others to want what you want—might be called cooptive, or soft power behavior. Soft power can rest on such resources as the attraction of one's ideas or on the ability to set the political agenda in a way that shapes the preferences others express. Parents of teenagers know that if they have structured their children's beliefs and preferences, their power will be greater and will last longer than if they had relied only on active control. Similarly, political leaders and philosophers have long understood the power that comes from setting the agenda and determining the framework of a debate. The ability to establish preferences tends to be associated with intangible power resources such as culture, ideology, and institutions.

What resources are the most important sources of power today? A look at the five centuries of modern state systems shows that different power resources played critical roles in different periods. The sources of power are never static and they continue to change in today's world.

In an age of information-based economies and transnational interdependence, power is becoming less transferable, less tangible, and less coercive. However, the transformation of power is incomplete. The twenty-first century will certainly see a greater role for informational and institutional power, but as the 1991 Gulf War showed, military force remains an important factor. Economic scale, both in markets and in natural resources, will also remain important. As the service sector grows within modern economies, the distinction between services and manufacturing will continue to blur. Information will become more plentiful, and the critical resource will be the organizational capacity for rapid and flexible response. Political cohesion will remain important, as well as a universalistic popular culture.

The difficulty of measuring changing power resources is a major problem for statesmen trying to assess the balance of power. For analysts of international politics, there is an additional confusion when the same word is used for different things. We must try to separate and clarify the underlying concepts covered by the loose use of the same words. The term *balance of power* commonly refers to at least three different things.

Balances as Distributions of Power

Balance of power can mean, in the first sense, any distribution of power. Who has the power resources? Sometimes people use the term *balance of power* to refer to the status quo, the existing distribution of power. Thus in the 1980s, some Americans argued that if Nicaragua became a communist state, the balance of power would be changed. Such a use of the term is not very enlightening. If one little state changed sides, that might slightly alter the existing distribution of power, but it would be a rather trivial change and it would not tell us much about the deeper changes that were occurring in world politics.

Another way the term is used is to refer to a special (and more rare) set of situations where power is distributed equally. This usage conjures up the image of a set of scales in balance or equilibrium. Some realists argue that stability occurs when there is an equal balance, but others argue that stability occurs when one side has a preponderance of power so that the others dare not attack it. Hegemonic theory holds that imbalanced power produces peace. When there is a strong dominant power, there will be stability, and when that strong power begins to slip, and a new challenger rises, war is more likely. Consider Thucydides's explanation of the Peloponnesian War: The rise of the power in Athens and the fear it created in Sparta fits this hegemonic transition theory. As we see later, so does World War I.

However, we must be cautious about such theories, for they tend to overpredict conflict. In the 1880s, the United States passed Great Britain as the largest economy in the world. In 1895, there was a dispute between the United States and Britain over borders in South America, and it looked as if there might be war. There was a rising challenger, an old hegemon, and a cause of conflict, but you do not read about the great British-American War of 1895 because it did not occur. As Sherlock Holmes pointed out, we can get important clues from dogs that do not bark. In this case, the absence of war leads us to look for other causes. Realists point to the rise of Germany as a more proximate threat to Britain. Liberals point to the increasingly democratic nature of the two countries and to transnational cultural ties between the old leader and the new challenger. The best we can conclude about the balance of power in the first sense of the term is that changes in the unequal distribution of power among leading states may be a factor, but not the sole factor, in explaining war and instability.

Balance of Power as Policy

The second use of the term refers to balance of power as a policy of balancing. Balance of power predicts that states will act to prevent any one state from developing a preponderance of power. This prediction has a long pedigree. Lord Palmerston, British foreign secretary in 1848, said that Britain had no eternal allies or perpetual enemies; Britain thought only of its interests. Sir Edward Grey, the British foreign minister in 1914, did not want to go to war, but eventually did because he feared that Germany would gain preponderance in Europe by controlling the Continent. And in 1941, when Hitler invaded the Soviet Union, Prime Minister Winston Churchill said that Britain should make an alliance with Stalin, against whom he had been fulminating just a few years before. Churchill said, "If Hitler invaded Hell, I would make at least a favorable reference to the Devil in the House of Commons."[2] These are good examples of balance of power as policy.

Predicting such behavior rests on two basic assumptions: (1) The structure of international politics is an anarchic system of states and (2) states value their independence above all else. A balance of power policy does not necessarily assume that states act to maximize power. In fact, a state might choose a very different course of action if it wished to maximize power. It might choose to bandwagon, that is, join whoever seems stronger and share in the victor's gains. Bandwagoning is common in domestic politics where politicians flock to an apparent winner. Balance of power, however, predicts that a state will join whoever seems *weaker* because states will act to keep any one state from developing a preponderance of power. Bandwagoning in international politics carries the risk of losing independence. In 1939 and 1940, Mussolini joined Hitler's attack on France as a way to get some of the spoils, but Italy became more and more dependent on Germany. That is why a balance of power policy says join the weaker side. Balance of power is a policy of helping the underdog because if you help the top dog, it may eventually turn around and eat you.

States can try to balance power unilaterally by developing armaments or by forming alliances with other countries whose power resources help to balance the top dog. This is one of the more interesting and powerful predictions in international politics. The contemporary Middle East is a good example. As we see in Chapter 6, when Iran and Iraq went to war in the early 1980s, some observers thought all Arab states would support Saddam Hussein's Iraq, which represented the Ba'ath party and Arab forces, against the Ayatollah Khomeini's Iran, which represented Persian culture and the minority Shi'ite version of Islam. But Syria, despite having a secular leader from the Ba'ath party, became an ally of Iran. Why? Because Syria was worried about the growing power in the Arab world of its neighbor Iraq. Syria choose to balance Iraqi power regardless of its ideological preferences. Efforts to use ideology to predict state behavior are often wrong whereas counterintuitive predictions based on balancing power often get the answer right.

Of course, there are exceptions. Human behavior is not fully determined. Human beings have choices, and they do not always act as predicted. Certain situations predispose people toward a certain type of behavior, but we cannot always predict the details. If someone shouts "Fire!" in a crowded lecture hall, we could predict that students would run for the exits, but not *which* exits. If all choose one exit, the stampede may prevent many from getting out. Theories in international politics often have large exceptions. Even though balance of power in a policy sense is one of the strongest predictors in international politics, its record is far from perfect.

Why do countries sometimes eschew balance of power and join the stronger rather than the weaker side or stand aloof, thus ignoring the risks to their independence? Some countries may see no alternatives or believe they cannot affect the balance. If so, a small country may decide that it has to fall within the sphere of influence of a great power while hoping that neutrality will preserve some freedom of action. For example, after World War II, Finland was defeated by the Soviet Union and far away from the center of Europe. The Finns felt that neutrality was safer than trying to become part of the European balance of power. They were in the Soviet sphere of influence, and the best they could do was bargain away independence in foreign policy for a large degree of control over their domestic affairs.

Another reason that balance of power predictions are sometimes wrong has to do with perceptions of threat. For example, a mechanical accounting of the power resources of countries in 1917 would have predicted that the United States would join World War I on the side of Germany because Britain, France, and Russia had 30 percent of the industrial world's resources while Germany and Austria had only 19 percent. It did not happen that way because the Americans perceived the Germans as militarily stronger and the aggressor in the war and because the Germans underestimated America's military potential.

Perceptions of threat are often influenced by the *proximity* of the threat. A neighbor may be weak on some absolute global scale, but threatening in its region or local area. Consider Britain and the United States in the 1890s: Britain could have fought, but instead chose to appease the United States. It gave in on many things, including the building of the Panama Canal, which allowed the United States to improve its naval position. One reason is that Britain was more worried about its neighbor Germany than it was about the distant Americans. The United States was larger than Germany but proximity affected which threat loomed larger in British eyes. Proximity also helps explain the alliances after 1945. The United States was stronger than the Soviet Union, so why didn't Europe and Japan ally with the Soviet Union against the United States? The answer lies partly in the proximity of the threat. From the point of view of Europe and Japan, the Soviets were an immediate threat and the United States was far away. The Europeans and the Japanese called in the distant power to rebalance the situation in their immediate neighborhood. The fact that proximity often affects how threats are perceived qualifies any predictions based on simple mechanical toting up of power resources.

Another exception to balance of power predictions relates to the growing role of economic interdependence in world affairs. According to a balance of power policy, France should not wish to see Germany grow, but because of economic integration, German growth stimulates French growth. French politicians are more likely to be reelected when the French economy is growing. Therefore, a policy of trying to hold back German economic growth would be foolish because the French and German economies are so interdependent. In economic considerations, there are often joint gains that would be lost by following too simple a balance of power policy.

Finally, ideology will sometimes cause countries to join the top dog rather than the underdog. Even in Thucydides's day, democratic city-states were more likely to align with Athens and oligarchies with Sparta. Britain's appeasement of the United States in the 1890s, or the Europeans joining with the Americans in an alliance of democracies after 1945, owed something to the influence of ideology, as well as to the proximity of the threat. On the other hand, we must be careful about predicting too much from ideology, because it often leads to colossal mistakes. Many Europeans believed that Stalin and Hitler could not come together in 1939 because they were at opposite ends of the ideological spectrum; but balance of power considerations led

STRUCTURE OF THE PRE-WORLD WAR I
BALANCE OF POWER

1815–1870	Loose Multipolarity
1870–1907	Rise of Germany
1907–1914	Bipolarity of Alliances

them to an alliance against the countries in the middle of the ideological spectrum. Likewise, in the 1960s, the United States mistakenly treated China, the Soviet Union, Vietnam, and Cambodia as similar because they were all communist. A policy based on balance of power would have predicted that those communist states would balance each other (as they eventually did), which would have been a less expensive way to pursue stability in the East Asian region.

Balance of Power as Multipolar Systems

The third way in which the term *balance of power* is used is to describe multipolar historical cases. Europe in the nineteenth century is sometimes held up as the model of a moderate multipolar balance of power system. Historians such as Edward Gulick use the term *classical balance of power* to refer to the European system of the eighteenth century. In this sense, a balance of power requires a number of countries, usually five or six, that follow a set of rules of the game which are generally understood. Since this use of the term balance of power refers to historical systems, we look at the two dimensions of systems, *structure* and *process,* which we introduced in Chapter 2. It is true that the multipolar balance of power system in the nineteenth century produced the longest interval without world war in the modern state system—1815 to 1914—but we should not romanticize or oversimplify a complex story.

The structure of the nineteenth-century European balance of power changed toward the end of the century. From 1815 to 1870, there were five major powers that often shifted alliances to prevent any one from dominating the Continent. From 1870 to 1907, there were six powers after the unification of Germany and Italy, but the growing strength of Germany eventually led to the problems that brought about the end of the system. As we have seen, from 1907 to 1914, the two alliance systems polarized into tight blocs whose loss of flexibility contributed to the onset of World War I.

In terms of process, the nineteenth-century balance of power system divides into five periods. At the Congress of Vienna, the states of Europe brought France back into the fold and agreed on certain rules of the game to equalize the players. From 1815 to 1822, these rules formed the "Concert of Europe." The states concerted their actions, meeting frequently to deal with disputes and to maintain an equilibrium. They accepted certain interventions to keep governments in power domestically when their replacements might lead to a destabilizing reorientation of policy. This became more difficult with the rise of nationalism and democratic revolutions, but a truncated concert persisted from 1822 to 1854. This concert fell apart

PROCESS OF THE PRE-WORLD WAR I BALANCE OF POWER	
1815–1822	Concert of Europe
1822–1854	Loose Concert
1854–1870	Nationalism and the Unification of Germany and Italy
1870–1890	Bismarck's Balance of Power
1890–1914	The Loss of Flexibility

in mid-century when the revolutions of liberal nationalism challenged the practices of providing territorial compensation or restoring governments to maintain equilibrium. Nationalism became too strong to allow such an easy cutting up of cheeses.

The third period in the process, from 1854 to 1870, was far less moderate and was marked by five wars. One, the Crimean War, was a classic balance of power war in which France and Britain prevented Russia from pressing the declining Ottoman Empire. The others, however, were related to the unification of Italy and Germany. Political leaders dropped the old rules and began to use nationalism for their expedient purposes. Bismarck, for example, was not an ideological German nationalist. He was a deeply conservative man who wanted Germany united under the Prussian monarchy. But he was quite prepared to use nationalist appeals and wars to defeat Denmark, Austria, and France in bringing this about. Once he had accomplished his goals, he returned to a more conservative style.

The fourth period, 1870 to 1890, was the Bismarckian balance of power in which the new Prussian-led Germany played the key role. Bismarck played flexibly with a variety of alliance partners and tried to divert France overseas into imperialistic adventures and away from its lost province of Alsace and Lorraine. He limited German imperialism in order to keep the balancing act in Europe centered on Berlin. Bismarck's successors, however, were not as agile. From 1890 to 1914, there was a balance of power, but flexibility was gradually lost. Bismarck's successors did not renew his treaty with Russia; Germany became involved in overseas imperialism, challenged Britain's naval supremacy, and did not discourage Austrian confrontations with Russia over the Balkans. These policies exacerbated the fears of rising German power, polarized the system, and led to World War I.

Alliances

Balance of power as a multipolar system is intimately related to the concept of alliances. Alliances are formal or informal arrangements that sovereign states enter into with each other in order to ensure their mutual security. An alliance might be motivated by military concerns: Two medium sized states might decide that they will be more secure against threats from a larger state by forming an alliance. Traditionally, military alliances have been one of the focal points of international politics.

States might also ally for nonmilitary reasons. As mentioned earlier, ideology often draws states together, though it can also cause conflicts. Economic concerns might be another reason for an alliance, particularly in those parts of the modern world where purely military concerns are receding.

Alliances collapse for as many reasons as they form, but in general states cease to ally when they come to see each other as threats to their security. That might occur because the regime in one state changes. Where before, the two states might have shared a common ideology, now they are opposed. Thus, China and the United States were allies when the Nationalists were in power before 1949 and enemies after the Communists came to power in 1949. Of course, there may be other reasons for an alliance to end. One state may grow more powerful. It might view the other state as a rival, while the other state might view it as a threat and look for alliances elsewhere to balance that threat.

The hallmarks of Bismarck's alliance system were its flexibility and its complexity. The former made the resulting balance of power system stable because it allowed for occasional crises or conflicts without causing the whole edifice to crumble. Germany was at the center of the system, and Bismarck can be likened to an expert juggler who keeps several balls in the air. If one ball falls, the juggler can continue to keep the others aloft and even bend down to retrieve the errant one.

Yet, complexity was also the system's weakness. When Bismarck was succeeded by leaders less adroit, the alliance system could not be maintained. Rather than channeling conflict away from Germany, as Bismarck did by encouraging France to expend its energies on colonial ventures in Africa, German leaders in the years leading up to 1914 allowed alliances to lapse and tension to grow. Instead of renewing the German entente with Russia, the kaiser let Russia float into an alliance with the British. What was once a fluid, multipolar alliance system gradually evolved into two alliance blocs, with dangerous consequences for European peace.

THE ORIGINS OF WORLD WAR I

World War I killed some 15 million people. In one battle, the Somme, there were 1.3 million killed and wounded. Compare that to 36,000 casualties when Bismarck defeated Austria in 1866. The United States lost about 55,000 each in Korea and in Vietnam. World War I was a horrifying war of trenches, barbed wire, machine guns, and artillery that ground up a generation of Europe's youth. It not only destroyed people, it destroyed three European empires: the German, Austro-Hungarian, and Russian. Until World War I, the global balance of power was centered in Europe. After World War I, Europe still mattered, but the United States and Japan had become major players. World War I also ushered in the Russian Revolution and the beginning of the ideological battles that racked the twentieth century.

How could such an event happen? Prince Bernhard von Bülow, the German chancellor from 1900 to 1909, met with his successor, Bethmann Hollweg, in the chancellor's palace in Berlin shortly after the war broke out. Here is how von Bülow described what he remembered:

> Bethmann stood in the center of the room; shall I ever forget his face, the look in his eyes? There is a picture by some celebrated English painter which shows the wretched scapegoat with a look of ineffable anguish in its eyes, such pain as I now saw in Bethmann's. For an instant we neither of us spoke. At last I said to him,

"Well, tell me, at least, how it all happened." He raised his long, thin arms to heaven and answered in a dull, exhausted voice: "Oh, if I only knew!" In many later polemics on war guilt I have often wished it had been possible to produce a snapshot of Bethmann Hollweg standing there at the moment he said those words. Such a photograph would have been the best proof that this wretched man had never wanted war.[3]

Generations of historians have examined the origins of World War I and tried to explain why war came. As we will see, it is impossible to isolate one cause, but it is possible to break the question down into distinct levels. At each of these levels, the balance of power—as *a multipolar system* and as the *policy* of separate states and individual leaders—is essential to an understanding of the war's outbreak. As the alliance system became less flexible, the balance of power became less multipolar and the likelihood of war increased.

Three Levels of Analysis

Parts of the answer lie at each of the three levels of analysis. Parsimony suggests that we start with the simplest causes, see how much they explain, and go on to more complexity as needed. Thus we look first at the system level explanations, both the structure and the process; then at the domestic societal level; and finally turn to the individuals. Then we use counterfactual thought experiments to see how the pieces fit together in an explanation of World War I.

At the structural level, there were two key elements: the rise of German power and the increased rigidity in the alliance systems. The rise of German power was truly impressive. German heavy industry surpassed that of Great Britain in the 1890s, and the growth of German GNP at the beginning of the century was twice that of Great Britain's. In the 1860s, Britain had one-quarter of the world's industrial production, but by 1913 that had shrunk to 10 percent, and Germany's share had risen to 15 percent. Germany transformed some of its industrial strength into military capability, including a massive naval armaments program. As a result of the increase in Germany's power, Britain began to fear becoming isolated. Britain began to worry about how it would defend its far-flung empire. These fears were exacerbated in the Boer War by German sympathy for the Boers, the Dutch settlers in South Africa, against whom Britain was fighting at the end of the century.

In 1907, Sir Eyre Crowe, permanent secretary of the British foreign office, wrote a document famous in the history of British foreign policy, a long memorandum in which he tried to interpret German foreign policy. He concluded that although German policy was vague and confused, Britain clearly could not allow one country to dominate the continent of Europe. Crowe argued that the British response was nearly a law of nature.

Britain's response to Germany's rising power contributed to the second structural cause of the war: the increasing rigidity in the alliance systems in Europe. In 1904, parting from its geographically semi-isolated position as a balancer off the coast of Europe, Britain moved toward an alliance with France. In 1907, the Anglo-French partnership broadened to include Russia and became known as the Triple Entente. Germany, seeing itself encircled, tightened its relations with Austria-Hungary. As the alliances became more rigid, diplomatic flexibility was lost. No more were there the

Either Germany is definitely aiming at a general political hegemony and maritime ascendency, threatening the independence of her neighbours and ultimately the existence of England;

Or Germany, free from any such clear-cut ambition, and thinking for the present merely of using her legitimate position and influence as one of the leading Powers in the council of nations, is seeking to promote her foreign commerce, spread the benefits of German culture, extend the scope of her national energies, and create fresh German interests all over the world wherever and whenever a peaceful opportunity offers. . . . It will, however, be seen, upon reflection, that there is no actual necessity for a British Government to determine definitely which of the two theories of German policy it will accept. For it is clear that the second scheme (of semi-independent evolution, not entirely unaided by statecraft) may at any stage merge into the first, or conscious-design scheme. Moreover, if ever the evolution scheme should come to be realized, the position thereby accruing to Germany would obviously constitute as formidable a menace to the rest of the world as would be presented by any deliberate conquest of a similar position by "malice aforethought."

—Eyre Crowe, Memorandum, January 1, 1907[4]

shifting alignments that characterized the balance of power during Bismarck's day. Instead, the major powers wrapped themselves around two poles.

What about changes in the process? The structural shift to bipolarity affected the process by which the nineteenth-century balance of power system had worked. In addition, there were three other reasons for the loss of moderation in the early twentieth-century balance of power. These included transnational ideas that were common to several countries. One was the rise of nationalism. In Eastern Europe there was a movement calling for all Slavic-speaking peoples to come together. Pan-Slavism threatened both the Ottoman and Austro-Hungarian Empires, which each had large Slavic populations. A nationalistic hatred of Slavs arose in Germany. German authors wrote about the inevitability of the Teutonic-Slavic battles and schoolbooks inflamed nationalist passions. Nationalism proved to be stronger than socialism when it came to bonding working classes together, and stronger than the capitalism that bound bankers together. Indeed, it proved stronger than family ties among the monarchs. Just before the war broke out, the kaiser wrote to the czar and appealed to him to avoid war. He addressed his cousin as "Dear Nicky" and signed it "Yours, Willie." The kaiser hoped that because war was impending over the assassination of a fellow royal family member, the Austrian Archduke Franz Ferdinand, the czar would see things the same way he did. But by then nationalism had overcome any sense of aristocratic or monarchical solidarity, and that family telegram had no effect at all.

A second cause for the loss of moderation in the early twentieth-century balance of power was a rise in complacency about peace. For 40 years, the great powers had not been involved in a war in Europe. There had been crises—in Bosnia in 1908, in Morocco again in 1911, and the Balkan wars in 1912, but they had been mastered. However, the diplomatic compromises caused frustration. Afterward,

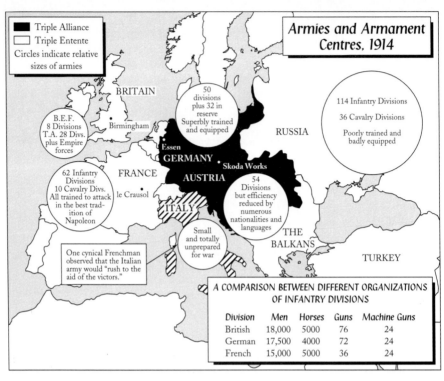

Armies and Armament Centres, 1914

Triple Alliance (black)
Triple Entente (white)
Circles indicate relative sizes of armies

BRITAIN

B.E.F.
8 Divisions
T.A. 28 Divs.
plus Empire forces

Birmingham

50 divisions plus 32 in reserve. Superbly trained and equipped

RUSSIA

114 Infantry Divisions
36 Cavalry Divisions
Poorly trained and badly equipped

Essen
GERMANY

Skoda Works

FRANCE

AUSTRIA

62 Infantry Divisions
10 Cavalry Divs.
All trained to attack in the best tradition of Napoleon

le Crausol

ITALY

54 Divisions but efficiency reduced by numerous nationalities and languages

THE BALKANS

TURKEY

Small and totally unprepared for war

One cynical Frenchman observed that the Italian army would "rush to the aid of the victors."

A COMPARISON BETWEEN DIFFERENT ORGANIZATIONS OF INFANTRY DIVISIONS

Division	Men	Horses	Guns	Machine Guns
British	18,000	5000	76	24
German	17,500	4000	72	24
French	15,000	5000	36	24

Navies and Naval Bases, 1914

✠ German naval base
▲ Allied naval base
Triple Alliance (black)
Triple Entente (white)
(Italy did not fight on Germany's side in 1914 and later joined the allies)

Scapa Flow

Rosyth
BRITAIN *North Sea*
Heligoland
Harwich
Plymouth
Portsmouth
Brest

Baltic Sea

Kiel Konigsberg
Wilhelmshaven

RUSSIA

Atlantic Ocean

FRANCE

GERMANY

AUSTRIA

ITALY

THE BALKANS

Sevastopol
Black Sea

Toulon

Mediterranean Sea

Gibraltar

Malta

Type	Br.	Ger.
Dreadnoughts	20	13
Older Battleships	40	22
Battlecruisers	8	5
Cruisers	58	7
Light Cruisers	44	34
Destroyers & MTBs	300	144
Submarines*	78	28

*Notice that even here Britain had a marked numerical advantage

Figure 3.1

there was a tendency to ask, "Why should my side back down? Why didn't we make the other side give up more?" There was growing acceptance of social Darwinism. Charles Darwin's ideas of survival of the fittest made good sense as a statistical construct about genetics of natural species over generations, but they were misapplied to human society and unique events. Darwin's ideas were used to justify the view that "the strong *should* prevail." And if the strong should prevail, why worry about peace? Long wars seemed unlikely, and many leaders believed that short decisive wars won by the strong would be a welcome change.

A third contributor to the loss of flexibility in the early twentieth-century balance of power was German policy. As Eyre Crowe said, it was vague and confusing. There was a terrible clumsiness about the kaiser's policy. The Germans were no different in having "world ambitions," but they managed to press them forward in a way that antagonized everybody at the same time—just the opposite of the way Bismarck played the system in the 1870s and 1880s. The Germans antagonized the British by starting a naval arms race. They antagonized the Russians over issues in Turkey and the Balkans; and they antagonized the French over a protectorate in Morocco. The kaiser tried to shock Britain into a friendship, believing that if he scared Britain enough, it would realize how important Germany was and the need for good relations with Germany. Instead, he scared the British into the arms of the French, first, and then of the Russians. So by 1914, the Germans felt they had to break out of this encirclement and thereby deliberately accepted the risk of war. Thus the rise of nationalism, increased complacency, social Darwinism, and German policy all contributed to the loss of moderation in the process of the international system and helped contribute to the onset of World War I.

The second level of analysis provides a look at what was happening in domestic society and politics. At that level, there is one explanation we can safely reject: Lenin's argument that the war was caused by the financial capitalists. In Lenin's view, World War I was simply the final stage of capitalist imperialism. But the war did not arise out of imperialist conflicts on the colonial peripheries as Lenin had expected. In 1898, Britain and France confronted each other at Fashoda in the Sudan as the British tried to complete a north-south line from South Africa to Egypt, while the French tried to create an east-west line of colonies in Africa. If war had occurred then, it might have fit Lenin's explanation. But, in fact, the war broke out 16 years later in Europe, and the bankers' activity on the eve of World War I strongly resisted it. Bankers believed that the war would be bad for business. Sir Edward Grey, the British foreign minister, felt he had to follow Eyre Crowe's advice and that Britain had to prevent Germany from gaining mastery of the balance of power in Europe, but Grey worried about getting the London bankers to go along with declaring war.

We can reject the Leninist explanation, but there are two other domestic causes that need to be taken more seriously. One was the internal crises of the declining Austro-Hungarian and Ottoman Empires; the other was the domestic political situation in Germany.

Both Austria-Hungary and Ottoman Turkey were multinational empires and were therefore threatened by the rise of nationalism. In addition, the Ottoman government was very weak, very corrupt, and an easy target for nationalist groups in the Balkans that wanted to free themselves from centuries of Turkish rule. The Balkan wars of 1912 pushed the Turks out, but in the next year the Balkan states then fell to war among themselves in dividing the spoils. The wars whetted the appetite of some Balkan states to fight Austria: If the Turks could be pushed out, then why not the Austrians too?

Serbia took the lead among the Balkan states. Austria feared disintegration from this nationalistic pressure and worried about the loss of status that would result. In the end, Austria went to war against Serbia not because of the assassination of its Archduke Franz Ferdinand by a Serbian terrorist, but because Austria wanted to weaken Serbia and prevent it from becoming a magnet for nationalism among the Balkan Slavs. General Conrad, the Austrian chief of staff, exposed his motives very clearly: "For this reason, and not as vengeance for the assassination, Austria-Hungary must draw the sword against Serbia. . . . The monarchy had been seized by the throat and had to choose between allowing itself to be strangled, and making a last effort to prevent its destruction."[5] Disintegration of an empire because of nationalism was the real precipitating cause of the war; Franz Ferdinand was a pretext.

Another important domestic level explanation lay in the domestic politics of Germany. German historian Fritz Fischer and his followers argue that the German social problems were a key cause of the war. According to Fischer, Germany's efforts toward world hegemony were an attempt by the German elites to distract attention from the poor domestic integration of German society. According to this school of thought, Germany was ruled by a domestic coalition of landed aristocrats and some very large industrial capitalists, called the Coalition of Rye and Iron. This ruling coalition used expansionist policies to provide foreign adventures instead of domestic reform, circuses in place of bread. Expansionism was an alternative to social democracy. This is not sufficient to explain World War I, but it does help to explain the source of the pressure that Germany put on the international system after 1890.

What about the first level of analysis, the role of individuals? What distinguished the leadership on the eve of World War I was its mediocrity. The Austro-Hungarian emperor, Franz Josef, was a tired old man who was putty in the hands of General Conrad and Count Berchtold, the duplicitous foreign minister. Ironically, Franz Ferdinand, the crown prince who was assassinated at Sarajevo, would have been a restraining force, for the potential heir had liberal political views. In Russia, Czar Nicholas II was an isolated autocrat who spent most of his time resisting change at home. He was served by incompetent foreign and defense ministers and was strongly influenced by his sickly and neurotic wife. Most important was the kaiser, who had a great sense of inferiority. He was a blusterer, a weak man and extremely emotional. He led Germany into a risky policy without any skill or consistency. To quote von Bülow:

> William II did not want war, if only because he did not trust his nerves not to give way under the strain of any really critical situation. The moment there was danger, his majesty would become uncomfortably conscious that he could never lead an army into battle. He was well aware that he was neurasthenic. His more menacing jingo speeches were intended to give the foreigner the impression that here was another Frederick the Great or Napoleon.[7]

GERMANY'S REACTION TO BRITAIN'S DECLARATION OF WAR

Edward VII [the kaiser's uncle and former king of England] in the grave is still stronger than I, who am alive! And to think there have been people who believed England could be won over or pacified with this or that petty measure!!! . . . Now this whole trickery must be ruthlessly exposed and the mask of Christian pacifism roughly and publicly torn from the face [of Britain], and the pharisaical sham peace put in the pillory!! And our consuls in Turkey and India, agents and so forth, must fire the whole Mohammedan world to fierce revolt against this hateful, lying, unprincipled nation of shopkeepers; for if we are to bleed to death, England will at least lose India.

—Kaiser Wilhelm II[6]

Personality did make a difference. There was something about the leaders, the kaiser in particular, that made them significant contributory causes of the war. The relationship among some of the systemic, societal, and individual causes are illustrated in Figure 3.2.

Was War Inevitable?

When there are several causes, each of which could be sufficient, we call a situation *overdetermined.* If World War I was overdetermined, does that mean it was inevitable? The answer is no, war was not inevitable until it actually broke out in August 1914. And even then it was not inevitable that four years of carnage had to follow.

Let us distinguish three types of causes in terms of their proximity in time to the event we are studying. The most remote are deep causes, then come intermediate causes, and those immediately before the event are precipitating causes. By analogy, ask how the lights came to be on in your room. The precipitating cause is that you flicked the switch, the intermediate cause is that someone wired the building, and the deep cause is that Thomas Edison discovered how to deliver electricity. Another anology is building a fire: The logs are the deep cause, the kindling and paper the intermediate cause, and the actual striking of the match is the precipitating cause.

In World War I, the deep causes were changes in the structure of the balance of power and certain aspects of the domestic political systems. Especially important reasons were the rise of German strength, the development of a bipolar alliance system, the rise of nationalism and the resultant destruction of two declining empires, and German politics. The intermediate causes were German policy, the rise in complacency about peace, and the personal idiosyncrasies of the leaders. The precipitating cause was the assassination of Franz Ferdinand at Sarajevo by a Serbian terrorist.

Looking back, things always look inevitable. Indeed, we might say that if it had not been the assassination, it would have been some other incident. Some say that precipitating events are like trolley cars: They come along every ten minutes. Thus the specific event at Sarajevo was not all that important; some incident would probably have occurred sooner or later. This type of argument can be tested by counterfactual

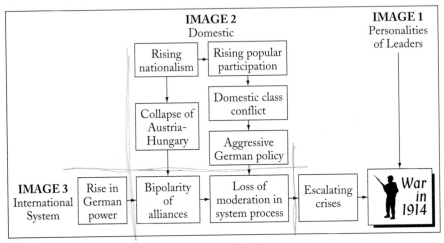

Figure 3.2   Three images of the causes of World War I

history. We can ask "what if" and "what might have been" as we look carefully at the history of the period. What if there had been no assassination in Sarajevo? What if the Social Democrats had come to power in Germany? There is also the issue of probability. Given the deep and intermediate causes, there was a high probability of war, but a high probability is not the same as inevitability. Using the metaphor of the fire again, logs and kindling may sit for a long time and never be lit. Indeed, if it rains before somebody comes along with a match, they may not catch fire even when a Sarajevo occurs.

Suppose there had been no Sarajevo in 1914, and no crisis occurred until 1916; what might have happened? One possibility is that the growth in Russian strength might have deterred Germany from recklessly backing Austria. In 1914, General von Moltke and Foreign Secretary Jagow, two of the German leaders who were most influential in precipitating the war, believed that war with Russia was inevitable. They knew that Germany would have a problem fighting a war on two fronts and would have to knock out one side before fighting the other. Russia, although larger, was technologically backward and had a poor transportation system, so it could be put off for the second strike. Germany ought first to rush westward to knock out the French. After victory in the west, Germany could turn east and take its time to beat the Russians. Indeed, that was the Schlieffen Plan, the war plan of the German general staff, which called for a rapid sweep through Belgium (violating Belgian neutrality in the process) to knock out France quickly, and then to turn east.

But this strategy might have become obsolete by 1916 because Russia was using French money to build railroads. In the 1890s, it would have taken the Russians two or three months before they could have transported all their troops to the German front, giving Germany ample time to fight France first. By 1910, that time had shrunk to 18 days, and the German planners knew they no longer had a large margin of safety. By 1916, the margin would have been gone and Germany might have had to drop its two-front strategy. Some German leaders thought that a war in 1914 was better than a war later. They wanted to seize the crisis to wage and win a preventive war.

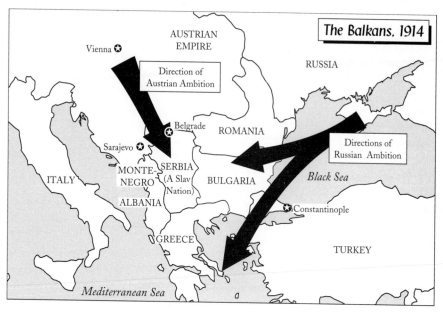

The Balkans, 1914

AUSTRIAN EMPIRE

Vienna ✪

Direction of Austrian Ambition

RUSSIA

✪ Belgrade

ROMANIA

Sarajevo ✪

Directions of Russian Ambition

ITALY

MONTE-NEGRO

SERBIA (A Slav Nation)

BULGARIA

Black Sea

ALBANIA

✪ Constantinople

GREECE

TURKEY

Mediterranean Sea

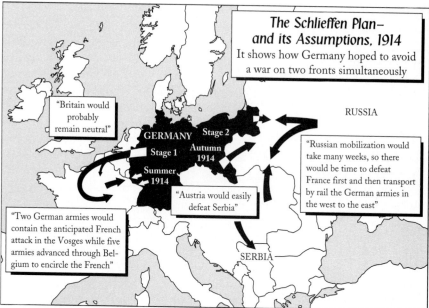

The Schlieffen Plan – and its Assumptions, 1914
It shows how Germany hoped to avoid a war on two fronts simultaneously

"Britain would probably remain neutral"

RUSSIA

GERMANY

Stage 2

Stage 1

Autumn 1914

Summer 1914

"Russian mobilization would take many weeks, so there would be time to defeat France first and then transport by rail the German armies in the west to the east"

"Austria would easily defeat Serbia"

"Two German armies would contain the anticipated French attack in the Vosges while five armies advanced through Belgium to encircle the French"

SERBIA

Figure 3.3

If there had been no assassination and crisis in 1914, and the world had made it to 1916 without a war, it is possible that the Germans might have felt deterred, unable to risk a two-front war. They might have been more careful before giving Austria a blank check, as they did in 1914. Or they might have dropped the Schlieffen Plan and concentrated on a war in the east only. Or they might have come to terms with Great Britain or changed their view that the offense had the advantage. In summary, in another two years, a variety of changes related to Russian strength might have prevented the war. Without war, German industrial strength would have continued to grow. Ironically, without war, the British historian A. J. P. Taylor has speculated, Germany might have won mastery over Europe. Germany might have become so strong that France and Britain would have been deterred.

We can also raise counterfactuals about what might have happened in Britain's internal affairs if two more years had passed without war. In *The Strange Death of Liberal England,* historian George Dangerfield tells of Britain's domestic turmoil. The Liberal Party was committed to getting out of Ireland while the Conservatives, particularly in Northern Ireland, were bitterly opposed. There was a prospect of mutiny in the British army. If the Ulster Revolt had developed, it is quite plausible that Britain would have been so internally preoccupied, it would not have been able to join the coalition with France and Russia. Certainly many historically significant changes could have occurred in two more years of peace.

What Kind of War?

Another set of counterfactuals raises questions about what *kind* of a war would have occurred rather than whether some war would have occurred. It is true that Germany's policies frightened its neighbors and that Germany in turn was afraid of being encircled by the Triple Entente, so it is reasonable to assume that some war was more likely than not. But what kind of war? The war did not have to be what we now remember as World War I. Counterfactually, four other wars were possible.

One was a simple local war. Initially, the kaiser expected a replay of the Bosnian crisis of 1908–1909 when the Germans backed the Austrians, and Austria was therefore able to make Russia stand down in the Balkans. On July 5, 1914, the kaiser promised full support to Austria-Hungary. And with that, he went on vacation. When the kaiser returned from his cruise, he found that the Austrians had filled in the blank check he left them by issuing an ultimatum to Serbia. When he realized that, the kaiser made great efforts to keep the war from escalating, thus the Nicky-Willie telegrams referred to earlier. If his efforts had been successful, we might today recall not World War I, but merely a little Austrian-Serbian War of August 1914.

A second counterfactual possibility was a one-front war. When the Russians mobilized their troops, the Germans also mobilized. The kaiser asked General von Moltke whether he could limit the preparations to just the eastern front. Von Moltke replied that it was impossible because any change in the timetables for assembling the troops and supplies would create a logistical nightmare. He told the kaiser that if he tried to change the plans, he would have a disorganized mass instead of an army. However, after the war, General von Staab of the railway division of the German army admitted that it might have been possible after all to have altered the mobilization schedules successfully. Had the kaiser known that and insisted, there might have been a one-front war.

A third counterfactual is to imagine a two-front war without Britain: Germany and Austria versus France and Russia. If the British had not been there to make the difference, Germany might well have won. It is possible that Britain might not have joined if Germany had not invaded Belgium, although Belgium was not the main cause of Britain entering the war. For some people, like Sir Edward Grey and the Foreign Office, the main reason for entering the war was the danger of German control of the Continent. But Britain was a democracy, and the Liberal Party in the Cabinet was split. The left Liberals opposed war, but when Germany swept through Belgium and violated Belgian neutrality, it allowed the prowar Liberals to overcome the reluctance of the antiwar Liberals and to repair the split in the British Cabinet.

Finally, a fourth counterfactual is a war without the United States. By early 1918, Germany might have won the war if the United States had not tipped the military balance by its entry in 1917. One of the reasons the United States became involved was the German submarine campaign against Allied and American shipping. There was also some German clumsiness: Germany sent a message, now known as the Zimmerman telegram, instructing its embassy in Mexico to stir up trouble against Americans there, and the United States regarded this as a hostile act. These factors ensured that the United States would enter the war.

Our counterfactual analysis first suggests ways in which the war might not have occurred in 1914, and second, ways in which the war that occurred did not have to become four years of carnage, which destroyed Europe as the heart of the global balance of power. It suggests that World War I was probable, but not inevitable. Human choices mattered.

The Funnel of Choices

History is path-dependent. Events close in over time, degrees of freedom are lost, and the probability of war increases. But the funnel of choices available to leaders might open up again, and degrees of freedom could be regained (see Figure 3.4). If we start in 1898 and ask what was the most likely war in Europe, the answer would have been war between France and Britain, which were eyeball-to-eyeball in a colonial dispute in Africa. But after the British and French formed the Entente in 1904, and included the Russians in 1907, a Franco-British war looked less likely. The first Moroccan crisis in 1905 and the Bosnian crisis in 1908 made war with Germany look more likely. But some interesting events occurred in 1910. Bethmann Hollweg, the German chancellor, sought détente with Britain. Britain implied that it would remain neutral in any European war if Germany would limit its navy. At that same time, it looked as if renewed colonial friction between Britain and Russia in Asia and between the British and the French threatened a collapse or erosion of the Triple Entente. In other words, in 1910 the funnel of choices started to widen again.

But the funnel closed once more in 1911 with the second Moroccan crisis. When France sent troops to help the Sultan of Morocco, Germany demanded compensation in the French Congo and sent a gunboat to Agadir on the coast of Morocco. Britain prepared its fleet. French and German bankers lobbied against

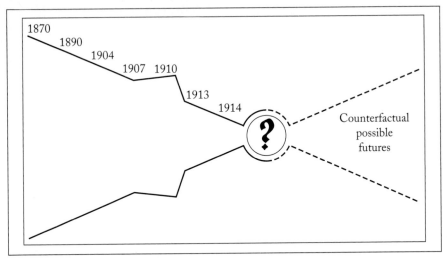

Figure 3.4   The narrowing funnel of choices

war, and the kaiser pulled back. But these events deeply affected public opinion and raised fears about German intentions.

Although the Balkan wars in 1912 and 1913 and the increased pressure on Austria set the scene for 1914, there was also a renewed effort at détente in 1912. Britain sent Lord Haldane to Berlin, and the British and Germans agreed on a number of the issues. Also, by this time it was clear that Britain had won the naval arms race. Perhaps the funnel would open up again.

In June 1914, the feeling that relations were improving was strong enough for Britain to send four of its great Dreadnought battleships to Kiel, Germany, for a state visit. If Britain had thought war was about to occur, the last thing it would have done was put four of its prime battleships in an enemy harbor. Clearly, the British were not thinking about war at that point. In fact, on June 28, British and German sailors were walking together along the quay in Kiel when they heard the news that some strange Serbian terrorist had shot an Austrian archduke in a far-away place called Sarajevo. History has its surprises, and "probable" is not the same as "inevitable."

Lessons of History Again

Are there any lessons we can draw from this history? We must be careful about lessons. Analogies can mislead, and many myths have been created about World War I. For example, some say that World War I was an accidental war. World War I was not purely accidental. Austria went to war deliberately. And if there was to be a war, Germany preferred a war in 1914 to a war later. There were miscalculations over the length and depth of the war, but that is not the same as an accidental war.

It is also said that the war was caused by the arms race in Europe. But by 1912, the naval arms race was over, and Britain had won. While there was concern in Europe about the growing strength of the armies, the view that the war was precipitated directly by the arms race is too simple.

On the other hand, there are some valid warnings. One lesson is to pay attention to the process of a balance of power system as well as to its structure or distribution of power. Moderation comes from the process. Stability is not assured by the distribution of power alone. Another useful lesson is to beware of complacency about peace or believing that the next crisis is going to fit the same pattern as the last crisis: 1914 was supposed to be a repeat of the Bosnian crisis of 1908, though clearly it was not. In addition, the experience of World War I suggests it is important to have military forces that are stable in crisis, without any feeling that one must use them or lose them. The railway timetables were not the major determinants of World War I, but they did make it more difficult for political leaders to buy time for diplomacy.

The world in the 1990s is different from the world in 1914 in two important ways: One is that nuclear weapons have made preventive wars disastrous, and the other is that the ideology of war, the acceptance of war, is much weaker. In 1914, war was thought to be inevitable, a fatalistic view compounded by social Darwinism's argument that war should be welcome because it would clear the air like a good fresh storm. On the eve of World War I that was indeed the mood. Winston Churchill's book, *The World in Crisis,* captures this feeling very well:

> There was a strange temper in the air. Unsatisfied by material prosperity, the nations turned fiercely toward strife, internal or external. National passions, unduly exalted in the decline of religion, burned beneath the surface of nearly every land with fierce, if shrouded, fires. Almost one might think the world wished to suffer. Certainly men were everywhere eager to dare.[8]

They dared and they lost, and that is the lesson of 1914.

NOTES

1. Richard Cobden, *The Political Writings of Richard Cobden* (London: T. Fisher Unwin, 1903); reprinted (New York: Kraus Reprint, 1969).
2. Winston Churchill, June 22, 1941, to his private secretary Colville, in Robert Rhodes James, M. P., ed., *Churchill Speaks 1897–1963* (New York: Chelsea House, 1980).
3. Bernhard von Bülow *Memoirs of Prince Von Bülow 1909–1919* (Boston: Little, Brown, 1932), pp. 165–166.
4. G. P. Gooch and Harold Temperly, eds., *British Documents on the Origins of the War, 1898–1914,* Vol. III (London: His Majesty's Stationary Office, 1928).
5. Baron Conrad von Hotzendorff in Sidney Fay, *The Origins of the World War,* Vol. II (New York: Macmillan, 1928), pp. 185–186.
6. Richard Ned Lebow, *Between Peace and War: The Nature of International Crisis* (Baltimore: Johns Hopkins University Press, 1981), p. 139.
7. Ibid., p. 144.
8. Winston Churchill, *The World Crisis* (New York: Scribner's, 1923), p. 188.

SELECTED READINGS

1. Gulick, Edward, *Europe's Classical Balance of Power* (New York: Norton, 1967), pp. 1–34, 184–218.
2. Joll, James, *The Origins of the First World War* (New York: Longman, 1984), pp. 9–147.

3. Kennedy, Paul, "The Kaiser and German *Weltpolitik*," in John Rohl and Nicholas Sombart, eds., *Kaiser Wilhelm II: New Interpretations* (Cambridge, England: Cambridge University Press, 1982), pp. 143–168.

FURTHER READINGS

Fischer, Fritz, *World Power or Decline: The Controversy over Germany's Aims in the First World War* (New York: Norton, 1951).

Kennedy, Paul M., *The Rise of the Anglo-German Antagonism: 1870–1914* (London: Allen & Unwin, 1980).

Kupchan, Charles, *The Vulnerability of Empire* (Ithaca: Cornell University Press, 1994).

Lebow, Richard Ned, *Between Peace and War: The Nature of International Crisis* (Baltimore: Johns Hopkins University Press, 1981).

Maier, Charles S., "Wargames: 1914–1919," in Robert Rotberg and Theodore Rabb, eds., *The Origin and Prevention of Major Wars* (New York: Cambridge University Press, 1989), pp. 249–280.

Miller, Steven, Sean Lynn-Jones, and Stephen Van Evera, eds., *Military Strategy and the Origins of the First World War* (Princeton, NJ: Princeton University Press, 1991).

Organski, A. F. K., and Jacek Kugler, *The War Ledger* (Chicago: University of Chicago Press, 1980).

Rock, Stephen R., *Why Peace Breaks Out: Great Power Rapprochement in Historical Perspective* (Chapel Hill: University of North Carolina Press, 1989).

Sagan, Scott, "1914 Revisited: Allies, Offense, and Stability," *International Security*, Vol. 2, No. 2 (Fall 1986), pp. 151–176.

Snyder, Jack L., *Myths of Empire: Domestic Politics and International Ambition* (Ithaca, NY: Cornell University Press, 1991).

Trachtenberg, Marc, *History and Strategy* (Princeton, NJ: Princeton University Press, 1991), Chapter 2.

Tuchman, Barbara, *The Guns of August* (New York: Macmillan, 1962).

Turner, L. C. F., *The Origins of World War I* (New York: Norton, 1970).

Walt, Stephen, *The Origins of Alliances* (Ithaca: Cornell University Press, 1987).

Williamson, Samuel R., "The Origin of World War I," in Robert Rotberg and Theodore Rabb, eds., *The Origin and Prevention of Major Wars* (New York: Cambridge University Press, 1989), pp. 225–248.

STUDY QUESTIONS

1. Was World War I inevitable? If so, why and when? If not, when and how could it have been avoided?
2. How might you apply Waltz's images to the origins of World War I?
3. Which of the following factors do you consider most significant in explaining the outbreak of World War I?
   a. alliance system
   b. public opinion
   c. military doctrine or military leadership (specify countries)
   d. political leadership (specify countries)
   e. economic pressures or forces

    f. misperception

    g. other

4. Thucydides argues that the underlying cause of the Peloponnesian War was the "growth of Athenian power and the fear which this caused in Sparta." To what extent was World War I caused by the growth of German power and the fear this caused in Britain? Or the growth of Russian power and the fear this caused in Germany?

5. To what extent, if any, was World War I "accidental"? Does it make sense to talk about "accidental" wars? What about "unintended" ones?

6. What might be some "lessons" of 1914 that might help policymakers avoid war today?

CHRONOLOGY: THE ROAD TO WORLD WAR I

1905–1906	First Moroccan crisis: Kaiser visits Tangier as Germany attempts to supplant France; settled to France's satisfaction at the Algeciras conference
1908	Austria proclaims annexation of Bosnia and Herzegovina, Slavic territories it had administered since 1878; Serbia threatens war but powerless without Russian backing; Germany supports Austria-Hungary, deterring Russia
1911	Second Moroccan crisis: German gunboat *Panther* appears at Agadir in attempt to force France into colonial concessions in other areas in return for German recognition of French claims in Morocco
1912	First Balkan War: Bulgaria, Serbia, and Greece defeat Turkey and gain Thrace and Salonika; Austria-Hungary helps create Albania as check to Serbian power
1913	Second Balkan War: Serbia, Greece, and Romania defeat Bulgaria and gain territory at the latter's expense
1914	
June 28	Assassination of Archduke Franz Ferdinand and his wife at Sarajevo
July 5	Austria seeks and obtains German backing against Serbia
July 23	Austria sends harsh ultimatum to Serbia
July 25	Serbia rejects some terms of ultimatum; seeks Russian support
July 26	British Foreign Minister Sir Edward Grey proposes conference to resolve the crisis; Germany and Austria reject proposal
July 28	Austria declares war on Serbia
July 29	Austrian forces bombard Belgrade; Russia mobilizes against Austria
July 30	Russia and Austria order general mobilization; French troops withdraw 10 kilometers from German border
July 31	Germany delivers ultimatum to Russia, demanding demobilization; Russia does not reply
August 1	Germany declares war on Russia; British fleet mobilizes; France mobilizes as German forces invade Luxembourg
August 2	Germany demands unimpeded passage through Belgium
August 3	Belgium rejects German ultimatum; Germany declares war on France
August 4	German troops march into Belgium; Britain declares war on Germany

4

THE FAILURE OF COLLECTIVE SECURITY AND WORLD WAR II

The Allied leaders at Versailles (Woodrow Wilson at right)

THE RISE AND FALL OF COLLECTIVE SECURITY

World War I caused enormous social disruption and shock waves of revulsion at the senseless slaughter. Balance of power politics was widely blamed for the war. Woodrow Wilson, the American president during World War I, was a classic nineteenth-century liberal who regarded balance of power policies as immoral because they violated democracy and national self-determination. In Wilson's view, "The balance of power is the great game now forever discredited. It's the old and evil order that prevailed before this war. World War I was to do away with an old order, one that was unstable. The balance of power is a thing that we can do without in the future."[1]

Wilson had a point, because balance of power policies do not give priority to democracy or peace. As we have seen, the balance of power is a way to preserve the sovereign state system. States act to prevent any state from becoming preponderant. The resulting balance of power is consistent with war or violations of self-determination if that is the only way to preserve independence. However, World War I was so devastating, chaotic, and brutal that many people began to feel that war to preserve the balance of power was no longer tolerable. But if the world could not afford a balance of power system, what would take its place?

Sovereign states could not be abolished, Wilson admitted, but force could be tamed by law and institutions as it was at the domestic level. The liberal solution was to develop international institutions analogous to domestic legislatures and courts so that democratic procedures could be applied at the international level. Some liberals of the day thought that not only was World War I fought to make the world safe for democracy, but in turn democracy could make the world safe. In January 1918, the United States issued a 14-point statement of its reasons for joining in the war. The fourteenth point was the most important. It called for "a general association of nations to be formed under specific covenants for the purpose of affording mutual guarantees of political independence and territorial integrity to great and small states alike."

The League of Nations

Although critics called Wilson a utopian, he believed that organizing international security could be a practical approach to world politics. He knew that mere paper agreements would not be sufficient; organizations and rules were needed to implement the agreements. This was why Wilson put so much faith in the idea of a League of Nations. Moral force was important, but a military force was necessary to back it up. Security had to be a collective responsibility. If all nonaggressive states banded together, the preponderance of power would be on the side of the good. International security would be a collective responsibility in which nonaggressive countries would form a coalition against aggressors. Peace would be indivisible.

How could the states bring about such a new system of collective security? First, make aggression illegal and outlaw offensive war. Second, deter aggression by forming a coalition of all nonaggressive states. If all pledged to aid any state that was a victim anywhere in the world, there would be a preponderance on the side of the nonaggressive forces. Third, if deterrence failed and aggression occurred, all states would agree to punish the state that committed aggression. This doctrine of collective security bore some similarities to balance of power policies in that states tried to deter aggression by developing a powerful coalition and if deterrence failed, they were willing to use force.

But there were three important differences between the collective security and balance of power approaches. First, in collective security, the focus was on the aggressive policies of a state rather than its capacity, whereas in balance of power politics, alliances were created against any state that was becoming too strong; that is, the focus was on the capacity of states. Second, in a collective security system, alliances were not formed in advance, since it would not be known which states would be aggressive. It would be all against one, once the one committed aggression, whereas in balance of power, the alliances were formed in advance. Third, collective security was designed to be global and universal with no neutrals or free riders. If too many countries were neutral, the coalition of the good might appear weak and diminish the coalition's ability to deter or punish the aggressor.

The doctrine of collective security was embodied in the Covenant of the League of Nations, which, in turn, was part of the treaties that ended World War I. Several of the articles of the League of Nations Covenant were especially noteworthy. In Article 10, states pledged to protect all members against aggression. In Article 11, any war or threat of war was declared to be of concern to all states. In Articles 12 and 15, states agreed to submit their disputes to arbitration and not to go to war until three months after arbitration failed. Article 16, the critical article, said that any war disregarding the League of Nations procedures would be regarded as at war against all the members of the League of Nations. The state that started a war would be immediately subject to economic sanctions, and the Council of the League of Nations might recommend further military measures.

This sounds tough, but there were ambiguities. All members had to agree to apply collective security. Thus each state had a veto. When they signed the Covenant, states agreed to abide by Article 16, but in practice, it was up to each state to decide what kinds of sanctions to apply and how to implement them; they were not bound by any higher authority. Thus the League of Nations was not a move toward world government in which a higher authority could commit the member states. It was not the end of the anarchic system of states, but an effort to make the states collectively discipline unruly members of the system.

Collective security involves two related concepts: *sovereignty* and *international law*. The definition of sovereignty is very simple: legal supremacy within a given territory. As championed by state moralists and established by the League of Nations, the sovereignty of the state is absolute and inviolable; a state government has full authority within its borders. It can limit that authority only with its own consent; that is, if a government signs a treaty allowing another government to have some influence in its domains, which is an agreed limitation rather than an invasion of sovereignty. Thus, by signing the pact of the League of Nations, states would voluntarily give up some sovereignty to the international community in return for the guarantees of collective security and international law.

As understood by Wilson and implied in the League of Nations charter, international law transcended national law and hence sovereignty in particular situations. A central tenet of international law is that states are sovereign except that when they violate international law, they are subject to punishment. Collective security was to international law what the police are to domestic law. However, international law enjoyed far less acceptance among states than domestic law. Many states refused to be constrained by international law and saw compliance as voluntary rather than mandatory.

The United States and the League of Nations

The unwillingness of states to relinquish some sovereignty in exchange for collective security lay at the heart of one of the League's most notable weaknesses: the failure of the United States to join its own creation. The American Senate refused to ratify

> My conception of the League of Nations is just this, that it shall operate as the organized moral force of men throughout the world, and that whenever or wherever wrong and aggression are planned or contemplated, this searching light of conscience shall be turned upon them.
>
> —Woodrow Wilson[2]

the Covenant. As a result, the collective security system had to function without what would have been its biggest player.

Why did the United States hold back when, to a large extent, the League was an American liberal plan to reorder world politics? After World War I, most Americans wanted to return to "normalcy." Many defined "normal" as avoiding involvement in international affairs. Opponents claimed that the Monroe Doctrine of 1823 limited American interests to the Western Hemisphere. Opposition to "entangling alliances" went back all the way to George Washington. The leader of the opposition to the League of Nations, Senator Henry Cabot Lodge of Massachusetts, feared that Article 16 of the Covenant would dilute both American sovereignty and the constitutional power of the Senate to declare war. Lodge suspected that the United States might be drawn into distant wars on the basis of the League's decisions to enforce collective security rather than by the Senate's decision or the will of the American people.

The debate between President Wilson and Senator Lodge is sometimes portrayed as a clash between an idealist and a realist, but it can also be seen as a debate between different forms of American moralism. Lodge's isolationism reflected a long-standing American attitude toward the balance of power in Europe: European states do nasty things in the name of balance of power, and Americans are better than that. In fact, however, the United States was able to ignore the balance of power in the nineteenth century because the Americans were enjoying a free ride behind Britain's fleet. Other European countries could not get to the Western Hemisphere to threaten Americans. In fact, the United States was not at all isolationist when it came to interfering in the affairs of its weak neighbors in Central America or Mexico. Americans at the end of World War I were torn between two forms of moralism, and it was the isolationist impulse toward the European balance of power that won. The result was the country that had tipped the balance of power in World War I refused to accept responsibility for the postwar order.

The Early Days of the League

What France wanted more than anything else at the end of World War I were military guarantees that Germany could not rise again. Since the United States would not join the League of Nations, France pressed Britain for a security guarantee and wanted military preparations in case Germany recovered. Britain resisted on the grounds that such an alliance would be against the spirit of collective security because it would identify the aggressor in advance. Moreover, Britain saw France as stronger than Germany, so there was no need for an alliance, even on traditional balance of power terms. Britain said it was important to reintegrate Germany, just as the Congress of Vienna had brought France back into the Concert of Europe at the end of the Napoleonic Wars. War passions had abated more quickly in Britain than in France, and the British felt it was time to appease the Germans by bringing them back into the process.

Unmoved by these arguments, France formed alliances with Poland, which had been reborn at the end of World War I, and with the "Little Entente," the states of Yugoslavia, Czechoslovakia, and Romania that had been created out of the former Austro-Hungarian Empire. The French policy fell between two stools: Not only were these alliances against the spirit of collective security, but they did not do very much for France in terms of the balance of power. Poland was on bad terms with its neighbors and no substitute for Russia, which had been ostracized because of the Bolshevik Revolution. The Little Entente states were destabilized by ethnic problems and domestic divisions.

Germany came out of World War I enormously weakened. It lost 25,000 square miles of territory and 7 million of its population. The Treaty of Versailles forced it to reduce its army to only 100,000 and prohibited it from having an air force. The treaty contained the famous "war guilt clause," which said that Germany caused the war. Since Germany was blamed, Germany should pay. The reparations bill was $33 billion, a sum that Germans thought impossibly high in their damaged position. When the Germans did not pay, France sent troops to occupy the Ruhr industrial area of Germany until the Germans did pay. After engaging in passive resistance, Germany suffered an enormous inflation that wiped out the savings of the middle class. That in turn removed one of the sources of internal stability as the Weimar Republic struggled to create democracy.

Italy had never been keen on the Paris peace treaties or the League of Nations. Italy had originally been allied with Germany and Austria-Hungary, but at the beginning of the war, the Italians decided they would get a better payoff from the Allies and switched sides. In the secret Treaty of London signed in 1915, it was promised compensation at the expense of the part of the Austro-Hungarian Empire that became postwar Yugoslavia. The Italians expected that these promises would be honored, but Woodrow Wilson objected to such old-fashioned spoils of war behavior. In addition, after Mussolini and the fascists took power in 1922, one of the motivating forces in Italian foreign policy was to gain glory: to finally fulfill the destiny of a new Roman Empire.

With such a start, it is remarkable the League was able to do anything at all. Yet, 1924 to 1930 was a period of relative successes. Plans were made to scale down the reparations Germany had to pay. In 1924, governments signed a protocol on the peaceful settlement of disputes in which they promised to arbitrate their differences. Perhaps most important, in 1925, the Treaty of Locarno allowed Germany to enter the League of Nations and gave Germany a seat on its Council.

The Treaty of Locarno had two aspects. In the west, Germany guaranteed that its borders with France and Belgium would be inviolable. Alsace and Lorraine, taken by Bismarck in the War of 1870, had been returned to France by the Treaty of Versailles, and Germany promised to demilitarize a zone along the Rhine. Locarno reaffirmed those results. In the east, Germany promised to arbitrate before pursuing

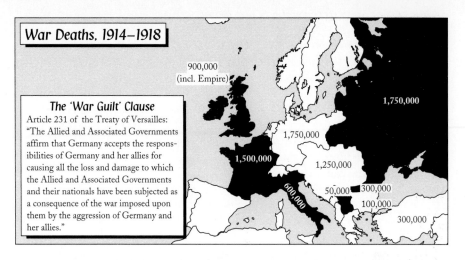

War Deaths, 1914–1918

900,000
(incl. Empire)

1,750,000

1,750,000

1,500,000

1,250,000

600,000

50,000   300,000

100,000

300,000

The 'War Guilt' Clause

Article 231 of the Treaty of Versailles:
"The Allied and Associated Governments
affirm that Germany accepts the responsibilities of Germany and her allies for
causing all the loss and damage to which
the Allied and Associated Governments
and their nationals have been subjected as
a consequence of the war imposed upon
them by the aggression of Germany and
her allies."

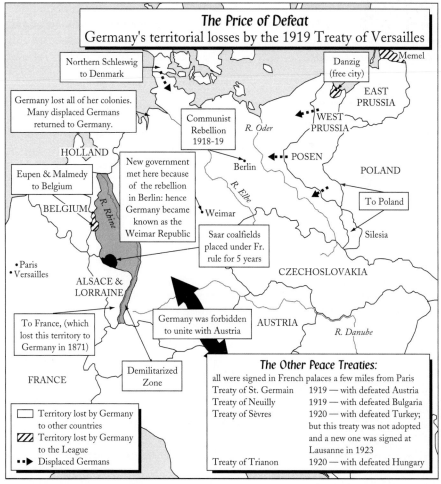

The Price of Defeat
Germany's territorial losses by the 1919 Treaty of Versailles

Memel

Northern Schleswig
to Denmark

Danzig
(free city)

EAST
PRUSSIA

Germany lost all of her colonies.
Many displaced Germans
returned to Germany.

Communist
Rebellion
1918-19

R. Oder

WEST
PRUSSIA

HOLLAND

Berlin

POSEN

POLAND

Eupen & Malmedy
to Belgium

New government
met here because
of the rebellion
in Berlin: hence
Germany became
known as the
Weimar Republic

R. Elbe

To Poland

BELGIUM

R. Rhine

Weimar

Silesia

Saar coalfields
placed under Fr.
rule for 5 years

• Paris
• Versailles

ALSACE &
LORRAINE

CZECHOSLOVAKIA

To France, (which
lost this territory to
Germany in 1871)

Germany was forbidden
to unite with Austria

AUSTRIA

R. Danube

FRANCE

Demilitarized
Zone

□ Territory lost by Germany
  to other countries
▨ Territory lost by Germany
  to the League
■■▶ Displaced Germans

The Other Peace Treaties:

all were signed in French palaces a few miles from Paris

Treaty of St. Germain	1919 — with defeated Austria
Treaty of Neuilly	1919 — with defeated Bulgaria
Treaty of Sèvres	1920 — with defeated Turkey; but this treaty was not adopted and a new one was signed at Lausanne in 1923
Treaty of Trianon	1920 — with defeated Hungary

Figure 4.1

changes in its eastern border with Poland and Czechoslovakia. That second clause should have set off a warning bell, however, for there were now two kinds of borders around Germany—an inviolable part in the west and a negotiable part in the east— but at that time, these agreements looked like progress.

The League managed to settle some minor disputes, such as one between Greece and Bulgaria, and it began a process of disarmament negotiations. Following up on the 1921 Washington Conference, in which the United States, Britain, and Japan had agreed to a measure of naval disarmament, the League organized a preparatory commission for broader disarmament talks. They set the scene for a worldwide conference that finally met (too late) in 1932. In addition, in 1928, states agreed to outlaw war in the Kellogg-Briand Pact, named after the American and French foreign ministers. Most important, the League became a center of diplomatic activity. Although not members, the Americans and the Russians began to send observers to the League meetings in Geneva. The world financial collapse in October 1929 and the success of the National Socialist Party in the 1930 German elections were harbingers of problems to come, yet there was still a sense of progress at the September 1930 annual assembly of the League of Nations. That optimism about the collective security system was dispelled by two crises in the 1930s over Manchuria and Ethiopia.

The Manchurian Failure

The Manchurian episode tested the League, and it failed. To understand the Manchurian case, we must understand the situation in Japan. Japan had transformed itself from a potential victim of imperialist aggression in the mid-nineteenth century to a very successful imperialist by the century's end. Japan defeated Russia in a war of 1904–1905, colonized Korea in 1910, and joined the Allies in World War I. After the war, Japan sought recognition as a major power. Europeans and Americans resisted. At Paris, the Western governments rejected a Japanese proposal that the Covenant of the League affirm the principle of racial equality. In the 1920s, the Americans passed racist laws excluding Japanese immigrants, and Britain ended its bilateral treaty with Japan. Many Japanese felt that just as they were about to enter the club of the great powers, the rules were changed.

China was the other actor in the Manchurian crisis. In the 1920s, China was in chaos, with civil war between regions controlled by different warlords. Manchuria was part of China, though somewhat independent under a separate warlord. The Chinese Nationalist Movement was trying to unify the country, and it bitterly criticized the unequal treaties that had been imposed on China in the imperialist era. As the Chinese Nationalists gained strength in the 1920s, friction with Japan increased. The Nationalists declared a boycott against Japanese goods. Inside Japan, civilian and military factions contended for dominance. As the global economic crisis deepened and friction with China increased, the military faction in Japan gradually increased its strength.

In September 1931, the Japanese army staged an incident along the Manchurian Railway, where they had had a right to station troops since the Russo-Japanese War of 1904–1905. Sabotage on the Manchurian Railway gave the Japanese troops a pretext to take over all of Manchuria. Although Japan said its actions were to protect the Manchurian Railway, it went further and set up a Japanese-controlled puppet state that was called Manchukuo. China appealed to the League of Nations, but Japan prevented passage of a resolution asking it to withdraw its troops. In December, the League agreed to send a committee under the British Lord Lytton to investigate the events in Manchuria.

Lord Lytton finally reported to the League in September 1932, and he rejected Japan's pretext as an unjustified intervention. Although his report recommended that the members of the League of Nations should not recognize the state of Manchukuo, it did not call for applying Article 16 sanctions against Japan. In February 1933, the Assembly of the League of Nations voted 42 to 1 to accept Lytton's report on the Japanese invasion of Manchuria. The one opposing vote was Japan, which then withdrew from the League of Nations. Overall, the Manchurian case showed the procedures of the League of Nations to be slow, cautious, and totally ineffective.

The Ethiopian Debacle

The last great test of the League of Nations's collective security system came in Ethiopia in 1935. This time, sanctions were applied, but the outcome was again failure. Italy had long planned to annex Ethiopia; not only was it near Italy's colonies in Eritrea on the Red Sea, but the fascists felt affronted that the Ethiopians had defeated an Italian effort to colonize them during the imperialist era in the nineteenth century. Fascist ideologists argued that this historic "wrong" should be rectified. Between 1934 and 1935, Italy provoked incidents on the border between Ethiopia and Eritrea. It did so despite the existence of a peace treaty between Ethiopia and Italy, and despite the fact that Italy had signed the Kellogg-Briand Pact outlawing war, and that as a member of the League of Nations, it was committed to arbitrate for three months before doing anything.

In October 1935, Italy invaded Ethiopia. The invasion was a clear-cut case of aggression, and the Council of the League avoided an Italian veto by the procedural device of calling for a special conference to decide what sanctions to impose against Italy. Fifty states attended, and eight days after the invasion the conference recommended to member states that they impose four sanctions: an embargo on the sale of all military goods to Italy; a prohibition against loans to Italy; cessation of imports from Italy; and refusal to sell certain goods that could not be easily bought elsewhere, such as rubber and tin. But three things were missing: Italy was still allowed to buy steel, coal, and oil; diplomatic relations were not broken; and Britain did not close the Suez Canal, through which Italy shipped materials to Eritrea.

Why didn't the members of the League of Nations do more? There was general optimism that sanctions would force Italy to withdraw from Ethiopia. Sanctions certainly had an effect on the Italian economy: Italian exports declined by about one-third during the year, the value of the Italian lira declined, and there were estimates that Italy's gold reserves would be exhausted in nine months. But aside from stinging, sanctions did not cause Mussolini to change his policies toward Ethiopia. The anger of Britain and France over Ethiopia was more than offset by their concern for the European balance of power. Britain and France wanted to avoid alienating Italy because Germany was regaining its strength, and Britain and France thought it would be useful to have Italy in a coalition to balance Germany. In 1934, when it looked as though Hitler would take over Austria, Mussolini moved Italian troops to the Austrian border, and Hitler backed down. The British and French hoped that Mussolini could be persuaded to join a coalition against Germany.

Traditional diplomats did not fight the League of Nations' collective security system; they reinterpreted it. From a balance of power perspective, the last thing they wanted was to become involved in a distant conflict in Africa when there were pressing problems in the heart of Europe. Distant aggression in Africa, said the traditional realists, was not a threat to European security. Conciliation and negotiation were needed to bring the Italians back into the coalition. Not surprisingly, the British and French began to get cold feet about sanctions. Sir Samuel Hoare and Pierre Laval, the British and French foreign ministers, met in December 1935 and drew up a plan that divided Ethiopia into two parts, one Italian and the other a League of Nations zone. When someone leaked this plan to the press, there was outrage in Britain. Accused of having sold out the League of Nations and collective security, Hoare was forced to resign.

But within three months, British opinion turned again. In March 1936, Hitler denounced the Locarno treaties and marched German troops into the demilitarized Rhineland. Britain and France immediately stopped worrying about Ethiopia. They met with Italy to consult about how to restore the balance of power in Europe. The balance of power in Europe prevailed over the application of the collective security doctrine in Africa. In May 1936, the Italians were able to complete their military victory, and by July the sanctions were removed.

The best line in this tragedy was spoken by the Haitian delegate to the League of Nations: "Great or small, strong or weak, near or far, white or colored, let us never forget that one day we may be somebody's Ethiopia."[3] And, within a few years, most European nations were to be victims of Hitler's aggression in World War II. The world's first efforts at collective security were a dismal failure.

THE ORIGINS OF WORLD WAR II

World War II overshadows all other wars in terms of its human costs, estimated to be between 35 and 50 million people. The war was noted for advances in weaponry. Tanks and planes that had just been introduced and played an insignificant role in World War I dominated World War II. Radar played a significant role, for example, in the Battle of Britain, one of the turning points in World War II. And at the end of the war, of course, there was the atomic bomb and the dawn of the nuclear age.

World War II ended with unconditional surrender. Unlike World War I, the Western Allies occupied Germany and Japan and transformed their societies during the occupation. The "German problem" was solved for half a century by dividing Germany. World War II also created the bipolar world in which the United States and the Soviet Union emerged from the conflict much stronger than the rest. The war represented the replacement of Europe as the arbiter of the balance of power. Instead, Europe became an arena where outsiders contended, somewhat like Germany before 1870. The end of World War II created the framework of the world order until 1989.

> Here, it seems to me, is the key to the problem whether Hitler deliberately aimed at war. He did not so much aim at war as expect it to happen, unless he could evade it by some ingenious trick, as he had evaded civil war at home. Those who have evil motives easily attribute them to others; and Hitler expected others to do what he would have done in their place.
>
> —A. J. P. Taylor[4]

Hitler's War?

World War II is often called "Hitler's war." While true, it is too simple. World War II was also old business, Act II of the great war that ended Europe's hegemony in 1918; the interwar period was only an intermission. Hitler wanted war, but not the war we now know as World War II. He wanted a short sharp war, a blitzkrieg. Another reason it was not simply Hitler's war was the war in the Pacific. Hitler had continually, but unsuccessfully, urged the Japanese to attack the British colony of Singapore or to attack Siberia to divert Soviet troops away from Europe. Japan did neither; it surprised Hitler by attacking the American naval base at Pearl Harbor instead. The war in the Pacific, while part of World War II, had its own roots and was more a traditional imperial effort at regional hegemony.

On the other hand, we can go too far in stressing other causes. Some historians have nearly exonerated Hitler. A. J. P. Taylor argues that while Hitler was a terrible person and a very unpleasant adventurer, he was merely an opportunist stepping into the power vacuums created by the appeasement policies of the Western democracies. But Taylor goes too far. For example, Hitler's 1924 book, *Mein Kampf,* set forth a vague plan that Taylor dismisses as Hitler's ranting in resentment of the French invasion of the Ruhr. But Hitler wrote another, secret book in 1928 that repeated many of the arguments in *Mein Kampf.* Even if it was not a detailed plan, it was a clear indication of where he wanted to go.

Taylor also deals too lightly with the "Hossbach memorandum." Colonel Hossbach, an aide to Hitler, took notes at a meeting at Berchtesgaden in 1937 that reported Hitler planning to take territory by 1943, before Germany's preeminence became obsolete. Hitler felt it was important to take opportunities when they arose in the east, and that Austria and Czechoslovakia would be first. Taylor dismisses the importance of this memo by saying that it was not an *official* memorandum. Since Taylor wrote, additional evidence has come to light. We know that Hitler talked often of this timetable and of these objectives. The Hossbach memorandum generally predicted Hitler's actions.

Hitler's Strategy

Hitler had four options after he came to power in 1933, and he rejected three of them. He could have chosen passivity, accepting Germany's international position. He could have tried expansion through economic growth (like Japan after World War II) and led Germany to international influence through industrial expansion.

He could have limited his goals to revision of the Versailles treaty and regained some of Germany's 1918 losses. By the 1930s, the Western democracies were sensitive to the injustice of blaming Germany for *all* of World War I. But these three strategies were rejected by Hitler, who chose instead a breakout. In his view, Germany, stuck in the middle of Europe, could not live forever encircled. It had to gain land. He would go east for living space, expand his base, and at a later stage go for a larger world role.

Hitler followed this fourth option through four phases. First, he set out to destroy the Versailles framework by a very clever set of diplomatic maneuvers. In October 1933, he withdrew from the League of Nations and from the disarmament conference that the League had convened. He blamed the withdrawal on the French, who he said were not willing to cut their forces in the disarmament conference, thereby making it impossible for Germany to continue in the League or the conference. In January of 1934, he signed a treaty with Poland, disrupting the arrangements France had been trying to make with Poland and the smaller Eastern European states. In March 1935, Hitler denounced the military clauses of the Versailles treaty, saying Germany would no longer be restricted to an army of 100,000. Instead he announced plans to triple the army and build an air force.

The British, French, and Italians met at Stresa (in Italy) to respond to Hitler's activities, but before they could get organized, Hitler offered Britain negotiations on a naval treaty. Britain leapt at the opportunity, thereby disrupting any coordinated response from the Stresa meeting. In March 1936, when events in Ethiopia diverted attention from central Europe, Hitler moved his troops into the Rhineland, which had been demilitarized by the Locarno Pact. He blamed France for forcing him to do this. He said France had destroyed the Locarno treaty by developing an arrangement with the Soviet Union. He dropped hints that he might return to the League of Nations after the other states in Europe accepted his views about the revisions of the Versailles treaty, a clever maneuver that played on guilt and uncertainty in the Western democracies.

The second phase (1936 to 1940) was Hitler's expansion into the small neighboring countries. In 1936, Hitler laid out a four-year economic plan for a military buildup in order to be ready for war by 1940. He signed the Axis Pact with Italy and an anti-Comintern (the Communist International) pact with Japan. He also intervened on the side of the fascists in the Spanish civil war. Hitler justified sending troops to support the fascist general Francisco Franco in Spain's civil war as part of the protection of the West against the threat of bolshevism. In 1938, Chancellor Schuschnigg of Austria called for a plebiscite on whether Austria should reunite with Germany, hoping that the Austrian people would vote against it before Hitler forced it upon them. But Hitler intervened. German troops marched into Vienna, ending Austrian independence.

Czechoslovakia was next. Hitler pressured Czechoslovakia by pushing the issue of national self-determination for the 3 million Germans in the Sudetenland section of Czechoslovakia. This area where Czechoslovakia borders Germany was militarily important because it included the Bohemian massif, the natural line of defense for Czechoslovakia and the logical place for Czechs to start their defense against potential German attack. Hitler argued that the post–World War I settlement that put these German-speaking people in Czechoslovakian territory was a violation of their self-determination and another example of the perfidy of the Western countries. He demanded the German-speaking territory be permitted to leave Czechoslovakia to join the German fatherland. The Czechs became worried and mobilized portions of their reserves. That infuriated Hitler, who vowed to crush Czechoslovakia.

These events also alarmed Britain, which did not want war to break out in Europe. Neville Chamberlain, the British prime minister, made three trips to Germany to try to stave off the war. Chamberlain believed that it was not possible for Britain to defend Czechoslovakia because of the distance and because Britain had no troops on the Continent. More important, he did not think Czechoslovakia was worth war and he knew that Britain was not ready for war. Air power was becoming more significant, fear of bombing campaigns was growing, and Chamberlain realized that the British air defense and radar systems were not ready for an air war. For this combination of reasons, Chamberlain met with Hitler at Munich in September 1938 and agreed to the partition of Czechoslovakia, giving the Sudetenland to Germany if Hitler would promise to leave the rest of Czechoslovakia alone. Hitler promised, and Chamberlain returned to Britain claiming that he saved Czechoslovakia and achieved "peace in our time."

Only six months later, in March 1939, German troops rolled into the rest of Czechoslovakia and took the capital city, Prague. A shocked Britain realized Hitler might seek further conquests and that his next target might be Poland. Divided in the eighteenth century, Poland was recreated as a state after World War I and given a corridor to the port of Danzig on the Baltic Sea, though the area included German-speaking people. Once again, Hitler used the same tactics. He claimed that having German-speaking people inside Polish territory was a violation of self-determination, another example of the perfidy of the Versailles system. This time, Britain and France tried to deter Hitler by issuing a guarantee to defend Poland.

Hitler then pulled off a brilliant diplomatic coup. Despite having said he would protect the West against bolshevism, Hitler suddenly signed a treaty with Stalin in August 1939. The pact gave Hitler a free hand to do what he wanted in the west. It also included a secret protocol for another partition of Poland. Stalin and Hitler each agreed to take a part. Hitler seized his part by starting a war against Poland on September 1, 1939. This time, he was not looking for another Munich agreement in which the British would step in and give him part of Poland in return for promises of moderation.

Phase three was short. Hitler achieved military mastery on the Continent in 1940. After Hitler took Poland, things were temporarily quiet; this period was called the "phony war." Hitler expected Britain to sue for peace. In the spring of 1940, however, Hitler feared that Britain was going to move troops to Norway. He preempted a British landing in Norway by sending his troops there first. Then he launched his blitzkrieg into Holland, Belgium, and France. Sending his tanks through the supposedly impenetrable Ardennes Forest, Hitler took the French and British by surprise. He had skirted the Maginot line of French fortifications that lined most of the French border with Germany. He drove the British troops back to Dunkirk, where they had to leave their equipment and evacuate what was left of the

> Now Poland is in the position in which I wanted her. . . . I am only afraid that at
> the last moment some swine or other will submit to me a plan for mediation.
>
> —Adolf Hitler, August 27, 1939[5]

men across the Channel. Thus Hitler became master of the European continent west of the Soviet Union through a brilliant set of moves in 1940.

The fourth phase, "the phase of overreaching," unleashed the full-scale war. Hitler had long wanted to move east against the Soviet Union. But he wanted to dispose of Britain first to avoid the possibility of a war on two fronts. If he could gain air supremacy, he could then cross the Channel and invade Britain. But Hitler's air force was defeated in the Battle of Britain. Unable to gain air supremacy, Hitler was faced with a conundrum: Should he put off his plans to attack the Soviet Union?

Hitler decided to attack the Soviet Union even though he had been unable to defeat Britain, thinking that he could beat Stalin quickly and then go at Britain once again. Furthermore, he would have deprived the British of any potential alliance with the Soviet Union. In June 1941, Hitler attacked the Soviet Union, a massive mistake. In December 1941, after the Japanese attacked Pearl Harbor, he made another huge mistake: He declared war on the United States. Hitler did this to keep Japan locked into the war, since he had been urging Japan to join him, and he took the occasion to unleash his U-boat campaign against American shipping. In doing so, he also unleashed the global war that ended his Third Reich.

The Role of the Individual

What role did Hitler's personality play? It was probably not the crucial factor in the first phase. The Western democracies were so guilt-ridden, weak, and internally divided that any clever German nationalist probably would have been able to revise the Versailles system. But the second and third phases that brought mastery over Europe depended on Hitler's skill, audacity, and bellicose ideology. He often overruled his conservative generals and staff. Hitler wanted war and was willing to take risks. The fourth phase, which brought on global war and failure, is also attributable to two aspects of Hitler's personality. First, Hitler's appetite grew with the eating. He was convinced of his own genius, but that conviction led him to two crucial mistakes: invading the Soviet Union before he finished off Britain and declaring war on the United States, which gave Franklin Roosevelt, the American president, a pretext to become engaged in a war in Europe as well as in the Pacific.

Hitler's other great flaw was his racist ideology, which deprived him of critical assets. For example, when Germany first invaded the Soviet Union, many Ukrainians and others revolted against Stalin's brutality. But Hitler regarded them as Slavic underpeople, unworthy of an alliance with him against Stalin. He also thought the United States was weak because of its population of blacks and Jews. He used to joke about Roosevelt having a Jewish ancestor. He failed to understand that American pluralism could be a source of strength. Moreover, his anti-Semitism led him to expel some of the scientists crucial to developing the atomic bomb. In

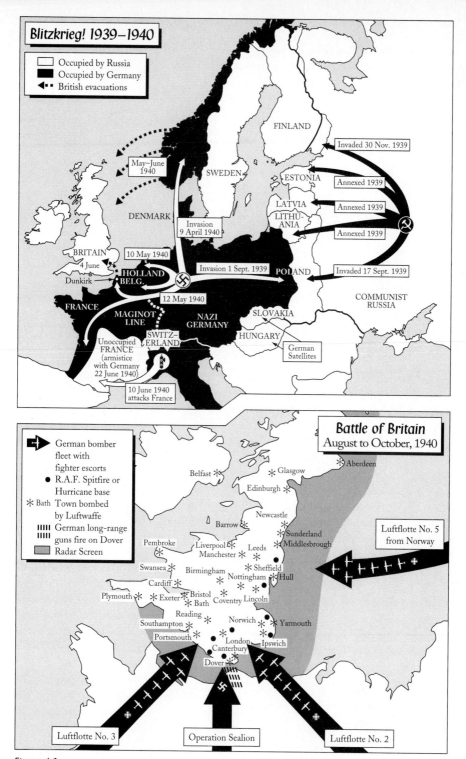

Blitzkrieg! 1939–1940

Occupied by Russia
Occupied by Germany
British evacuations

FINLAND

Invaded 30 Nov. 1939

SWEDEN

ESTONIA

Annexed 1939

May–June 1940

DENMARK

LATVIA
LITHU-
ANIA

Annexed 1939

Annexed 1939

Invasion 9 April 1940

BRITAIN
4 June

10 May 1940

Dunkirk

HOLLAND
BELG.

Invasion 1 Sept. 1939

POLAND

Invaded 17 Sept. 1939

COMMUNIST
RUSSIA

FRANCE

MAGINOT
LINE

12 May 1940

SWITZ-
ERLAND

NAZI
GERMANY

SLOVAKIA

HUNGARY

German
Satellites

Unoccupied
FRANCE
(armistice
with Germany
22 June 1940)

10 June 1940
attacks France

Battle of Britain
August to October, 1940

German bomber
fleet with
fighter escorts

● R.A.F. Spitfire or
Hurricane base

✳ Bath Town bombed
by Luftwaffe

⦀ German long-range
guns fire on Dover

Radar Screen

Belfast ✳

Glasgow ✳

Aberdeen ✳

Edinburgh ✳

Newcastle

Barrow ✳

Sunderland ✳
Middlesbrough ✳

Luftflotte No. 5
from Norway

Pembroke
✳

Liverpool ✳
Manchester ✳

Leeds
✳

Sheffield ✳

Swansea ✳

Birmingham ✳

Nottingham ✳ Hull ✳

Cardiff ✳

Coventry Lincoln

Plymouth ✳

✳ Exeter ✳ Bristol
✳ Bath

Reading
✳

Southampton ✳

Norwich ✳ Yarmouth ✳

Portsmouth ✳

London
Canterbury

Ipswich

Dover ✳ ⦀

Luftflotte No. 3

Operation Sealion

Luftflotte No. 2

Figure 4.2

short, an individual was one of the crucial causes of World War II. The kind of war it was and its outcome depended very much on Hitler.

Systemic and Domestic Causes

Of course, there were also other causes. World War II was more than just Hitler's war, and that is the value of A. J. P. Taylor's interpretation. There were systemic causes, both structural and procedural. At the structural level, World War I did not solve the German problem. The Versailles treaty was both too harsh because it stirred up German nationalism and too lenient because it left the Germans the capability to do something about it. Furthermore, the absence of the United States and the Soviet Union from the balance of power until very late in the game meant that Germany was not deterred. In addition, the process of the international system was immoderate. Germany was a revisionist state bound on destroying the Versailles treaty system. In addition, the growth of ideologies, the great "isms" of fascism and communism, engendered hatreds and hindered communication in the 1930s.

Three domestic level changes were also particularly important. First, the Western democracies were torn apart by class cleavages and ideological disputes. Coordinated foreign policymaking was nearly impossible. For example, when Leon Blum, a French socialist, came to power after 1936, French conservatives used the slogan, "Better Hitler than Blum." In 1939, the British conservative government sent a mission to Moscow to see whether they could sign a treaty with Stalin, but both the mission and the government were internally divided. Before they decided, Hitler had beat them to it. One reason for the delay was the British upper-class reluctance to deal with communists.

A second domestic-level cause of the war was economic collapse. The Great Depression was systemic in the sense that it affected all countries and grew out of the inability of the major capitalist states to establish effective international economic coordination to deal with imbalances in transnational trade and financial flows. But the depression had powerful effects on domestic politics and class conflict. The enormous amount of unemployment had the political effect of pouring gas on a fire: It contributed to the Nazi takeover in Germany and weakened the governments of the democracies.

The third domestic cause was the U.S. policy of isolationism. The United States came out of World War I with the world's strongest economy, but it refused to accept the responsibilities of that position. In the 1930s, the Great Depression increased internal preoccupation and deepened isolationism. In his first term, President Franklin Roosevelt, along with other Americans, paid little attention to Europe. After his reelection in 1936, Roosevelt began to realize that if Hitler became too strong, he might dominate Europe and eventually threaten the United States. In 1937, Roosevelt began to speak about events in Europe, but the American public did not want to get involved. In 1940, Roosevelt traded destroyers to the British in return for base rights on British territories in the Western Hemisphere. In 1941, he persuaded Congress to approve "lend-lease" war supplies to Britain to prevent it from being defeated by Hitler. However, Roosevelt was limited by domestic opinion on how far he could go in resisting Hitler. Only Japan's attack on Pearl Harbor and Hitler's declaration of war ended America's isolationism.

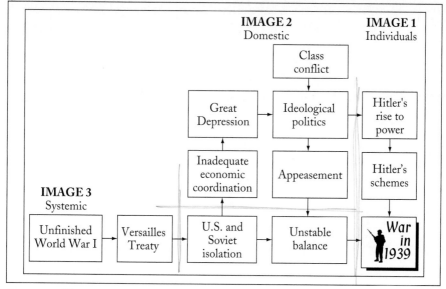

Figure 4.3 Three images of the causes of World War II in Europe

How do these domestic, personal, and systemic causes fit together? We could say that the deep causes of World War II were systemic—the unfinished business of World War I. The intermediate causes were largely domestic—the social and ideological disruptions that produced Hitler in Germany and the weakness in the democracies. The precipitating cause was Adolf Hitler's strategy for domination (see Figure 4.3).

Was War Inevitable?

Was a second world war inevitable? No, but it became increasingly likely as time passed. In 1918, there was already some probability of a second world war. In 1926 (after the Locarno treaties), that probability diminished, but after the Great Depression in 1929 and Hitler's ascent to power in 1933, the funnel of choices closed down until the war became global in 1941 (see Figure 4.4).

The failure of World War I to solve the German problem meant there was some probability of a second war already in 1918. If the Western democracies had chosen to appease Germany in the 1920s, however, the democratic government of the Weimar Republic might have been preserved. Or if the United States had signed the Treaty of Versailles and stayed in Europe to preserve the balance of power (as it did after 1945), Hitler might not have risen to power. There might have been some war in Europe, but not necessarily the global World War II. In the 1930s, the shock of the economic depression fueled the rise of ideologies that glorified aggression, which made war more likely.

Counterfactually, suppose Britain and France had confronted Germany and made an alliance with the Soviet Union early in the 1930s. Or imagine that the United States had joined the League of Nations. Hitler might have been deterred or

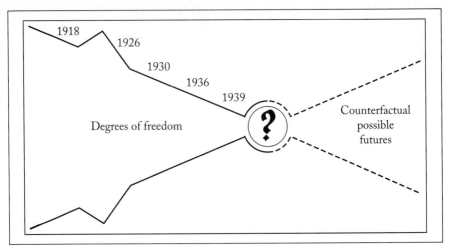

Figure 4.4   The narrowing funnel of choices in Europe

delayed. He might not have had such dramatic early successes and might have been overthrown by his own generals, who several times had contemplated such a coup. But since these things did not happen, Hitler's personality and strategy became the key precipitating cause. By the late 1930s, once Hitler began to plan war, it became almost inevitable. Even so, some historians believe that if France and Britain had launched an offensive in September 1939, they might have defeated Germany.

The Pacific War

The war in the Pacific had separate origins. Japan was a much more traditional society and not so deeply involved in European events. In the 1920s, Japan was far from being a perfect democracy, but it did have a parliamentary system. In the 1930s, the military and extreme nationalists gained control of the government. Their policy of imperialist expansion was widely popular. Japan had always worried about being prevented from obtaining the raw materials it had to import. When the depression of the 1930s cut Japan's trade, the Japanese feared that if they did not change their situation, they would face a bleak future. The Japanese tried to create a regional hegemony, which they called the Greater East Asia Co-Prosperity Sphere (a wonderful euphemism for conquest of one's neighbors). Japan believed the sphere would allow them to resist threats from Britain and the United States, who were still major naval powers in the Pacific.

Japan first expanded at the expense of China. The brutal war in China brought Japan into diplomatic conflict with the United States, which supported China. After France fell to Hitler in 1940, the Japanese took advantage of the opportunity to seize the French colonies in Southeast Asia, Vietnam, and Cambodia. At this point, the Japanese expansionists had three options. One was to strike westward against the Soviet Union. Since there had already been clashes between Japanese and Soviet forces along the border in Manchuria, some people thought a Japanese-Soviet war along the Manchurian border was most likely. The second option for the Japanese was to strike south, for although they had already taken the French colonies in Southeast Asia, the biggest prize was the Dutch East Indies (today's Indonesia), which had the oil Japan needed. Option three was to strike east against the United States, by far the riskiest of the three options.

The Japanese eventually chose both options two and three. On December 7, 1941, they struck east against the United States and south toward Indonesia and the Philippines. While the move south was for raw materials, the attack on the United States is more difficult to explain. Given the disparity in power resources, the Japanese knew that they could not ultimately win a war against the United States, but they hoped that the surprise attack on Pearl Harbor would so demoralize the United States that full-scale war would never erupt. That was a miscalculation on the part of the Japanese, but from the perspective of the Japanese government, it was the wisest available option.

By the fall of 1941, Japanese expansionists no longer considered the Soviet Union a viable target. Hitler's attack on the Soviet Union had removed the Soviet threat to Japan, and until the last weeks of World War II, Japan and the USSR maintained a neutrality of convenience. At the same time, the Americans tried to deter the Japanese from striking south by putting an embargo on oil shipments to Japan. As President Roosevelt put it, "The U.S. would slip a noose around Japan's neck and give it a jerk now and then." Assistant Secretary of State Dean Acheson was quoted at the time as saying this would not lead to war because "no rational Japanese could believe that an attack on us could result in anything but disaster for his country."[6] But the Japanese felt that if they did not go to war, they would eventually suffer defeat in any case. With 90 percent of their oil imported, they calculated that their navy could not last for even a year if they were cut off; therefore they concluded that it was better to go to war than to be slowly strangled.

In addition, the United States demanded that Japan withdraw from China. The Japanese believed this would cut them off from the area they viewed as their economic hinterland. As a Japanese military officer explained to Emperor Hirohito, the situation was like that of a patient with a serious illness: "An operation, while it might be extremely dangerous, would still offer some hope of saving his life."[7] From their point of view, it was *not* totally irrational for Japan to go to war because it was the least bad of the alternatives they saw. If Germany defeated Britain and American opinion was discouraged by the suddenness of the attack, there might be a negotiated peace. A poorly reasoned form of the Japanese leaders' mood was expressed by Vice Army Chief of Staff Tsukuda:

> In general, the prospects if we go to war are not bright. We all wonder if there isn't some way to proceed peacefully. There is no one who is willing to say, "Don't worry, even if the war is prolonged, I will assume all responsibility." On the other hand, it is not possible to maintain the status quo. Hence, one unavoidably reaches the conclusion that we must go to war.[8]

Of course, Japan had the option of reversing its aggression in China and Southeast Asia, but that was unthinkable for the military leaders. Thus on December 7, 1941, the Japanese bombed Pearl Harbor.

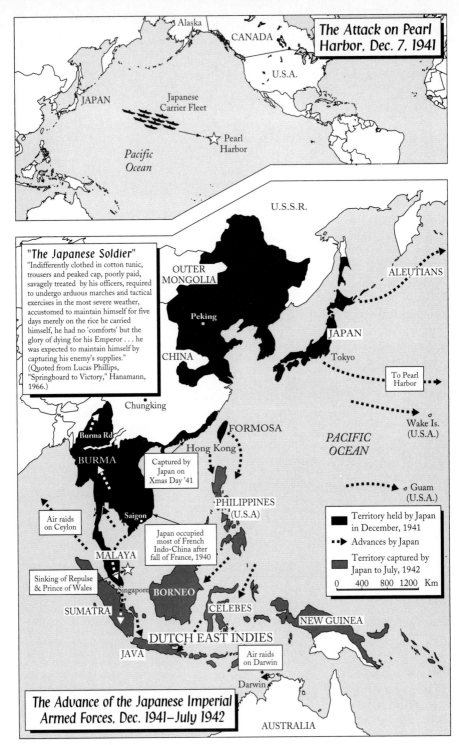

The Attack on Pearl Harbor, Dec. 7, 1941

Alaska

CANADA

JAPAN

Japanese
Carrier Fleet

U.S.A.

☆ Pearl
Harbor

*Pacific
Ocean*

U.S.S.R.

"The Japanese Soldier"
"Indifferently clothed in cotton tunic, trousers and peaked cap, poorly paid, savagely treated by his officers, required to undergo arduous marches and tactical exercises in the most severe weather, accustomed to maintain himself for five days merely on the rice he carried himself, he had no 'comforts' but the glory of dying for his Emperor . . . he was expected to maintain himself by capturing his enemy's supplies."
(Quoted from Lucas Phillips, "Springboard to Victory," Hanamann, 1966.)

OUTER
MONGOLIA

ALEUTIANS

Peking

JAPAN

Tokyo

To Pearl
Harbor

CHINA

Chungking

FORMOSA

*PACIFIC
OCEAN*

Wake Is.
(U.S.A.)

Burma Rd

Hong Kong

BURMA

Captured by
Japan on
Xmas Day '41

Guam
(U.S.A.)

Air raids
on Ceylon

Saigon

PHILIPPINES
(U.S.A)

Japan occupied
most of French
Indo-China after
fall of France, 1940

■ Territory held by Japan
in December, 1941

∙■▶ Advances by Japan

▒ Territory captured by
Japan to July, 1942

MALAYA

0   400   800 1200 Km

Sinking of Repulse
& Prince of Wales

Singapore

BORNEO

CELEBES

NEW GUINEA

SUMATRA

DUTCH EAST INDIES

JAVA

Air raids
on Darwin

Darwin

**The Advance of the Japanese Imperial
Armed Forces, Dec. 1941–July 1942**

AUSTRALIA

Figure 4.5

> Even if we should make concessions to the United States by giving up part of our national policy for the sake of a temporary peace, the United States, its military position strengthened, is sure to demand more and more concessions on our part; and ultimately our empire will lie prostrate at the feet of the United States.
>
> —Records of Japan's 1941 Policy Conferences

What about the three levels of analysis as applied to the Pacific War? The *role of the individual* is certainly less pronounced than it was with Hitler in Europe, but individual policymakers nonetheless influenced the trajectory of events. In Japan, expansionist generals and admirals wanted to increase Japan's regional dominance and actively sought an expanded war, west to China, south to Singapore, Indonesia, and the Philippines, and east to U.S. possessions in the Pacific. Military leaders such as Hideki Tojo played a leading role in determining government policy. However, Tojo supported policies identical to many other high-ranking military and political leaders. While Hitler was also supported by many of the leading generals and industrialists in Germany, he made decisions largely on his own. In Japan, there was a greater diffusion of power at the top and decisions were more the result of consensus amongst the political and military elite.

The role of the individual was also important for determining U.S. policy. Franklin Roosevelt was willing to impose punitive sanctions in response to Japanese aggression in Southeast Asia, but many in Congress and throughout the country were uneasy with Roosevelt's activist and confrontational foreign policy. There was still strong isolationist sentiment in the United States in 1940 and 1941, and many people still rejected U.S. involvement in international politics. If someone like Senator Burton Wheeler of Montana or Hiram Johnson of California had been president, the United States might have tried to appease Japanese aggression rather than confront it, and consequently, Japan may never have felt the need to attack the United States. Of course, Japanese aggression would then have been unchecked, and Japan would have established itself as the regional power in the western Pacific.

In terms of *systemic and domestic causes,* we have seen how at a domestic level, the increased militarism of Japan's government made war more likely. And as with Europe in the 1930s, the economic collapse in both Japan and the United States affected the foreign policies of both countries. Japan became more expansionist, while until 1940, the United States became even more isolated. In addition, the domestic chaos in Nationalist China in the 1930s made China more susceptible to Japanese expansion, which in turn increased the influence of the militarists within Japanese domestic politics.

At the system level, the Versailles treaty had left the ambitions of Japan in China unsated, while the economic problems of the 1930s made it more difficult for Japan to obtain its needed raw materials by trade alone. And the breakdown between 1931 and 1933 of the already weak League of Nations' collective security system in Asia removed any institutional constraints on Japan's imperial ambitions. Unlike the war in Europe, both the deep and intermediate causes of the war in the Pacific were largely domestic—the shift toward expansion in Japan, toward greater isolationism in the United States, and the chaos of 1930s China. The precipitating causes were the decision of Roosevelt to implement a full embargo in July 1941 and the resulting decision of the Japanese military to attack the United States on December 7.

Appeasement and Two Types of War

What lessons can we draw from this? Some say that the key lesson of the 1930s is the evil of *appeasement*. But appeasement is not bad per se; it is a classic tool of diplomacy. It is a policy choice to allow for changes in the balance of power that benefit a rival state. Rather than attempting to deter or contain the aggression of adversaries, a state might decide that it is preferable to allow its adversaries modest gains. On the eve of the Peloponnesian War, Corinth argued to the Athenians that it should be allowed to absorb Corcyra. The Athenians, however, refused to appease Corinth and chose instead to fight. Given subsequent events, it is possible that Athens would have done better to appease Corinthian ambitions than to challenge them over Corcyra. Appeasement was used successfully in 1815 when the victorious powers appeased the defeated but still strong France. In the 1890s, Britain appeased the rising United States. We could even argue that appeasement might have been the right policy for the Western Allies to have taken toward Germany in the 1920s. One of the great ironies of the interwar period is that the West confronted Germany in the 1920s when it should have been appeased and appeased Germany in the 1930s when it should have been confronted.

Appeasement was the wrong approach to Hitler, but British Prime Minister Neville Chamberlain was not such a coward as the Munich experience makes him out to be. He wanted to avoid another World War I. In July 1938, he said,

> When I think of those four terrible years and I think of the 7 million young men who were cut off in their prime and 13 million who were maimed and mutilated, the misery and suffering of the mothers and fathers, sons and daughters, I must say that there are no winners in a war, but all losers. It is those thoughts which make me feel that it is my prime duty to strain every nerve to avoid repetition of the Great War in Europe.[9]

Chamberlain's sins were not his intentions, but his ignorance and arrogance in failing to appraise the situation properly. And in that failure, he was not alone.

World Wars I and II are often cast as two quite different models of war: accidental war versus planned aggression. World War I was an unwanted spiral of hostility. To some extent, it might have been avoided with appeasement. As political scientist David Calleo has said, "The proper lesson is not so much the need for vigilance against aggressors, but the ruinous consequences of refusing reasonable accommodation of upstarts."[10] World War II was not an unwanted spiral of hostility—it was a failure to deter Hitler's planned aggression. In that sense, the policies appropriate for preventing World Wars I and II were almost opposite. Appeasement of Germany might have helped forestall World War I and deterrence of Germany might have prevented World War II, but the policies were reversed. In trying to avoid a repetition of World War I, British leaders in the 1930s helped to bring on World War II. At the same time, the efforts of U.S. leaders to deter Japan helped to bring on war in the Pacific. Deterrence failed because the Japanese felt cornered in a situation where the alternative of peace looked worse than losing a war.

Of course, these two models of war are too simple. World War I was not purely accidental, and World War II, in the Pacific at least, was not merely Hitler's planned aggression. The ultimate lesson is to be wary of overly simple historical analogies. Always ask whether a model is true to the facts of history and whether it really fits the current reality. It helps to remember the story of Mark Twain's cat. As Twain pointed out, a cat that sits on a hot stove will not sit on a hot stove again, but neither will it sit on a cold one. It is necessary to know which stoves are cold and which are hot when using historical analogies or political science models based on World Wars I and II.

NOTES

1. Woodrow Wilson in Ray S. Baker and William E. Dodd, eds., *The Public Papers of Woodrow Wilson,* Vol. I (New York: Harper, 1925), pp. 182–183.

2. Quoted in Inis L. Claude, *Power and International Relations* (New York: Random House, 1962), p. 104.

3. Quoted in F. P. Walters, *A History of the League of Nations* (London: Oxford University Press, 1952), p. 653.

4. A. J. P. Taylor, *The Origins of the Second World War,* 2nd ed. (Greenwich: Fawcett, 1961), p. 281.

5. Adolf Hitler on August 27, 1939, in Gordon Craig, *Germany, 1866–1945* (New York: Oxford University Press, 1978), p. 712.

6. Quoted in Scott Sagan, "The Origins of the Pacific War," in Robert Rotberg and Theodore Rabb, eds., *The Origin and Prevention of Major Wars* (New York: Cambridge University Press, 1989), pp. 335, 336.

7. Sagan, "The Origins of the Pacific War," p. 325.

8. Quoted in Scott Sagan, "Deterrence and Decision: An Historical Critique of Modern Deterrence Theory" (Ph.D. thesis, Harvard University, 1983), p. 280.

9. Neville Chamberlain, *In Search of Peace: Speeches 1937–38* (London: Hutchinson, n.d.), p. 59.

10. David P. Calleo, *The German Problem Reconsidered: Germany and the World Order, 1870 to the Present* (Cambridge, England: Cambridge University Press, 1978), p. 6.

SELECTED READINGS

1. Ross, Graham, *The Great Powers and the Decline of the European States System, 1919–1945* (London: Longman, 1983), pp. 109–126.

2. Bell, P. M. H., *The Origins of the Second World War in Europe* (London: Longman, 1986), pp. 14–38.

3. Sagan, Scott, "The Origins of the Pacific War," *Journal of Interdisciplinary History,* Vol. 18, No. 4 (Spring 1988), pp. 893–922.

4. Taylor, A. J. P., *The Origins of the Second World War* (London: Hamilton, 1961), pp. xi–xxviii, 102–109, 272–278.

5. Bullock, Alan, "Hitler and the Origins of the Second World War," in W. R. Louis, ed., *The Origins of the Second World War: A. J. P. Taylor and His Critics* (New York: Wiley, 1972), pp. 117–145.

FURTHER READINGS

Barkin, J. Samuel, and Bruce Cronin, "The State and the Nation: Changing Norms and the Rules of Sovereignty," *International Organization* (Winter 1994), pp. 107–130.

Barnhart, Michael A., *Japan Prepares for Total War* (Ithaca, NY: Cornell University Press, 1987).

Bell, P. M. H., *The Origins of the Second World War in Europe* (London: Longman, 1986).

Bullock, Alan, *Hitler: A Study in Tyranny* (New York: Harper & Row, 1964).

Carr, E. H., *The Twenty Years' Crisis 1919–1939: An Introduction to the History of International Relations* (London: Macmillan, 1940).

Claude, Inis L., *Power and International Relations* (New York: Random House, 1962).

Heinrichs, Waldo, Jr., *Threshold of War: Franklin D. Roosevelt and American Entry into World War II* (New York: Oxford University Press, 1988).

Hilderbrand, Klaus, *Foreign Policy of the Third Reich,* trans. Anthony Fothergill (Berkeley: University of California Press, 1973).

Hughes, Jeffrey, "The Origins of World War II in Europe: British Deterrence Failure and German Expansionism," in Robert Rotberg and Theodore Rabb, eds., *The Origin and Prevention of Major Wars* (Cambridge, England: Cambridge University Press, 1989), pp. 281–322.

Iriye, Akira, *The Origins of the Second World War in Asia and the Pacific* (London: Longman, 1987).

Jervis, Robert, Richard Ned Lebow, and Janice Gross Stein, *Psychology and Deterrence* (Baltimore: Johns Hopkins University Press, 1985).

Middlemas, Keith, *The Strategy of Appeasement: The British Government and Germany* (Chicago: Quadrangle, 1962).

Ross, Graham, *The Great Powers and the Decline of the European States System, 1914–1945* (London: Longman, 1983).

Storry, Richard, *A History of Modern Japan* (Baltimore: Penguin, 1960).

Utley, Jonathan, *Going to War with Japan, 1937–1941* (Knoxville: University of Tennessee Press, 1985).

Walters, F. P., *A History of the League of Nations* (London: Oxford University Press, 1952).

Wolfers, Arnold, *Discord and Collaboration: Essays on International Politics* (Baltimore: Johns Hopkins University Press, 1962).

STUDY QUESTIONS

1. What "lessons" of World War I did policymakers draw at the time? How did it affect their behavior in the interwar period?

2. How did the concept of collective security differ from balance of power politics? Is the notion of collective security utopian? If not, how might collective security have worked better during the interwar period?

3. Was World War II inevitable? If so, why and when? If not, when and how could it have been avoided?

4. To what extent can the outbreak of World War II be attributed to the personalities of the leaders involved?

5. What might be some lessons of the interwar period that might help policymakers avoid war today?

6. Was Japan irrational to attack the United States?

CHRONOLOGY: BETWEEN THE WORLD WARS

1919	Peace Conference opens at Versailles; adoption of Weimar Constitution
1920	Creation of the League of Nations
1921–1922	Washington conference on naval armaments
1922	Permanent Court of Justice at the Hague established; Treaty of Rapallo between Germany and the Soviet Union; Mussolini assumes power in Italy
1923	France and Belgium occupy the Ruhr in response to German default on coal deliveries; Nazi Beer Hall *Putsch* aborted
1924	Dawes Plan for reparations accepted; Geneva Protocol for the peaceful settlement of international disputes adopted
1925	Locarno Conference and treaties
1926	Germany admitted to the League of Nations
1928	Kellogg-Briand Pact signed
1930	London Naval Conference
1931	Japanese invasion of Manchuria; failure of the Austrian Credit-Anstalt; Bank of England forced off the gold standard
1932	Disarmament conference; Lausanne Conference on German reparations
1933	Adolf Hitler becomes chancellor of Germany; Reichstag fire; Enabling Act passed establishing Nazi dictatorship; Germany withdraws from the disarmament conference and League of Nations
1934	Soviet Union joins the League of Nations
1935	Germany renounces the disarmament clauses of the Versailles treaty; Franco-Russian alliance formed; Anglo-German naval agreement reached; Italian invasion of Ethiopia; Hoare-Laval Pact
1936	Germany renounces Locarno Pacts and reoccupies the Rhineland; Italy wins the war in Ethiopia; League of Nations discredited as a political instrument; Rome-Berlin axis formed; Anti-Comintern Pact formed
1936–1939	Civil war in Spain
1937	Hostilities begin between China and Japan
1938	German invasion and annexation of Austria; Chamberlain meets Hitler at Berchtesgaden, Godesberg, and Munich to resolve the German-Czech crisis; Munich agreement signed
1939	Crisis in Czechoslovakia; Germany occupies all of Czechoslovakia; British and French pledges to Poland and guarantees to Greece and Romania; Italy invades Albania; German-Russian Pact; Germany invades Poland; Britain and France declare war on Germany
1940	Hitler invades France; Battle of Britain; Japan occupies French Indochina
1941	Hitler invades Soviet Union; Japan attacks Pearl Harbor

THE COLD WAR

Winston Churchill, Franklin Roosevelt, and Josef Stalin at Yalta

Given its violent first half, a most remarkable feature of the second half of the twentieth century was the absence of World War III. Instead, there was a *cold war*, a period of intense hostility without actual war. The hostility was so intense that many expected armed conflict between the superpowers. Fighting occurred, but it was on the peripheries and not directly between the United States and the Soviet Union. The Cold War lasted four decades, from 1947 to 1989. The height of the Cold War was from 1947 to 1963, when there were few serious negotiations between the United States and the Soviet Union. There were not even any summit meetings between 1945 and 1955. In 1952, George Kennan, the U.S. ambassador in Moscow, compared his isolation in the American embassy to his experience of being interned during World War II in Berlin. The later phases of the Cold War in the 1970s and 1980s were very different. The Americans and Soviets had many contacts, and they constantly negotiated on arms control treaties. The end of the Cold War occurred quite quickly with the change in Soviet policies after Mikhail Gorbachev came to power in 1985. Soviet hegemony over Eastern Europe collapsed in 1989, and the Soviet Union itself disintegrated in 1991.

DETERRENCE AND CONTAINMENT

What makes the Cold War exceptional is that it was a period of protracted tension that did not end in a war between the two rival states. There are a variety of explanations for why this was the case, and these will be discussed below. Because of its unusual trajectory, the Cold War offers a unique perspective on international relations, and it illuminates the dynamics of several possible foreign policy choices that states might make: the choice to *deter* and the choice to *contain*.

To deter is to discourage through fear, and it is not new to the Cold War. Throughout history, countries built armies, formed alliances, and issued threats to deter other countries from attacking. During the Cold War and with the advent of nuclear weapons, the superpowers depended more on discouraging by threat than on denying by defense after an attack occurred. Cold War deterrence was tied to the whole question of nuclear deterrence, but it was also an extension of balance of power logic. Deterrence by nuclear threat was one way each superpower tried to prevent the other from gaining advantage and hence upsetting the balance of power between them. As we shall see, deterrence often aggravated the tension between the United States and the Soviet Union, and it is not necessarily easy to demonstrate that deterrence worked. There is always the danger of spurious causation. If a professor said her lectures kept elephants out of the classroom, it would be difficult to disprove her claim if no elephants ever came to class. We can test such claims by using counterfactuals: How likely is it that elephants would come to class?

The concept of deterrence was linked to the policy of *containment*. During the Cold War, containment referred to a specific American policy of containing Soviet communism so as to promote a liberal economic and political world order. But like deterrence, containment did not originate with the Cold War, even if the term did. Containment has been a primary tool of foreign policy for centuries. In the eighteenth century, the conservative monarchic states of Europe attempted to contain the ideology of freedom and equality espoused by the French Revolution, and even before, the Catholic Church in the Counter-Reformation attempted to contain the spread of the Reformation and the ideals of Martin Luther. There are different forms of containment. It can be offensive or defensive. It can be military in the form of war or alliances, and it can be economic in the form of trading blocs or sanctions. During the Cold War, the United States wavered between an expansive policy of containing communism and a more limited policy of containing the Soviet Union.

THREE APPROACHES TO THE COLD WAR

Who or what caused the Cold War? Almost since it began, those questions have been the subject of fierce debate among scholars and policymakers. There are three main schools of opinion: *traditionalists, revisionists,* and *postrevisionists*.

The *traditionalists* (also known as the orthodox) argue that the answer to the question of who started the Cold War is quite simple: Stalin and the Soviet Union. At the end of World War II, American diplomacy was defensive, while the Soviets were aggressive and expansive. The Americans only slowly awoke to the nature of the Soviet threat.

What evidence do the traditionalists cite? Immediately after the war, the United States was proposing a universal world order and collective security through the United Nations. The Soviet Union did not take the United Nations very seriously because it wanted to expand and dominate its own sphere of influence in Eastern Europe. After the war, the United States demobilized its troops, whereas the Soviet Union left large armies in Eastern Europe. The United States recognized Soviet interests; for example, when Roosevelt, Stalin, and Churchill met in February 1945 at Yalta, the Americans went out of their way to accommodate Soviet interests. Stalin, however, did not live up to his agreements, particularly by not allowing free elections in Poland.

Soviet expansionism was further confirmed when the Soviet Union was slow to remove its troops from northern Iran after the war. Eventually they were removed, but only under pressure. In 1948, the communists took over the Czechoslovakian government. The Soviet Union blockaded Berlin in 1948 and 1949, trying to squeeze the Western governments out. In 1950, communist North Korea's armies crossed the border into South Korea. According to the traditionalists, these events gradually awakened the United States to the threat of Soviet expansionism and launched the Cold War.

The *revisionists*, who wrote primarily in the 1960s and early 1970s, believe the Cold War was caused by American rather than Soviet expansionism. Their evidence is that at the end of World War II, the world was not really bipolar—the Soviets were much weaker than the United States, which was strengthened by the war and had nuclear weapons while the Soviets did not. The Soviet Union lost up to 30 million people, and industrial production was only half of its 1939 level. Stalin told American Ambassador Averell Harriman in October 1945 that the Soviets would turn inward to repair their domestic damage. What is more, say the revisionists, Stalin's external behavior early in the post-war period was quite moderate: In China, Stalin tried to restrain Mao Tse-tung's communists from taking power; in the Greek civil war, he tried to restrain the Greek communists; and he allowed noncommunist governments to exist in Hungary, Czechoslovakia, and Finland.

Revisionists come in two varieties: "soft" and "hard." Soft revisionists stress the importance of individuals and feel that Roosevelt's death in April 1945 was a critical event because American policy became more harsh after President Harry S. Truman took office. In May 1945, the United States so precipitously cut off the lend-lease program of wartime aid that some ships bound for Soviet ports had to turn around in mid-ocean. At the Potsdam Conference near Berlin in July 1945, Truman tried to intimidate Stalin by mentioning the atomic bomb. In the United States, the Democratic Party gradually shifted from the left and center to the right. In 1948, Truman fired Henry Wallace, his secretary of agriculture, who urged better relations with the Soviets. At the same time, James Forrestal, Truman's new secretary of defense, was a strong anticommunist. Soft revisionists say that these personnel changes help explain why the United States became so anti-Soviet.

The hard revisionists have a different answer. They see the problem not in individuals, but in the nature of U.S. capitalism. Gabriel and Joyce Kolko and William A. Williams, for example, argue that the American economy required expansionism and that the United States planned to make the world safe, not for democracy, but for capitalism. American economic hegemony could not tolerate any country that might try to organize an autonomous economic area. American leaders feared a repeat of the 1930s because without external trade, there would be another Great Depression. The Marshall Plan of aid to Europe was simply a way to expand the American economy. The Soviets were correct to reject it as a threat to their sphere of influence in Eastern Europe. In Williams's words, Americans always favored an open door policy in the international economy because they expected to walk through it.

The *postrevisionists* of the late 1970s and 1980s, as exemplified by John Lewis Gaddis, have yet another explanation. They argue that the traditionalists and revisionists are both wrong because nobody was to blame for starting the Cold War. It was inevitable, or nearly so, because of the bipolar structure of the postwar balance of power. In 1939, there was a multipolar world with seven major powers, but after the destruction wreaked by World War II, only two superpowers were left: the United States and the Soviet Union. Bipolarity plus the postwar weakness of the European states created a power vacuum into which the United States and the Soviet Union were drawn. They were bound to come into conflict and, therefore, say the postrevisionists, it is pointless to look for blame.

The Soviets and the Americans had different goals at the end of the war. The Soviets wanted tangible possessions, territory. Americans had intangible or milieu goals; they were interested in the general context of world politics. Milieu goals clashed with possession goals when the United States promoted the global UN system while the Soviets sought to consolidate their sphere of influence in Eastern Europe. But these differences in style were no reason for Americans to feel sanctimonious, say the postrevisionists, for the United States benefited from the United Nations and, with a majority of allies voting, was not very constrained by it. The Soviets may have had a sphere of influence in Eastern Europe, but the United States also had a sphere of influence in the Western Hemisphere.

The United States and the Soviet Union were both bound to expand, say the postrevisionists, not because of the economic determinism that the revisionists stress, but because of the age-old security dilemma of states in an anarchic system. Neither the Americans nor the Soviets could allow the other to dominate Europe any more than Athens could afford to let the Corinthians gain control of Corcyra's navy. As evidence, postrevisionists cite Stalin's comment to a Yugoslav leader, Milovan Djilas, in 1945: "This war is not as in the past; whoever occupies a territory also imposes on it his own social system. Everyone imposes his own system as far as his army can reach."[1] In other words, in an ideological bipolar world, a state uses its military forces to impose societies similar to its own in order to ensure its security. Roosevelt had said something similar to Stalin in the fall of 1944: "In this global war there is literally no question, political or military, in which the United States is not interested."[2] Given this bipolar structure, say the postrevisionists, a spiral of hostility set in: Hard lines in one country bred hard lines in the other. Both began to perceive the enemy as analogous to Hitler in the 1930s. As perceptions became more rigid, the Cold War deepened.

> The President acted as if genuine cooperation as the Americans understood the term were possible both during and after the war. Roosevelt apparently had forgotten, if indeed he ever knew, that in Stalin's eyes, he was not all that different from Hitler, both of them being heads of powerful capitalist states whose longterm ambitions clashed with those of the Kremlin.
>
> —William Taubman, *Stalin's American Policy*.[4]

ROOSEVELT'S POLICIES

Franklin Roosevelt wanted to avoid the mistakes of World War I, so instead of a Versailles-like peace, he demanded Germany's unconditional surrender. He wanted a liberal trade system to avoid the protectionism that had damaged the world economy in the 1930s and contributed to the onset of war. The United States would avoid its tendency toward isolationism that had been so damaging in the 1930s. It would join a new and stronger League of Nations in the form of a United Nations with a powerful security council. Cordell Hull, secretary of state during most of the war, was a committed Wilsonian, and public opinion in the United States was strongly in favor of the United Nations.

To promote his great design, Roosevelt needed to maintain bipartisan domestic support for his international position. Externally, he needed to reassure Stalin that his security needs would be met by joining the United Nations. Roosevelt has been accused of a naive approach to postwar planning. His design was not naive, but some of his tactics were. He placed too much faith in the United Nations, overestimated the likelihood of American isolationism, and, most important, he underestimated Stalin. Roosevelt thought that he could treat Stalin the way he would treat a fellow American politician, throwing his arm around him, bonding politician to politician.

Roosevelt did not realize that Stalin, along with his men, was a totalitarian "who in the name of the people, murdered millions of them; who to defend against Hitler, signs a pact with him, divides the spoils of war with him, and like him, expels, exterminates, or enslaves neighboring peoples; who stands aside and fulminates against the democracies as Germany moves west, and then blames them for not helping enough when Hitler moves east."[3]

Roosevelt misinterpreted Stalin, but Roosevelt did not sell out American interests at the Yalta Conference in 1945. Roosevelt was not naive in all aspects of his policy. He tried to tie economic aid to political concessions by the Soviets, and refused to share the secrets of the atomic bomb with the Soviets. He was simply realistic about who would have troops in Eastern Europe at the end of the war, and, therefore, who would have leverage in that region. Roosevelt's mistakes were in thinking that Stalin saw the world his way, that he understood domestic politics in the United States, and that the same American political skills in which a leader blurred differences and appealed to friendship would work in dealing with Stalin.

STALIN'S POLICIES

Stalin's immediate postwar plans were to tighten domestic control. World War II inflicted tremendous damage on the Soviet Union, not just the terrible losses of life and industry already described, but also to the ideology of communism. Many in the Soviet Union collaborated with the Germans because of their deep resentment over the harshness of communist rule. Germany's invasion seriously weakened Stalin's control. Indeed, Stalin had to increase his appeals to Russian nationalism during the war as the weakened communist ideology was insufficient to motivate his people. Stalin's isolationist policy at the end of the war was designed to cut off external influences from Europe and the United States. Stalin used the United States as an objective enemy, urging the Soviet people to tighten down, pull in, to mistrust the outsiders. But it does not follow that Stalin wanted the Cold War that actually developed.

Stalin preferred some cooperation, especially if it helped him to pursue his goals in Eastern Europe and brought him some economic assistance from the United States. As a good communist, he believed the United States would have to give him economic assistance because the capitalist system had to export capital due to insufficient demand at home. Stalin also believed that in 10 or 15 years, the next crisis of the capitalist system would come along, and at that time the Soviet Union would have recovered and be ready to benefit in the inevitable conflict with the capitalists.

In foreign policy terms, Stalin wanted to protect himself at home, as well as maintain the gains the Soviet Union had made in Eastern Europe from the 1939 pact with Hitler. Stalin also wanted to probe soft spots, something better done when there is no crisis. In 1941, Stalin told the British foreign minister Anthony Eden that he preferred arithmetic to algebra; in other words, he wanted a practical rather than a theoretical approach. When Winston Churchill proposed a formula on the postwar division of influence in the Balkans, that is, some countries under British control, some under Soviet control, and others 50-50, Stalin was quite receptive to the idea. Some of Stalin's early caution in imposing communist governments right away in China, Czechoslovakia, and Hungary fit quite well with this arithmetic rather than algebraic approach to achieving his objectives. Stalin was a committed communist who, although he saw the world within the framework of communism, often used pragmatic tactics.

PHASES OF THE CONFLICT

The early stages of the Cold War can be divided into three phases: 1945 to 1947—the gradual onset; 1947 to 1949—the declaration of the Cold War; and 1950 to 1962—the height of the Cold War.

Neither Stalin nor Truman was looking for a cold war. At the end of World War II, Truman sent Roosevelt's former aide, Harry Hopkins, to Moscow to see if some arrangements could be worked out. Even after the Potsdam Conference, Truman continued to see Stalin as a moderate. Indeed, as late as 1949, he compared Stalin to his old friend Boss Pendergast in Kansas City. In 1946, George Kennan was trying to warn the United States about Stalin's true nature and intentions and Winston

Churchill gave a famous speech in Fulton, Missouri, warning that an "iron curtain" was falling across Europe. While Secretary of State James Byrnes was still trying to negotiate a postwar treaty with the Soviets, Truman asked his aide, Clark Clifford, to prepare a report on what the Soviets were really planning. Clifford talked with a variety of people and came to the conclusion that Kennan was right: The Soviets were going to expand whenever they found an inexpensive opportunity. When Truman received the report in December 1946, however, he told Clifford he did not want its results widely known, for he was still trying to follow Roosevelt's great design and had not yet developed a new strategy.

Phase I

① Six issues contributed to eventual change of American strategy and the onset of the Cold War. One was Poland and Eastern Europe. Poland, of course, had been one of the precipitating causes of World War II, and Americans believed that Stalin broke a clear commitment to hold free elections in Poland after the war. However, it was not clear what Stalin had agreed to do. When Stalin and Roosevelt met at Tehran in 1943, Roosevelt raised the Polish issue, but he appealed to Stalin in the context of the 1944 American election: He had an election coming up, there were many Polish voters, and he needed to tell them there would be elections in Poland after the war. Stalin, who never worried about elections in the Soviet Union, did not take Roosevelt's concerns seriously. The February 1945 Yalta agreement was also somewhat ambiguous, and Stalin stretched the meaning as far as he could by setting up a puppet government in Warsaw after Soviet troops had driven out the Germans. The Americans felt cheated, but Stalin felt the Americans would adjust to the reality that it was Soviet troops that had liberated Poland.

② In May 1945, the lend-lease aid program was abruptly stopped, and the economic relationship between the United States and the Soviet Union became strained. The precipitous termination of lend-lease was to some extent a bureaucratic mistake, but the overall situation was not improved when in February 1946 the United States refused Soviet requests for loans. The Soviets interpreted those acts as economic leverage for hostile purposes.

③ Germany was a third problem. At the Yalta meeting, the Americans and the Soviets agreed that Germany should pay $20 billion in reparations and half would go to the Soviet Union. The details of how and when the payments would be made were not worked out at Yalta, although both sides agreed they would be negotiated later. At the Potsdam meeting in July 1945, the Soviets demanded their $10 billion; furthermore, they wanted it from the western zones of Germany that the Americans, British, and French had occupied. Harry Truman, worried about how Germany would be reconstructed, said that if the Soviets wanted to take $10 billion out of Germany, they should take it out of the eastern zone they occupied; if there was anything left over after the reconstruction of the western side of Germany, he would let the Soviets know. Thus began a series of divisions between the Americans and the Soviets about how to reconstruct Germany. The Americans, along with the British and French, created a single currency in the western zones, starting the process of West German integration, which in turn caused the Soviets to tighten control of the eastern zone of Germany.

④ The Far East was also an issue. The Soviets were neutral in the Pacific until the last week of the war. Then the Soviets declared war on Japan, seizing Manchuria and

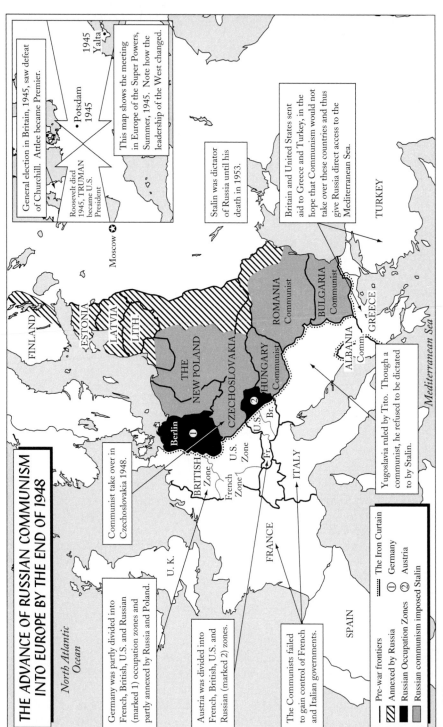

THE ADVANCE OF RUSSIAN COMMUNISM INTO EUROPE BY THE END OF 1948

General election in Britain, 1945, saw defeat of Churchill. Attlee became Premier.

This map shows the meeting in Europe of the Super Powers, Summer, 1945. Note how the leadership of the West changed.

Roosevelt died 1945, TRUMAN became U.S. President

• Potsdam 1945
1945 Yalta

Stalin was dictator of Russia until his death in 1953.

Britain and United States sent aid to Greece and Turkey, in the hope that Communism would not take over these countries and thus give Russia direct access to the Mediterranean Sea.

North Atlantic Ocean

Communist take over in Czechoslovakia 1948.

Germany was partly divided into French, British, U.S. and Russian (marked 1) occupation zones and partly annexed by Russia and Poland.

Austria was divided into French, British, U.S. and Russian (marked 2) zones.

The Communists failed to gain control of French and Italian governments.

Yugoslavia ruled by Tito. Though a communist, he refused to be dictated to by Stalin.

Moscow ✪

FINLAND
ESTONIA
LATVIA
LITH.
THE NEW POLAND
CZECHOSLOVAKIA
HUNGARY Communist
ROMANIA Communist
BULGARIA Communist
ALBANIA A. Comm.
GREECE
TURKEY
Mediterranean Sea

Berlin ①
BRITISH Zone
U.S. Zone
French Zone
Fr.
Br.
U.S. ②
ITALY
FRANCE
SPAIN
U.K.

Legend:
——	Pre-war frontiers
▨	Annexed by Russia
■	Russian Occupation Zones
▧	Russian communism imposed Stalin
⋯⋯	The Iron Curtain
①	Germany
②	Austria

Figure 5.1

four islands from the north of Japan. At Potsdam, the Soviets asked for an occupation zone in Japan, like the American occupation zone in Germany. Truman's response was, in effect, that the Soviets arrived at the party late, so no zone. From an American point of view, this seemed perfectly reasonable, but the situation reminded the Soviets of Eastern Europe, where the Americans wanted free elections and influence, but the Soviet armies had arrived there first. So the Soviets saw the Far Eastern situation as analogous to Eastern Europe, while the Americans saw it as one more example of the Soviets pressing for their own expansion.

A fifth issue was the atomic bomb. Roosevelt had decided not to share the secret of the atomic bomb with the Soviet Union. Most historians now agree that Truman dropped the bomb at Hiroshima and Nagasaki primarily to bring a quick end to the war with Japan, not to intimidate the Soviet Union, as some revisionists have claimed. But he did expect the bomb to have some political effects. At the Potsdam meeting when Truman told Stalin that America had an atomic bomb, Stalin remained poker-faced and seemingly unimpressed. Of course, Stalin already knew about it from his own spies, but his equanimity was a bit of a jolt to the Americans. In 1946, when the United States set forth the Baruch Plan for UN control of nuclear weapons, Stalin rejected it because he wanted to build his own bomb. As he saw it, a bomb under international control would still be an American bomb, for only the Americans knew how to build it. Far better for Soviet security to have their own (which they eventually exploded in 1949).

The sixth issue concerned countries in the eastern Mediterranean and the Middle East where the British had been influential before World War II. After the war, several things occurred. First, the Soviets refused to remove their troops from northern Iran in March 1946. The United States supported Iran in a debate within the United Nations. Eventually, the Soviets moved, but not without a good deal of bitterness over the event. Then the Soviet Union began to put pressure on Turkey, its neighbor to the south, and the Greek communists seemed to be winning the civil war in Greece. Once again, the West believed the Soviets were expanding.

These six issues were real, though there were some misperceptions involved in almost all of them. Could they have been solved by negotiation and appeasement? Would appeasement have worked? Probably not. Kennan argued that Stalin was intent on probing any soft spots. Appeasement would have been interpreted as a soft spot and invited more probing. In June 1946, Maxim Litvinov, the former Soviet foreign minister, warned an American counterpart against any concessions because the root cause of the tension was "the ideological conception prevailing here that conflict between Communist and capitalist worlds is inevitable." Concessions would merely lead "to the West's being faced, after a more or less short time, with the next series of demands."[5] Appeasement probably would not have worked, but harder bargaining might have limited some of the events that led to the onset of the Cold War. A tactical appeal to Stalin's pragmatism from a firmer American position, plus a willingness to negotiate, might have worked out better in that early period from 1945 to 1947.

The second phase, the declaration of the Cold War from 1947 to 1949, followed from the problems in Greece and Turkey. Britain, severely weakened by World War II, felt it could no longer provide security in the eastern Mediterranean.

The United States had to decide whether to let a vacuum develop or to replace British power by providing assistance to Greece and Turkey. This involved a considerable break from traditional American foreign policy. Truman was not sure that American public opinion would support such a move. There was still fear that isolationism would be the mainstay of America's postwar foreign policy. Truman asked Senator Arthur Vandenberg, the Republican leader from Michigan, whether the Senate would go along with aiding Greece and Turkey. Vandenberg said that Truman would have to "scare the hell out of them" to get congressional support for this break in traditional American policy. Thus, when Truman explained the policy change, he did not talk about the need to maintain a balance of power in the eastern Mediterranean by providing aid to Greece and Turkey. Instead, he talked about the need to protect free people everywhere. This moralistic, ideological explanation for American assistance became known as the Truman Doctrine.

George Kennan, by then back in the State Department, objected to the ideological way of formulating foreign policy, arguing that it was too open-ended and would get the country into trouble. Indeed, there were enormous ambiguities in the policy of containment that flowed from the Truman Doctrine. Was the United States interested in containing Soviet power or communist ideology? At the beginning, containing Soviet power and containing communist ideology seemed to be the same, but later in the Cold War when the communist movement split, the ambiguities became important.

Was Truman wrong to exaggerate the sense of threat and the ideological rationale for the policy change? Some observers feel it is harder to change public opinion in democracies than it is to change policies in totalitarian countries. They argue that exaggeration speeds up the process of change in democracies. It is necessary to tug harder on the reins when trying to turn an unruly team of horses. Regardless of whether the exaggeration was necessary or not, it helped to change the nature of the Cold War.

In June 1947, Secretary of State George Marshall announced a plan for economic aid to Europe. The initial proposal of the Marshall Plan invited the Soviet Union and the Eastern Europeans to join if they wished, but Stalin put strong pressure on the Eastern Europeans not to do so. Stalin saw the Marshall Plan not as American generosity, but as an economic battering ram to destroy his security barrier in Eastern Europe. When Czechoslovakia indicated it would like U.S. aid, Stalin tightened the screws in Eastern Europe, and the communists took full power in Czechoslovakia in February 1948.

Truman heard echoes of the 1930s in these events. He began to worry that Stalin would become another Hitler. The United States advanced plans for a West German currency reform; Stalin replied with the Berlin blockade. The United States answered with an airlift and began plans for the North Atlantic Treaty Organization (NATO). Hostility began to escalate in a tit-for-tat fashion.

The most rigid phase of the Cold War occurred after two shocks in 1949: The Soviet Union exploded an atomic bomb, much sooner than the Americans thought they could, and the Chinese Communist Party took control in China (except for the island of Taiwan). The alarm in Washington was illustrated by a secret government document, National Security Council Document 68 (NSC-68), which forecast a

> The purpose of NSC-68 was to so bludgeon the mass mind of "top government" that not only could the President make a decision but that the decision could be carried out. Even so, it is doubtful whether anything like what happened in the next few years could have been done had not the Russians been stupid enough to have instigated the attack against South Korea and opened the "hate America" campaign.
>
> —Secretary of State Dean Acheson, *Present at the Creation*[6]

Soviet attack in four to five years as part of a plan for global domination. NSC-68 called for a vast increase in the U.S. defense expenditure. Beset by budget problems, President Truman resisted NSC-68 until June 1950 after North Korea's troops crossed the border into South Korea.

The effect of the Korean War was like pouring gasoline onto a modest fire. It confirmed all the worst Western suspicions about Stalin's expansionist ambitions and led to a huge increase in the American defense budget of the type Truman had resisted up to that point. Why did Stalin permit North Korea to invade South Korea? Khrushchev gives an explanation in his memoirs: Kim Il Sung, the North Korean leader, pressed Stalin for the opportunity to unify the peninsula. The United States had said that Korea was outside its defense perimeter; Secretary of State Dean Acheson had articulated this position and the Joint Chiefs of Staff had planned accordingly. To Stalin, Korea looked like a soft spot. But when North Korea actually crossed into South Korea, Truman responded in an axiomatic rather than a calculating way: Truman remembered Hitler moving into the Rhineland and recalled the axiom that aggression must be resisted everywhere. Calculated plans about defense perimeters were overshadowed by the historical analogies triggered by North Korea's invasion. The United States was able to mobilize the Security Council to endorse collective security (which was possible because the Soviet Union was then boycotting the Security Council) and sent troops to Korea under the UN flag.

At first, North Korea's armies swept down the peninsula almost to the tip. In September, however, an American amphibious landing at Inchon, halfway up the peninsula, routed the North Koreans. Had the United States stopped there, the outcome might have been less painful, but Truman succumbed to pressures to pursue the retreating troops north of the 38th parallel. As the Americans approached the Yalu River, which divides Korea from China, the Chinese communists intervened, pushing the UN troops back to the middle of the peninsula. There the battle stalemated for three years until a truce was signed in 1953. The United States became embroiled with China, and communism appeared to be monolithic. At home, the frustrating war led to domestic division and the rise of McCarthyism, named after the harsh and poorly founded accusations of domestic subversion made by Senator Joseph McCarthy of Wisconsin. The Cold War blocs tightened and communication nearly ceased.

INEVITABILITY?

Was the onset of the Cold War inevitable? The postrevisionists are correct if we interpret inevitable to mean "highly probable." The bipolar structure made it likely that both sides would be sucked into a power vacuum in Europe and find it difficult to

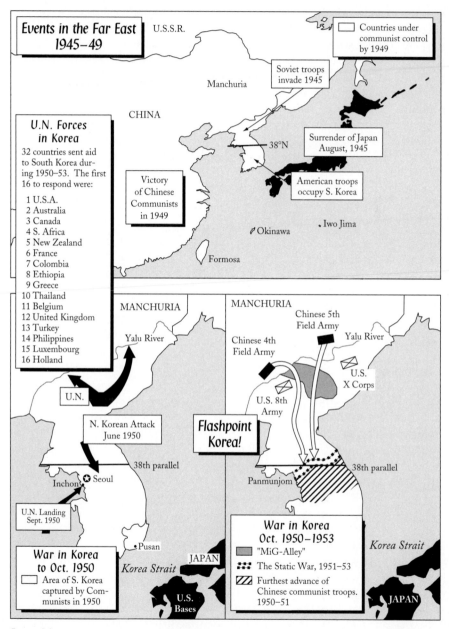

Events in the Far East 1945–49

U.S.S.R.

Manchuria

CHINA

38°N

Soviet troops invade 1945

Surrender of Japan August, 1945

American troops occupy S. Korea

Countries under communist control by 1949

Victory of Chinese Communists in 1949

• Iwo Jima

ℓ Okinawa

Formosa

U.N. Forces in Korea

32 countries sent aid to South Korea during 1950–53. The first 16 to respond were:

1 U.S.A.
2 Australia
3 Canada
4 S. Africa
5 New Zealand
6 France
7 Colombia
8 Ethiopia
9 Greece
10 Thailand
11 Belgium
12 United Kingdom
13 Turkey
14 Philippines
15 Luxembourg
16 Holland

MANCHURIA

Yalu River

U.N.

N. Korean Attack June 1950

38th parallel

Inchon ✪ Seoul

U.N. Landing Sept. 1950

• Pusan

JAPAN

Korea Strait

U.S. Bases

War in Korea to Oct. 1950

☐ Area of S. Korea captured by Communists in 1950

MANCHURIA

Chinese 5th Field Army

Yalu River

Chinese 4th Field Army

U.S. X Corps

U.S. 8th Army

Flashpoint Korea!

38th parallel

Panmunjom

Korea Strait

JAPAN

War in Korea Oct. 1950–1953

▓ "MiG-Alley"
⣿ The Static War, 1951–53
▨ Furthest advance of Chinese communist troops. 1950–51

Figure 5.2

disengage. The intense ideological climate hampered the working of the United Nations, restricted clear communication, and contributed to the immoderate process of the international system. Under such systemic conditions, conflicts would have arisen over the six issues just identified, or some others, and proven difficult to resolve.

The postrevisionists rely too heavily, however, on systemic explanation. Perhaps some Cold War was inevitable, but its depth was not. After all, there were different phases of the hostility, and since the bipolarity of the system did not change until 1989, structural explanations cannot explain the different phases or depth of the hostility. That is where individuals and domestic politics matter—Roosevelt and Truman, Stalin and Khrushchev. Domestic politics have to be considered to fully understand the extent of the Cold War. The revisionists are right to focus on domestic questions, but they are wrong to focus so strongly on economic determinism. More important was the role of exaggeration and ideology in domestic politics. Stalin used ideology because of Soviet domestic problems after the war, and Truman exaggerated in order to change American foreign policy. The use of 1930s analogies helped to reinforce rigidity on both sides.

Ironically, alternative strategies at different times might have alleviated the depths of hostility. For example, if the United States had followed Kennan's advice and responded more firmly in 1945 to 1947, and had tried more pragmatic negotiation and communication from 1947 to 1950, the Cold War might not have reached the depths of the early 1950s.

LEVELS OF ANALYSIS

The origins of the Cold War can be described in terms of the different images or levels of analysis as illustrated in Figure 5.3.

In the nineteenth century, Alexis de Tocqueville predicted that Russia and the United States were bound to become two great continental-scale giants in the world. Realists might thus predict that these two would become locked in some form of conflict. And of course, in 1917, the Bolshevik Revolution added an ideological layer to the conflict. When Woodrow Wilson first heard of the Russian Revolution, he congratulated the Russian people for their democratic spirit. But it did not take long before the Americans were accusing the Bolsheviks of regicide, of expropriation, and cooperation with Germany in World War I. The United States intervened with troops, allegedly to keep the Russians in the war against Germany, but the Soviets saw it as an attempt to strangle communism in its cradle. Despite these differences, the United States and the Soviet Union avoided serious conflict in the interwar period and became allies in the early 1940s. The bipolarity that followed the collapse of all the other great powers in World War II and the resulting power vacuum changed the relationship. Earlier there had been distrust between the two countries, but they distrusted each other at a distance. Before World War II, they could avoid each other, but after 1945 they were face to face, Europe was divided, and deep conflict began after 1947. Some people wonder whether the bipolar structure had to have this effect. After all, the Soviet Union was a land-based power, while the United States was a maritime power; why could there not have been a division of labor between the elephant and the whale, each staying in its own domain?

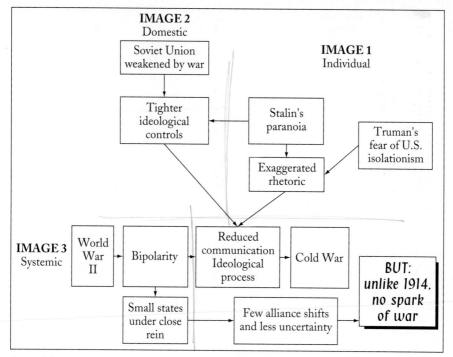

Figure 5.3

The answer is that the key stakes in world politics, the countries that could tip the balance of power, were located on the peripheries of the Soviet Union, particularly Europe and Japan. As George Kennan described the situation after the war, there were four great areas of technological and industrial creativity, which, if they were allied one way or the other, could tip the global balance of power. Those were the United States, the Soviet Union, Europe, and Japan. The fact that Europe and Japan became allied with the United States against the Soviet Union was of profound importance.

Structural explanations predicted conflict, not how deep it would go. For that we need to go beyond structural explanations to look at the societal and individual levels of analysis. At the societal level, the two countries were very different from each other. A thumbnail sketch of the Soviet Union's political culture and its expression in foreign policy showed two roots: Russian and communist. The Russian political culture emphasized absolutism rather than democracy, a desire for a strong leader, fear of anarchy (Russia had been a large unwieldy empire and the fear that anarchy and dissent could lead to disintegration was very real), fear of invasion (Russia was a geographically vulnerable land-based power that had invaded and been invaded by its neighbors throughout the centuries), a worry or shame about backwardness (ever since Peter the Great, Russians had been trying to prove their vitality in international competition), and secrecy (a desire to hide the seamy side of Russian life). In addition, the communist system treated class rather than individual rights as the basis for justice. The proper role for a person or for a society was to lead the proletariat or working class toward dominance because this was supposed to be the course of history.

The ideological overlay gave an additional outward thrust to traditional Russian imperialism and resulted in a secret and tightly held foreign policy process. It is interesting to note the strengths and weaknesses of that process. The strengths were evident in 1939 when Stalin was able quickly to sign the pact with Hitler. Public opinion did not constrain him, nor did he have to worry about a bureaucracy holding him back. He was free to rush into the pact with Hitler while the British and French were still dithering about whether or not to deal with him. The opposite side of the same coin became evident in 1941, however, when Hitler attacked the Soviet Union. Stalin was unable to believe Hitler would do such a thing and went into a deep depression for over a week. The result was disastrous for Soviet defenses in the early phases of the war.

In contrast, the American political culture stressed liberal democracy, pluralism, and fragmentation of power. Instead of shame of backwardness, the United States took pride in its technology and expanding economy. Instead of a fear of invasion, for much of its history, the United States had been able to isolate itself between two oceans (and the British navy) while it invaded its weaker neighbors. In terms of secrecy, the United States was so open that governmental documents often reached the press within a matter of days and weeks. Instead of a class basis for conceptions of justice, there was a strong emphasis on individual justice. The foreign policy that resulted from this political culture was moralistic, public, and tended to go through oscillations of inward and outward orientation. The result was that the American foreign policy process was often inconsistent and incoherent in many of its surface aspects. But there was also an opposite side to this coin. The strengths of openness and pluralism often protected the United States from deeper mistakes.

Thus, it is not surprising that these two societies, so differently constructed and with such different foreign policy processes, would confuse each other. We saw examples of that in the way both Truman and Roosevelt dealt with Stalin in the 1940s. It was hard for the Americans to understand the Soviet Union during the Cold War because the Soviet Union was like a black box. American leaders could see what went in and what came out of the box, but not what happened inside. The Americans confused the Soviets as well. The Americans were like a white noise machine that produced so much background noise that it was difficult to hear the true signals clearly. There were too many people saying too many things. Thus, the Soviets were often confused about what the Americans really wanted.

U.S. AND SOVIET GOALS IN THE COLD WAR

The Soviets were often accused of being expansive, of being a revolutionary power rather than a status quo power. The Soviet Union also tended to want tangible or possession goals such as territory, whereas the Americans tended to want intangible or milieu goals—ways of establishing the general setting of international politics. We can see this in the demands that Stalin, Churchill, and Roosevelt brought to the bargaining table at Yalta. Stalin had very clear objectives at Yalta: Germany and

Poland. Churchill wanted the restoration of France to help balance Soviet power in case the Americans went home. Roosevelt wanted the United Nations and an open international economic system. These goals were very different in their tangibility. In some ways, Stalin's postwar goals were classic Russian imperialist goals; he wanted to keep the gains he had made in the treaty with Hitler. His wish list would have been familiar to Peter the Great.

Some Americans felt the Soviets were as expansive as Hitler in desiring world domination. Others said the Soviets were basically security-oriented; their expansion was defensive. There were at least two ways in which Soviet expansionism was not like Hitler's. First, it was not bellicist; the Soviets did not want war. When Hitler invaded Poland, he worried he would be offered another Munich instead of the war he wanted for the glory of fascism. Another difference was that the Soviet Union was cautiously opportunistic, not recklessly adventuresome. Adventurism was seen as a sin against communism because it might disrupt the predicted course of history. During the Cold War, the Soviet Union was never as bellicist or as reckless as Hitler was.

Nonetheless, there are problems in portraying Soviet behavior as purely defensive. As we know from the Peloponnesian War, it is very hard in a bipolar world to distinguish offense from defense. Certain actions may have defensive motives but may look very threatening to the other side. Moreover, there is a long tradition of defensive expansion, or imperialism. For example, in the nineteenth century, Britain originally went into Egypt to protect the sea routes to India. After it took Egypt, it felt it had to take the Sudan to protect Egypt, and then it had to take Uganda to protect the Sudan. After it took Uganda, Britain felt it had to take Kenya to build a railway to protect Uganda. The appetite grows with the eating as the security dilemma is used to justify further and further expansion. Soviet communism added an ideological motive of freeing working classes in all areas of the world and that further legitimized expansion. In short, the Soviet Union was expansionist during the Cold War, but cautiously and opportunistically so.

CONTAINMENT

What about U.S. goals? During the Cold War, the U.S. government wanted to contain the Soviet Union. Yet, the policy of containment involved two large ambiguities. One was the question of the ends: whether to contain Soviet power or to contain communism. The second was a question of means: whether to spend resources to prevent any expansion of Soviet power or just in certain key areas that seemed critical to the balance of power. Those two ambiguities in the ends and means of containment were hotly debated in the period before the Korean War. George Kennan dissented from the rather expansive version of containment that Truman proclaimed. Kennan's idea of containment was akin to classical diplomacy. It involved fewer military means and was more selective. A good example was Yugoslavia, which had a communist totalitarian government under Josef Tito. In 1948, Tito split with Stalin over Soviet efforts to control Yugoslavia's foreign policy, including its support for the Greek communists. In an ideological view of containment, the United States should not help Yugoslavia because it was communist. In a

> It would be an exaggeration to say that American behavior unassisted and alone could exercise a power of life and death over the Communist movement and bring about the early fall of Soviet power in Russia. But the United States has it in its power to increase enormously the strains under which Soviet policy must operate, to force upon the Kremlin a far greater degree of moderation and circumspection than it has had to observe in recent years, and in this way to promote tendencies which must eventually find their outlet in either the break-up or the gradual mellowing of Soviet power.
>
> —George Kennan, "The Sources of Soviet Conduct"[7]

balance of power view of containment, the United States should help Yugoslavia as a means of weakening Soviet power. That, in fact, is what the United States did. It provided military aid to a totalitarian communist government despite the fact that the Truman Doctrine proclaimed the goal of defending free peoples everywhere. The United States did it for balance of power reasons, and the policy put a big dent in Soviet power in Europe.

After the Korean War, however, Kennan's approach to containment lost ground. Then it looked as though the NSC-68 predictions of Soviet expansionism had been justified. Communism seemed monolithic after the Chinese entered the Korean War, and the rhetoric of containment emphasized the ideological goal of preventing the spread of communism. It was in this context that the United States made the costly mistake of becoming involved in Vietnam's civil war. For nearly two decades, the United States tried to prevent communist control of Vietnam, at a cost of 58,000 American lives, perhaps a million Vietnamese lives, $600 billion, and domestic turmoil that undercut support for the policy of containment itself. In addition to containing communism in South Vietnam, the United States feared a defeat might weaken the credibility of its commitments, and thus containment in other parts of the world. Ironically, after the U.S. defeat and withdrawal in 1975, nationalist rivalries among the communist countries in Asia proved to be an effective force for maintaining the balance of power in the region.

THE REST OF THE COLD WAR

In 1952, Dwight Eisenhower was elected president on a campaign pledge to end the Korean War and to roll back communism. The Republican party argued that containment was a cowardly accommodation to communism. The right approach was to roll back communism. Within six months, however, it became clear that rolling back communism was too risky in terms of precipitating nuclear war. After Stalin died in 1953, the frozen relations of the Cold War thawed slightly. In 1955, there was a summit in Geneva and agreement to the establishment of Austria as a neutral state. In 1956, Khrushchev gave a secret speech exposing Stalin's crimes to the Twentieth Party Congress of the Soviet Union. The secret leaked out and contributed to a period of disarray in the Soviet sphere in Eastern Europe. Hungary attempted to revolt, but the Soviets intervened militarily to keep it within the communist camp.

Khrushchev decided that he needed to get the Americans out of Berlin and reach a final settlement of World War II so he could consolidate the Soviet hold on Eastern Europe and begin to take advantage of the decolonization occurring in the Third World. But Khrushchev's style and efforts to negotiate with the United States were reminiscent of the kaiser's style in trying to force the British to bargain before 1914, full of bluster and deception. Efforts to make the United States come to terms had the opposite effect. Khrushchev failed in the Berlin crisis of 1958–1961 and again in the Cuban missile crisis.

As we see later, the Soviet Union and the United States got so close to the nuclear brink during the Cuban missile crisis that they scared each other into a new phase in their relationship. From 1963 to 1978, there was a gradual détente, or relaxation of tensions. In the aftermath of the Cuban missile crisis, arms control negotiations produced the Limited Test Ban Treaty that limited atmospheric nuclear tests in 1963 and a Non-Proliferation Treaty in 1968. Trade began to grow gradually, and détente seemed to be expanding. The Vietnam War diverted U.S. attention more to the threat from Chinese communism.

From 1969 to 1974, the Nixon administration used détente as a means to pursue the goals of containment. After the Cuban missile crisis, the Soviets launched a major military buildup and gained parity in nuclear weapons. The Vietnam War led to a disillusionment in American public opinion with Cold War interventions. The Nixon strategy was (1) to negotiate a strategic arms control treaty to cap the nuclear relationship at relative parity; (2) to open diplomatic relations with China, and thus create a three-way balance of power in Asia (rather than pushing the Soviets and the Chinese together); (3) to increase trade so there would be carrots as well as sticks in the U.S.-Soviet relationship; and (4) to use "linkage" to tie the various parts of policy together. The high point of détente occurred in 1972 and 1973, but it did not last very long.

The Middle East War of 1973 and Soviet assistance to anti-Western movements in Africa led to bad feelings about who misled whom. American domestic politics contributed to the decline of détente when American legislators such as Senator Henry Jackson tried to link trade with the Soviet Union to human rights rather than to behavior in balance of power terms. In 1975, when Portugal decolonized Angola and Mozambique, the Soviet Union transported Cuban troops to help keep communist-oriented governments in power there. By the time of the 1976 presidential campaign, President Gerald Ford never used the word *détente*. His successor, Jimmy Carter, tried to continue détente with the Soviet Union during his first two years in office, but the Soviet Union (and Cuba) became involved in the Ethiopian civil war; the Soviets continued their defense buildup, and in December 1979, the Soviet Union delivered the coup de grace to détente by invading Afghanistan.

Why did the hostility come back? One argument is that détente was always oversold, that too much was expected of it. More to the point is that there were three trends in the 1970s that undercut it. One was the Soviet defense buildup in which the Soviets increased their defense budget nearly four percent a year, adding new heavy missiles that particularly worried American defense planners. Second was the Soviet interventions in Angola, Ethiopia, and Afghanistan. The Soviets felt they were justified by what they called the changing "correlation of forces" in history, their belief that history was moving in the directions that Marxism-Leninism predicted. Third were changes in American domestic politics, a rightward trend that tore apart the coalition supporting the Democratic Party. The result of the interaction of Soviet acts and U.S. political trends confirmed the view that the Cold War persisted, that détente could not last. However, the renewed hostility in the 1980s was *not* a return to the Cold War of the 1950s. There was a return to the rhetoric of the 1950s, but actions were quite different. Even as President Ronald Reagan talked about the Soviet Union as an "Evil Empire," he was planning arms control. There was increased trade, particularly in grain, and there were constant contacts between Americans and Soviets. The superpowers even evolved certain rules of prudence in their behavior toward each other: no direct wars, no nuclear use, and discussions of arms and the control of nuclear weapons. It was a different kind of Cold War in the 1980s than in the 1950s.

THE END OF THE COLD WAR

When did the Cold War end? Since the origins of the Cold War were very heavily related to the division of Europe by the United States and the Soviet Union, the end of the Cold War might be dated by when the division ended, that is 1989. When the Soviet Union did not use force to support the communist government in East Germany and the Berlin Wall was pierced by jubilant crowds in November 1989, the Cold War could be said to be over.

But why did it end? One argument is that containment worked. George Kennan argued right after World War II that if the United States could prevent the Soviet Union from expanding, there would be no successes to feed the ideology, and gradually Soviet communism would mellow. New ideas would arise, people would realize communism was not the wave of the future, that history was not on their side. In some larger prospect, Kennan was right. But the puzzle with that explanation is timing: Why 1989? Why did it last four decades? Why did it take so long to mellow? Alternatively, why didn't it last another ten years? Containment worked, but that does not give the full answer.

Another explanation is "imperial overstretch." The historian Paul Kennedy has argued that empires overexpand until that overexpansion saps the empire's internal strength. With over a quarter of its economy devoted to defense and foreign affairs (compared to six percent for the United States in the 1980s), the Soviet Union was overstretched. But Kennedy went on to say that none of the overexpanded multinational empires in history ever retreated to their own ethnic base until they had been defeated or weakened in a great power war. The Soviet Union, however, was not defeated or weakened in a great power war. A third explanation is that the U.S. military buildup in the 1980s forced the Soviets to surrender in the Cold War. There is some truth to that insofar as President Ronald Reagan's policies dramatized the extent to which the Soviets were imperially overstretched, but it does not really answer the basic question. After all, earlier periods of American military buildup did not have that effect. Why 1989? We must look for deeper causes, for to think that American rhetoric and policy in the 1980s were the prime cause of the Soviet Union's decline may be similar to the rooster who thought that his crowing before dawn caused the sun to come up.

We can gain better insights into the end of the Cold War by looking at our three types of causes: precipitating, intermediate, and deep. The most important precipitating cause of the end of the Cold War was an individual, Mikhail Gorbachev. He wanted to reform communism, not replace it. However, the reform snowballed into a revolution driven from below rather than controlled from above. In both his domestic and foreign policy, Gorbachev launched a number of actions that accelerated the existing Soviet decline and speeded the end of the Cold War. When he first came to power in 1985, Gorbachev tried to discipline the Soviet people as a way to overcome the existing economic stagnation. When discipline was not enough to solve the problem, he launched the idea of *perestroika,* or "restructuring," but he was unable to restructure from the top because the bureaucrats kept thwarting his orders. To light a fire under the bureaucrats, he used a strategy of *glasnost,* or open discussion and democratization. Airing people's discontent with the way the system was working would put pressure on the bureaucrats and let perestroika work. But once glasnost and democratization let people say what they were thinking, and vote on it, many people said, "We want out. There is no new form of Soviet man. This is an imperial dynasty, and we do not belong in this empire." Gorbachev unleashed the disintegration of the Soviet Union, which became increasingly evident after the failed old-line coup in August 1991. By December 1991, the Soviet Union ceased to exist.

Gorbachev's foreign policy, which he called "new thinking," also contributed to the end of the Cold War. This policy had two very important elements. One was the concept of common security in which the classical security dilemma is escaped by joining together to provide security. Gorbachev and the people around him said that in a world of increasing interdependence, security was a non-zero-sum game, and all could benefit through cooperation. The existence of the nuclear threat meant that all could perish together if the competition got out of hand. Rather than try to build as many nuclear weapons as possible, Gorbachev proclaimed a doctrine of "sufficiency," holding a minimal number for protection. The other dimension of Gorbachev's foreign policy change was his view that expansionism is on balance more costly than beneficial. The Soviet control over an empire in Eastern Europe was costing too much and providing too little benefit, and the invasion of Afghanistan had been a costly disaster. It was no longer necessary to impose a communist social system as a way to ensure security on Soviet borders.

Thus, by the summer of 1989, the Eastern Europeans were given more degrees of freedom. Hungary allowed East Germans to escape through Hungary into Austria. The exodus of East Germans put enormous pressure on the East German government. The Eastern European governments no longer had the nerve (or Soviet backing) to put down demonstrations. In November, the Berlin Wall was pierced—a dramatic conclusion to a crescendo of events occurring over a very short period. We can argue that these events stemmed from Gorbachev's miscalculations. He thought that communism could be repaired, but in fact, in trying to repair it, he punched a small hole in it. And like a hole in a dam, once the pent-up pressures began to escape, they rapidly increased the opening and tore apart the system.

That still leaves the question, why 1989? Why under this leader? To some extent, Gorbachev was an accident of history. In the early 1980s, there were three old Soviet leaders who died, one soon after the other. It was not until 1985 that the younger generation, the people who had come up under Khrushchev, the so-called generation of 1956, had their chance. But if the members of the Communist Party Politburo had chosen one of Gorbachev's hard-line competitors in 1985, it is quite plausible that the declining Soviet Union could have held on for another decade. It did not have to collapse so quickly. The personality of Gorbachev explains much of the timing.

As for the intermediate causes, Kennan and Kennedy are both on target. Two important intermediate causes were liberal ideas and imperial overstretch. The ideas of openness and democracy and new thinking that Gorbachev used were Western ideas that had been adopted by the generation of 1956. The growth of transnational communications and contacts helped spread liberal ideas, and the demonstration effect of Western economic success gave them additional appeal. As for imperial overstretch, the enormous Soviet defense budget began to affect other aspects of Soviet society. Health care declined and the mortality rate in the Soviet Union increased (the only developed country where that occurred). Eventually even the military became aware of the tremendous burden caused by imperial overstretch. In 1984, Marshall Ogarkov, the Soviet chief of staff, realized the Soviet Union needed a better civilian economic base and more access to Western trade and technology, but during the period of stagnation, the old leaders were unwilling to listen and Ogarkov was removed from his post.

Thus the intermediate causes of liberal ideas and imperial overstretch are important, but ultimately we must deal with the deep causes, which were the decline of communist ideology and the failure of the Soviet economy. Communism's loss of legitimacy over the postwar period was quite dramatic. In the early period, immediately after 1945, communism was widely attractive. Many communists had led the resistance against fascism in Europe, and many people believed that communism was the wave of the future. The Soviet Union gained a great deal of soft power from their communist ideology. But it was progressively undercut by the de-Stalinization in 1956 that exposed his crimes, by the repressions in Hungary in 1956, in Czechoslovakia in 1968, and in Poland in 1981, and by the growing transnational communication of liberal ideas.

Behind this, there was also decline in the Soviet economy, reflecting the diminished ability of the Soviet central planning system to respond to change in the world economy. Stalin had created a system of centralized economic direction that emphasized heavy metal and smokestack industries. It was very inflexible—all thumbs and no fingers. It tended to stockpile labor rather than transfer it to growing service industries. As the economist Joseph Schumpeter pointed out, capitalism is creative destruction, a way of responding flexibly to major waves of technological change. At the end of the twentieth century, the major technological change of the third industrial revolution was the growing role of information as the scarcest resource in an economy. The Soviet system was particularly inept at handling information. The deep secrecy of its political system meant that the flow of information was slow and cumbersome.

Soviet products could not keep up to world standards. There was a great deal of turmoil in the world economy at the end of the twentieth century, but the Western economies using market systems were able to transfer labor to services and to reorganize their heavy industries and to switch to computers. The Soviet Union could not keep up with the changes. For instance, when Gorbachev came to power in 1985, there were 50,000 personal computers in the Soviet Union; in the United States there were 30 million. Four years later, there were about 400,000 personal computers in the Soviet Union, and 40 million in the United States. Market-oriented economies and democracies proved more flexible in responding to technological change than the centralized Soviet system that Stalin created for the smokestack era of the 1930s. According to one Soviet economist, by the late 1980s, only eight percent of Soviet industry was competitive at world standards. It is difficult to remain a superpower when 92 percent of industry is subpar.

The end of the Cold War was one of the great transforming events of this century. It was equivalent to World War II in its effects on the structure of the international system, but it occurred without war. In the next chapters, we turn to what this means for international politics in the future.

The Cold War ended in 1989, but some scholars such as John Mearsheimer argue that the European peace may not be as lasting as most observers now suppose. Russia may never again occupy all its East European neighbors, but Russian nationalism combined with weak democracy could in the future lead to renewed expansionism. Once Russia passes through this period of domestic upheaval, it might turn its attention to the Baltic states, to Ukraine, and to Eastern Europe. If that happens, 1989 will be seen as a temporary calm in the midst of a long, drawn-out storm. However unlikely this scenario, a careful study of international politics dictates that it not be entirely ruled out.

Following the breakup of the Soviet Union, Russia has undergone a significant transformation. Renouncing the planned economy of the Soviet state, post–Cold War Russia tentatively embarked on a path of democratization and economic liberalization. That road has been fraught with peril, however. Following the advice of the World Bank, the Russian government at first embraced economic "shock therapy" as a way of making the transition from economic autocracy to liberal democracy. Yet, shock therapy so disrupted Russian society that it was quickly shelved in favor of a more gradualist approach. As the economic situation deteriorated, Russian nationalism was rejuvenated.

Theorists such as Michael Doyle, hypothesizing that liberal democracies do not fight wars with one another, have concluded that if Russia survives the transition to democracy, it will bode well for international peace. It remains to be seen whether the foreign policy of a democratic Russia will fit the model of the democratic peace, or whether there will be a resurgence of Russian nationalism that challenges the United States and Western Europe.

Regardless of what the future holds, one major puzzle remains: why the Cold War lasted so long without a "hot war" erupting between the two superpowers. Why did it not earlier turn into World War III?

THE ROLE OF NUCLEAR WEAPONS

Why didn't the Cold War turn hot? Some analysts believe that advanced developed societies learned from the lessons of World War I and World War II and simply outgrew war. Others believe that the "long peace" in the second half of the twentieth century stemmed from the limited expansionist goals of the superpowers. Still others credit what they consider the inherent stability of pure bipolarity in which two states (not two tight alliances) are dominant. But for most analysts, the largest part of the answer lies in the special nature of nuclear weapons and nuclear deterrence.

Physics and Politics

The enormous destructive power of nuclear weapons is almost beyond comprehension. A megaton nuclear explosion can create temperatures of 100 million degrees Celsius—four to five times the temperature in the center of the sun. The bomb dropped on Hiroshima in 1945 was relatively small, about the equivalent of 15,000 tons of TNT. Today's missiles can carry 30 times that explosive power. In fact, all of the explosive power used in World War II could fit in one three-megaton bomb, and that one bomb could fit in the nose cone of one large intercontinental missile. By the 1980s, the United States and the Soviet Union had more than 50,000 nuclear weapons.

Some physical effects of nuclear explosions are uncertain. For example, the theory of nuclear winter holds that a nuclear war would create so much carbon and dust in the atmosphere it would block plants from their photosynthesis, which would mean the end of life as we know it. A National Academy of Sciences study reported that nuclear winter is possible, but highly uncertain. Much would depend on whether the weapons were aimed at cities rather than at other weapons. Burning cities would cause smoke with a high carbon content that would block sunlight, but it is uncertain how long the smoke would stay aloft. If the bombs exploded in the Northern Hemisphere, would the smoke travel to the Southern Hemisphere? Some skeptics argued the worst result would not be nuclear winter, but nuclear autumn—a faint consolation. The certainty is that a large-scale nuclear war would destroy civilization as we know it, at least in the Northern Hemisphere. In their 1983 report on nuclear weapons, the American Catholic bishops engaged in only slight hyperbole when they said, "We are the first generation since Genesis with the capability of destroying God's creation."[8]

Nuclear weapons produced changes in the nature of warfare, but they did not change the basic way in which the world is organized. The world of anarchic states with no higher government above them continued in the nuclear age. In 1946, when the United States proposed the Baruch Plan to establish international control of nuclear weapons, the Soviet Union viewed it as just another American plot. After this failure, Albert Einstein lamented that everything changed except our thinking. Perhaps aprocryphally, he is supposed to have said that "physics is easier than politics."

There are both military and political reasons why nuclear weapons did not have a more dramatic effect right after 1945. For one thing, the early atomic weapon did not do significantly more damage than the most deadly uses of massed conventional weapons. The fire bombing of Dresden in Germany killed more people than the nuclear bombing of Hiroshima. Though one atomic weapon did the work of a entire air attack using conventional bombs, at first there were not that many nuclear weapons in the U.S. arsenal. The United States had only two in 1947, and 50 in 1948. Many military planners felt that atomic bombs were not totally different, just extensions of conventional warfare.

The emerging U.S.-Soviet rivalry also slowed change in political thinking. The Soviet Union mistrusted the United Nations as too reliant on the United States. The United States could not coerce the Soviets into cooperation because Europe was a hostage between the Soviets and the Americans. If the United States threatened nuclear attack, the Soviets could threaten to invade Europe with conventional forces. The result was a stalemate. The revolutionary physical effects of nuclear technology were initially not enough to change the ways states behaved in an anarchic system.

The second stage of the nuclear revolution occurred in 1952 when the hydrogen bomb was first tested. The hydrogen bomb relies on the fusion energy released when atoms are fused into one, instead of split apart as in the early fission bombs. The H-bomb increased the amount of destruction possible with a single weapon. The largest explosion on the earth's surface occurred in 1961 when the Soviet Union exploded a 60-megaton hydrogen bomb, 20 times all the explosive power used in World War II.

Ironically, the more important change that accompanied the development of the H-bomb was miniaturization. Fusion made it possible to deliver enormous amounts of destructive power in very small packages. The systems built to deliver the early atomic bombs got bigger and bigger as the bombs increased in size and took more and more space. The B-36 bomber was a huge eight-engine airplane with one big cavity to hold one bomb. A hydrogen bomb, on the other hand, could put the same potential destruction in a small package. Once that destructive power was mounted in the nose cone of a ballistic missile, an intercontinental nuclear war could occur with only 30 minutes warning, compared to the 8 hours it took a B-36 to fly the same distance.

The increased destructiveness of hydrogen bombs also dramatized the consequences of nuclear war. No longer could warfare be considered merely an extension of politics by other means. Karl von Clausewitz, the nineteenth-century philosopher of war said war is a political act, and therefore absolute war is an absurdity. The enormous destructive power of nuclear weapons meant there was now a disproportion between the military means and most of the political ends that a country might seek. This disjunction between ends and means caused a paralysis in the use of the ultimate force in most situations. Nuclear weapons have not been used since 1945; thus the view that nuclear weaponry is muscle-bound. It was just too powerful, too disproportionate.

The H-bomb had five significant political effects, even though it did not reorganize the anarchic way in which the world goes about its business. First, it revived the concept of limited war. The first half of the twentieth century saw a change from the limited wars of the nineteenth century to the two world wars, which took tens of millions of lives. At mid-century, analysts were referring to the twentieth century as "the century of total war." But war in the second half of the century has been more like the old wars of the eighteenth and nineteenth centuries; for instance, the

Korean and Vietnam wars each cost over 55,000 American deaths. In Vietnam and Afghanistan, the United States and the Soviet Union each accepted defeat rather than use their ultimate weapon.

Second, crises replaced central war as the moments of truth. In the past, war was the time when all of the cards were face up on the table. But in the nuclear age, war is too devastating and the old moments of truth are too dangerous. During the Cold War, the Berlin crisis, the Cuban missile crisis, and the Middle East crises of the early 1970s played the functional equivalent of war, a time to see the true correlation of forces in military power. Third, nuclear weapons made deterrence (discouragement by fear) the key strategy. It was now critical to organize military might to produce fear in advance so that attack would be deterred. In World War II, the United States relied on its ability to mobilize and gradually build a war machine after the war started, but that mobilization approach no longer worked when a nuclear war could be over in a matter of hours.

A fourth political effect was the development of a de facto regime of superpower prudence. The two superpowers, despite their bitter ideological differences, developed one common interest: avoiding nuclear war. During the Cold War, the United States and the Soviet Union engaged in proxy or indirect peripheral wars, but in no case did the two nations go head to head. In addition, the two sides developed spheres of influence. While the Americans talked about rolling back communism in Eastern Europe in the 1950s, in practice, when the Hungarians revolted against their Soviet rulers in 1956, the United States did not rush in to help them for fear of nuclear war. Similarly, with the exception of Cuba, the Soviets were relatively careful about incursions into the Western Hemisphere. Both countries adhered to a developing norm of nonuse of nuclear weapons. Finally, the superpowers learned to communicate. After the Cuban missile crisis, Washington and Moscow developed the hotline to allow instant communication between the Soviet and American leaders. They signed a number of arms control treaties, starting with the Limited Test Ban Treaty in 1963. Arms control negotiations became a way to discuss stability in the nuclear system.

Fifth, nuclear weapons in general and the H-bomb in particular were seen by most officials as unusable in time of war. It was not purely a matter of the destructive potential of the H-bomb. There was a stigma attached to the use of nuclear weaponry that simply did not apply to conventional weaponry. By the late 1960s, in fact, engineers and scientists had managed to shrink the payload of nuclear weapons so that some nuclear weapons could have been used by the United States in Vietnam and the Gulf War or the Soviet Union in Afghanistan without causing the type of unjustifiable damage of an H-bomb. Yet, both Americans and Russians refrained from using smaller payload nuclear weapons and opted instead for destructive tools such as napalm, incendiary bombs, and assorted conventional weapons. In part, that was because it was feared that using any nuclear weapon, no matter how similar to conventional weapons, would open the window to using all nuclear weapons, and that risk was unacceptable. Yet, there was another dimension. Ever since the first bomb was dropped by the United States on Hiroshima, there was a lingering sense that nuclear weapons were immoral, that they went beyond the realm of what was acceptable in war. Though that normative restraint is hard to measure, it clearly

---

NUCLEAR WEAPONS AND THE VIETNAM WAR

When President Kennedy made the first decision to increase significantly the American military presence in 1962–63, . . . he had in mind two things: What would have happened if Khrushchev had not believed him in the Berlin crisis of 1961–62, and what would have happened if Khrushchev did not believe Kennedy in the Cuban missile crisis of 1962?

I think we made a mistake in concluding that the Chinese would probably not intervene in the Korean War in 1950, and that influenced the American decision not to invade North Vietnam. The military said they did not think China would come in, but if it did, it would lead to nuclear war, and that decided that.

—Secretary of State Dean Rusk[9]

---

suffused the debates over nuclear weapons and was one reason for the unwillingness of states to use them.

Balance of Terror

Nuclear weapons produced a peculiar form of the balance of power that was sometimes called the "balance of terror." Tests of strength were more psychological than physical. Both sides followed a policy of preventing preponderance by the other, but the result was different from previous systems. Unlike the nineteenth-century balance of power system in which five great powers shifted alliances, the Cold War balance was very clearly organized around two very large states, each capable of destroying the other in an instant.

The problems raised by the classical security dilemma were not ended by the terror of nuclear weapons, but the superpowers acted prudently despite their ideological differences. Their prudence was similar to the effects of the constant communications that occurred in managing the multipolar nineteenth-century balance of power. At the same time, the superpowers tried to calculate balances of force, just as in the days when statesmen compared provinces, infantry, and artillery.

The nuclear balance of terror coincided with a period of bipolarity. Some political scientists like Kenneth Waltz define bipolarity as situations when two large states have nearly all the power, but that type of pure bipolarity is rare. More often bipolarity has occurred in history when alliances tighten so much that flexibility is lost, as happened in the Peloponnesian War. Even though they were independent states, the alliances around Athens and around Sparta coalesced tightly into a bipolar situation. Similarly, on the eve of World War I the alliance systems became tightly bound into bipolarity.

Waltz argues that bipolarity is a particularly stable type of system because it simplifies communication and calculations. On the other hand, bipolar systems lack flexibility and magnify the importance of marginal conflicts like the Vietnam War. The conventional wisdom in the past was that bipolarity either erodes or explodes. If so, why did bipolarity not explode after World War II? Perhaps the prudence produced by nuclear weapons provided the answer, and the stability that Waltz attributed to pure bipolarity was really the result of the bomb. The very terror of nuclear weapons may have helped to produce stability through the "crystal ball effect." Imagine that in August 1914 the kaiser, the czar, and the emperor of Austria-Hungary looked into a crystal ball and saw a picture of 1918. They would have seen that they had lost their thrones; their empires had been dismembered, and millions of their people had been killed. Would they still have gone to war in 1914? Probably not. Knowledge of the physical effects of nuclear weapons may be similar to the effect of giving statesmen in the post-1945 period a crystal ball. Since there were few political goals that would be proportionate to such destruction, they would not want to take great risks. Of course, crystal balls can be shattered by accidents and by miscalculations, but the analogy suggests why the combination of bipolarity and nuclear weapons produced the longest period of peace between the central powers since the beginning of the modern state system. (The previous record was 1871 to 1914.)

Problems of Nuclear Deterrence

Nuclear deterrence is a subset of general deterrence, but the peculiar qualities of nuclear weapons changed how the superpowers approached international relations during the Cold War. Nuclear deterrence encourages the reasoning, "If you attack me, I may not be able to prevent your attack, but I can retaliate so powerfully that you will not want to attack in the first place." Nuclear weapons have thus put a new twist on an old concept.

One way to assess the efficacy of nuclear deterrence is by counterfactual analysis. How likely was it that the Cold War would have turned hot in the absence of nuclear weapons? The political scientist John Mueller argues that nuclear weapons were irrelevant, that they were no more than the rooster crowing. He argues that the peoples of Europe had been turning away from war as a policy instrument ever since the horrors of World War I. The cause of peace was the increased recognition of the horror of war, at least in the developed world. According to Mueller, Hitler was an aberration, a rare person who had not learned the lessons of World War I and was still willing to go to war. After World War II, the general revulsion returned more strongly than before. Most analysts, however, believe that nuclear weapons had a lot to do with avoiding World War III. Crises over Berlin, Cuba, and perhaps the Middle East might have spiraled out of control without the prudence instilled by the crystal ball effect of nuclear weapons.

That raises a number of questions. One is, What deters? Effective deterrence requires both the capability to do damage and the credibility that the weapons will be used. Credibility depends on the stakes involved in a conflict. For example, an American threat to bomb Moscow in retaliation for a nuclear attack was probably credible. But suppose the United States had threatened to bomb Moscow in 1980 if the Soviets did not withdraw their troops from Afghanistan? The United States certainly had the capability, but the threat would not have been credible because the stakes were too low, and the Soviets could easily have threatened in return to bomb Washington. So deterrence is related not just to capability, but also to credibility.

That problem of credibility leads to a distinction between deterring threats against one's homeland and extending deterrence to cover an ally. For example, the United States could not stop the Soviet Union from invading Afghanistan by nuclear deterrence, but for the four decades of the Cold War it threatened to use nuclear weapons if the Soviet Union invaded the NATO countries of Western Europe. Thus to look for the effects of nuclear weapons in extending deterrence and averting war, we must look at major crises where the stakes are high.

Can history answer these questions about the effect of nuclear weapons? Not completely, but it can help. From 1945 to 1949, the United States alone had nuclear weapons, but did not use them. So there was some self-restraint even before mutual nuclear deterrence. Part of the reason was small arsenals, a lack of understanding of these new weapons, and the American fear that the Soviets would capture all of Europe with their massive conventional forces. By the 1950s, both the United States and the Soviet Union had nuclear weapons, and there were several crises in which American leaders considered their use. Nuclear weapons were not used in the Korean War, or in 1954 and 1958 when the Chinese communists mobilized forces to invade the Nationalist-held island of Taiwan. Presidents Truman and Eisenhower vetoed the use of nuclear weapons for several reasons. In the Korean War, it was not clear that dropping a nuclear weapon would stop the Chinese, and the United States was concerned about the Soviet response. There was always the danger that the threats might escalate and the Soviets might use a nuclear weapon to help their Chinese ally. So even though the Americans had superiority in the number of nuclear weapons, there was the danger of heading to a larger war involving more than Korea and China.

In addition, ethics and public opinion played a role. In the 1950s, U.S. government estimates of the number of citizens who would be killed were so high that the idea was put aside. President Eisenhower, when asked about using nuclear weapons, said, "We can't use those awful things against Asians for the second time in less than ten years. My God!"[10] Thus, even though the United States had more nuclear weapons than the Soviet Union in the 1950s, a combination of factors persuaded the Americans not to use them.

The Cuban Missile Crisis

The key case was the Cuban missile crisis of October 1962. This was probably the closest call in the nuclear age to a set of events that could have led to nuclear war. If a total outsider, a "man from Mars," had looked at the situation, he would have seen that the United States had a 17-to-1 superiority in nuclear weaponry. We now know the Soviets had only about twenty nuclear weapons on intercontinental missiles that could have reached the United States, but President Kennedy did not know it at the time. Why then didn't the United States try to preempt by attacking the Soviet missile sites, which were then relatively vulnerable? The answer was that if even one or two of the Soviet missiles had escaped and been fired at an American city, that was too much to risk and enough to deter. In addition, both Kennedy and Khrushchev feared that rational strategies and careful calculations might spin out of their control. Khrushchev came up with a nice metaphor for this in one of his letters to Kennedy: "Be careful as we both tug at the ends of the rope in which we have tied the knot of war."[11]

At a conference in Florida, 25 years after the event, Americans who had been involved in President Kennedy's Executive Committee of the National Security Council met with scholars to try to reconstruct the Cuban missile crisis. One of the most striking differences among the participants was how much each had been willing to take risks. That in turn depended on how likely each thought were the prospects of nuclear war. Robert McNamara, who was Kennedy's secretary of defense, became more cautious as the crisis unfolded. He said he thought the risks of nuclear war in the Cuban missile crisis were probably one chance out of fifty. Douglas Dillon, who was the secretary of the treasury, said he thought the risks of nuclear war were about zero. He did not see how the situation could possibly progress to nuclear war and as a result was willing to push the Soviets harder and to take more risks than McNamara was. General Maxwell Taylor, the chairman of the Joint Chiefs of Staff, also thought the risk of nuclear war was low, and he complained that the United States let the Soviet Union off too easily in the Cuban missile crisis. His view was the Americans could have pushed much harder and should have demanded the removal of Cuba's president, Fidel Castro. General Taylor said, "I was so sure we had 'em over a barrel, I never worried much about the final outcome."[12] But the risks of losing control weighed heavily on President Kennedy, who took a very cautious position, indeed, more prudent than some of his advisers would have liked. The moral of the story is that a little nuclear deterrence goes a long way. It is clear that nuclear deterrence made a difference in the Cuban missile crisis.

Nonetheless, there are still ambiguities about the missile crisis that make it difficult to attribute the whole outcome to the nuclear component. The public consensus was that the United States won. But the question of how much the United States won and why it won is overdetermined. There are at least three possible explanations. One view is that because the United States had more nuclear weapons than the Soviet Union, the Soviets gave in. A second explanation adds the importance of the relative stakes of the two superpowers in the crisis. Cuba was in America's backyard, but a distant gamble for the Soviets. Therefore, Americans not only had a higher stake in Cuba than the Soviets, but could also bring a third factor to bear: conventional forces. An American naval blockade and the possibility of an American invasion of Cuba also played a role. The psychological burden was on the Soviets because higher stakes and readily available conventional forces gave the Americans more credibility in their deterrent position.

Finally, although the Cuban missile crisis is called an American victory, it was also a compromise. The Americans had three options in the Cuban missile crisis. One was a shoot-out, that is, to bomb the missile sites; the second was a squeeze-out by blockading Cuba to convince the Soviets to take the missiles out; the third was a buy-out by offering to trade something the Soviets wanted, such as removal of American missiles from Turkey. For a long time, the participants did not say much about the buy-out aspects of the solution, but subsequent evidence suggests that a quiet American promise to remove its obsolete missiles from Turkey was probably more important than was thought at the time. We can conclude that nuclear deterrence mattered in the crisis and that the nuclear dimension certainly figured in John Kennedy's thinking. On the other hand, the number of weapons was less important. It was not the ratio of nuclear weapons that mattered so much as the fear that even a few nuclear weapons could wreak such devastation.

In 1962 President Kennedy insisted that each member of the National Security Council read Barbara Tuchman's *The Guns of August*. The book is the story of how the nations of Europe inadvertently blundered into World War I. The author begins by quoting Bismarck's comment that "some damned foolish thing in the Balkans" would ignite the next war. She then related the series of steps—following the assassination on June 28, 1914, of the Austrian heir apparent, Archduke Franz Ferdinand, by Serbian nationalists—each small and insignificant in itself, that led to the most appalling military conflict in the history of the world. Time and again, at the brink of hostilities, the chiefs of state tried to pull back, but the momentum of events dragged them forward.

President Kennedy reminded us of the 1914 conversation between two German chancellors on the origins of that war. One asked, "How did it happen?" and his successor replied, "Ah, if we only knew." It was Kennedy's way of stressing the constant danger of miscalculation.

—Robert McNamara, *Blundering into Disaster*[13]

Moral Issues

After the Cuban missile crisis there was a relative easing of the tension in the Cold War—almost as if the United States and the Soviet Union had stumbled to the brink of a cliff, looked over, and pulled back. In 1963, a hotline allowing direct communication between Washington and Moscow was installed, an arms control treaty limiting atmospheric nuclear tests was signed; Kennedy announced the United States would be willing to trade more with the Soviet Union, and there was some relaxation of tension. Through the late 1960s, the United States was preoccupied with the Vietnam War, yet there were still arms control efforts. Intense fear of nuclear war returned after the Soviet Union invaded Afghanistan in 1979. During "the little cold war" from 1980 to 1985, strategic arms limitation talks stalled, rhetoric became particularly harsh, military budgets and the number of nuclear weapons increased. President Ronald Reagan talked about nuclear war fighting, and peace groups pressed for a freeze and ultimate abolition of nuclear weapons.

In the climate of heightened anxiety, many people asked a basic question: "Is nuclear deterrence moral?" As we saw earlier, just war theory argues that certain conditions must be met in making moral judgments. Self-defense is usually regarded as a just cause, but the means and consequences by which a war is fought are equally important. In terms of the means, civilians must be distinguished from combatants; in terms of consequences, there has to be some proportionality, some relationship of the ends and the means.

Could nuclear war possibly fit the just war theory? Technically, it could. Low-yield nuclear weapons such as artillery shells that have explosive power near the range of the most advanced conventional weapons might be used against radar systems, ships at sea, or deep underground command bunkers. In that case, we could discriminate between combatants and noncombatants and keep the effects relatively limited. If the fighting stopped there, we could fit nuclear weapons within just war theory. But would fighting stop there or would it escalate? Escalation is the great risk, for what could be worth a hundred million lives or the fate of the earth? During the Cold War, some people answered, "It's better to be Red than dead."

But that may have been the wrong way to pose the question. Alternatively, we might ask, Is it ever justifiable to run a small risk of a large calamity? During the Cuban missile crisis, John Kennedy was reputed to have said he thought the chances of conventional fighting were perhaps one in three. And there was some smaller risk of nuclear escalation. Was he justified in taking such a risk? We can ask the counterfactual. If Kennedy had not been willing to take the risk in Cuba, would Khrushchev have tried something even more dangerous? What if a Soviet success had led to a later nuclear crisis or an even larger conventional war, for example, over Berlin or the Panama Canal?

Nuclear weapons probably played a significant role in preventing the Cold War from turning hot. During the 1980s, the American Catholic bishops said that nuclear deterrence could be justified on a conditional basis as a tolerable interim measure until something better was developed. But how long is the interim? So long as nuclear knowledge exists, some degree of nuclear deterrence will exist. Although the weapons produced prudence during the Cold War, complacency is a danger. It took the United States and the Soviet Union some time to learn how to control nuclear weapons, and it is far from clear that such control systems will exist among new aspirants to nuclear status.

Concern about the proliferation of nuclear weapons has played a central role in many international crises of the 1990s. While over 170 states have signed the Nuclear Non-Proliferation Treaty, the spread of nuclear weapons continues, with countries such as Iraq, Iran, and North Korea obtaining or seeking to obtain nuclear weapons. Also of concern are the spread of unconventional arsenals such as biological and chemical weapons; Libya for example continued to construct chemical weapons facilities even though it suffered from international sanctions as a result. The Gulf War in 1991, and the near confrontation between the United States and North Korea in 1994, as well as documented accounts of nuclear material making its way out of the former Soviet Union and into the international black market, demonstrate that these weapons still have the capacity to cause tension and bring nations to the brink of war.

The continued international animus against weapons of mass destruction has both a moral and a realist dimension. The moral opprobrium against nuclear weapons is shared not just by those states that do not have the capacity or desire to make such weapons, but even by the states that continue to build them, such as the United States, France, and Russia. Chemical and biological weapons have been condemned since World War I, when the use of mustard gas led to widespread outcries in both Allied and Axis countries. The realist dimension is simple: weapons of mass destruction carry great risk of escalation and enormous potential for devastation. Whenever these weapons are present, the dynamics of conflict change. Weak states with nuclear or unconventional weapons are better able to threaten strong states, while strong states with these weapons are able to more effectively threaten and deter adversaries. At the same time, the risk that these devices will be used if a crisis spins out of control raises the level of tension, whether it is between the United States and North Korea or between India and Pakistan. The Cold War may be over, but the era of nuclear and unconventional weapons is not.

NOTES

1. Milovan Djilas, *Conversations with Stalin,* trans. Michael B. Petrovich (San Diego: Harcourt Brace Jovanovich, 1962), p. 114.

2. Ralph B. Levering, *The Cold War, 1945–1972* (Arlington Heights, IL: Harlan Davidson, 1982), p. 15.

3. William Taubman, *Stalin's American Policy* (New York: Norton, 1982), p. 37.

4. Ibid., p. 36.

5. Ibid., p. 131.

6. Dean Acheson, *Present at the Creation* (New York: Norton, 1969), p. 375.

7. George Kennan, "The Sources of Soviet Conduct," *Foreign Affairs,* Vol. 25, No. 4 (July 1947), p. 581.

8. United States Catholic Conference, "The Challenge of Peace: God's Promise and Our Response," *Origins,* Vol. 13, No. 1 (May 19, 1983), p. 1.

9. Secretary of State Dean Rusk, *New York Times,* April 30, 1985, p. 6.

10. Stephen E. Ambrose, *Eisenhower* (New York: Simon & Schuster, 1983), p. 184.

11. Ronald R. Hope, ed., *Soviet Views on the Cuban Missile Crisis: Myth and Reality in Foreign Policy Analysis* (Washington, DC: University Press of America, 1982), p. 48.

12. James Blight and David Welch, *On the Brink: Americans and Soviets Reexamine the Cuban Missile Crisis* (New York: Hill and Wang, 1989), p. 80.

13. Robert McNamara, *Blundering into Disaster: Surviving the First Century of the Nuclear Age* (New York: Pantheon, 1986), p. 14

SELECTED READINGS

1. Schlesinger, Arthur, Jr., "The Origins of the Cold War," *Foreign Affairs,* Vol. 46, No. 1 (October 1967), pp. 22–53.

2. Yergin, Daniel, *The Shattered Peace* (Boston: Houghton Mifflin, 1977), pp. 69–86.

3. Gaddis, John L., *Russia, the Soviet Union, and the United States* (New York: Wiley, 1978), Chapters 6, 7.

4. Mueller, John, "The Essential Irrelevance of Nuclear Weapons," and Jervis, Robert, "The Political Effects of Nuclear Weapons," *International Security,* Vol. 13, No. 2 (Fall 1988), pp. 80–90.

5. Khong, Yuen F., "The Lessons of Korea and the Vietnam Decision of 1965," in George W. Breslauer and Philip E. Tetlock, eds., *Learning in U.S. and Soviet Foreign Policy* (Boulder, CO: Westview Press, 1991), pp. 302–349.

FURTHER READINGS

Allan, Charles T., "Extended Conventional Deterrence: In from the Cold and out of the Nuclear Fire?" *The Washington Quarterly,* Vol. 17, No. 3 (Summer 1994), pp. 203–233.

Allison, Graham T., *Essence of Decision: Explaining the Cuban Missile Crisis* (Boston: Little, Brown, 1971).

Blight, James G., and David A. Welch, *On the Brink: Americans and Soviets Reexamine the Cuban Missile Crisis* (New York: Hill and Wang, 1989).

Bundy, McGeorge, *Danger and Survival* (New York: Random House, 1988).

Fursenko, Aleksandr and Timothy Naftali, *"One Hell of a Gamble": Khrushchev, Castro & Kennedy, 1958–1964* (New York: Norton, 1997).

Gaddis, John L., *Strategies of Containment: A Critical Appraisal of Postwar American National Security Policy* (New York: Oxford University Press, 1982).

Gray, Colin S. *Weapons Don't Make War: Policy, Strategy, and Military Technology* (Lawrence: University Press of Kansas, 1993).

Herring, George C., *America's Longest War: The United States and Vietnam, 1950–75* (New York: Wiley, 1979).

Kagan, Donald, *On the Origins of War* (New York: Doubleday, 1995).

Kennan, George F., *Memoirs (1925–1950)* (Boston: Little, Brown, 1967).

Kennedy, Robert, *Thirteen Days* (New York: Norton, 1968).

Kolko, Gabriel, and Joyce Kolko, *The Limits of Power: The World and United States Foreign Policy, 1945–1954* (New York: Harper & Row, 1972).

Lafeber, Walter, *America, Russia, and the Cold War 1945–1975* (New York: Wiley, 1967).

Larson, Deborah W., *Origins of Containment: A Psychological Explanation* (Princeton, NJ: Princeton University Press, 1985).

Lebow, Richard Ned, and Thomas Risse-Kappen, eds., *International Relations Theory and the End of the Cold War* (New York: Columbia University Press, 1995).

Legvold, Robert, "Soviet Learning in the 1980s," in George W. Breslauer and Philip E. Tetlock, eds., *Learning in U.S. and Soviet Foreign Policy* (Boulder, CO: Westview Press, 1991), pp. 684–732.

Mandelbaum, Michael, *The Nuclear Revolution* (Cambridge, England: Cambridge University Press, 1986).

Mastny, Vojtech, *Russia's Road to the Cold War: Diplomacy, Warfare, and the Politics of Communism, 1941–1945* (New York: Columbia University Press, 1979).

Taubman, William, *Stalin's American Policy: From Entente to Détente to Cold War* (New York: Norton, 1982).

Williams, William A., *The Tragedy of American Diplomacy* (Cleveland: World, 1959).

Yergin, Daniel, *Shattered Peace: The Origins of the Cold War and the National Security State* (Boston: Houghton Mifflin, 1977).

STUDY QUESTIONS

1. When did the Cold War begin? When did it end? Why?

2. Was the Cold War inevitable? If so, why and when? If not, when and how could it have been avoided?

3. Why were statesmen unable to restore a concert system after World War II? What sort of system evolved?

4. How important were first and second image considerations in the development of the Cold War? What were the views of American and European statesmen on the Soviet Union and its international ambitions? What were Soviet views of the United States and the rest of the West?

5. Some historians argue that the real question is not why the Cold War occurred, but why it did not escalate into a "hot" war. Do you agree? Why didn't a hot war begin?

6. What is *containment?* How did this American policy emerge, and how was it implemented? What were Soviet responses?

7. How are nuclear weapons different from conventional weapons? Has the advent of nuclear weapons fundamentally changed the way nations behave?

8. Is Mueller correct that nuclear weapons are not the cause of the obsolescence of major wars among developed states? What other factors does he consider?

9. Is nuclear deterrence morally defensible? Or, in the words of one theorist, is it morally analogous to tying infants to the front bumpers of automobiles to prevent traffic accidents on Memorial Day? Might some strategies of deterrence be more ethical than others?

10. What is the relation of nuclear weapons to international relations apart from nuclear deterrence? How useful are they?

11. Does nuclear superiority matter? What role did it play in the Cuban missile crisis?

CHRONOLOGY: THE DEEP COLD WAR YEARS

November 1943	Teheran meeting between Stalin, Churchill, and Roosevelt
July 1944	Bretton Woods Conference: creation of International Monetary Fund and World Bank
August 1944	Dumbarton Oaks Conference: creation of United Nations
October 1944	Moscow meeting between Churchill and Stalin: spheres of influence plan for the Balkans
February 1945	Yalta Conference between Stalin, Churchill, and Roosevelt
April 1945	Roosevelt dies
May 1945	Germany surrenders
April–June 1945	San Francisco Conference—UN Organization Charter
July 1945	First test of A-bomb; Potsdam Conference: Truman, Churchill/Attlee, Stalin
August 1945	Hiroshima and Nagasaki destroyed by A-bombs; USSR enters war in Asia
September 1945	Japan surrenders
March 1946	Churchill's Iron Curtain speech; resumption of Greek civil war
March 1947	Truman Doctrine announced
June 1947	Marshall Plan announced
October 1947	Creation of Cominform by Moscow
February 1948	Coup by Czech Communist Party
March 1948	Partial blockade of Berlin begins
June 1948	Berlin airlift begins; Yugoslavia ousted from Cominform
November 1948	Truman reelected president
April 1949	North Atlantic Treaty signed in Washington
May 1949	End of the Berlin blockade
August 1949	USSR explodes first A-bomb
September 1949	Federal Republic of Germany comes into existence
October 1949	People's Republic of China proclaimed; German People's Republic proclaimed
February 1950	Sino-Soviet pact signed in Moscow
April 1950	NSC-68 drafted
June 1950	Beginning of Korean War

November 1952	First U.S. H-bomb exploded; Eisenhower elected president; Dulles becomes secretary of state
March 1953	Death of Stalin
June 1953	East Berlin uprising
July 1953	Armistice in Korea
August 1953	First Soviet H-bomb test
September 1953	Khrushchev becomes first secretary of Soviet Communist Party
September 1954	Chinese bombardment of Quemoy and Matsu
May 1955	West Germany admitted to NATO; Warsaw Pact signed; Austrian State Treaty signed; Austria neutralized
February 1956	Khrushchev denounces Stalin at Twentieth Party Congress
June 1956	Poznan uprising in Poland
October 1956	Start of Hungarian uprising
November 1956	USSR intervenes in Budapest
August 1957	Launching of first Soviet ICBM
October 1957	Sputnik satellite launched
February 1958	Launching of first U.S. satellite
August 1958	China threatens Taiwan
January 1959	Victory of Fidel Castro in Cuba
September 1959	Khrushchev visits United States
February 1960	First French A-bomb test
May 1960	American U-2 shot down over USSR; Paris summit fails
April 1961	Failure of Bay of Pigs landing in Cuba
June 1961	Khrushchev and Kennedy meet in Vienna
August 1961	Building of the Berlin Wall
October 1961	Incidents at Checkpoint Charlie in Berlin; tensions increase
October 1962	Cuban missile crisis

6 INTERVENTION, INSTITUTIONS, AND REGIONAL CONFLICTS

UN General Assembly meeting

SOVEREIGNTY AND INTERVENTION

With the end of the Cold War, major war has become less likely, but regional conflicts will persist, and there will be pressures for outside states and international institutions to intervene. Intervention is a confusing concept, partly because the word is both descriptive and normative. It not only describes what is happening, it casts value judgments. Nonintervention in the internal affairs of sovereign states is a basic norm of international law. Nonintervention is a powerful norm because it affects both order and justice. Order sets a limit on chaos. International anarchy—the absence of a higher government—is not the same as chaos if basic principles are observed. Sovereignty and nonintervention are two of the principles that provide order in an anarchic world system. At the same time, nonintervention affects justice. Nation-states are communities of people who deserve the right to develop a common

133

life within their own state boundaries. Outsiders should respect their sovereignty and territorial integrity. But not all states fit this ideal. There is often a tension between justice and order that leads to inconsistencies about whether to intervene or not.

Defining Intervention

In its broadest definition, intervention refers to external actions that influence the domestic affairs of another sovereign state. Some analysts use the term more narrowly to refer to *forcible* interference in the domestic affairs of another state. The narrow definition is merely one end of a spectrum of influences ranging from low coercion to high coercion (see Figure 6.1). At the low end of the scale, intervention may be simply a speech designed to influence domestic politics in another state. For example, in 1990, President Bush appealed to the Iraqi people to overthrow Saddam Hussein. His speech was designed to interfere in the domestic politics in another state. In the 1980s, the U.S. government established Radio Martí to broadcast its messages against Fidel Castro in Cuba.

Economic assistance is another way of influencing the domestic affairs of another country. For example, U.S. economic aid to El Salvador and Soviet aid to Cuba were designed to influence domestic affairs in those states. Bribery is illegal economic assistance. During the Cold War, American and Soviet intelligence agencies often poured resources into foreign elections. In the 1970s, the government of South Korea spent a great deal of money to help elect U.S. politicians who were more favorable to the interests of South Korea.

A little further along the spectrum of coercion is the provision of military advisers. In the early days of the Vietnam War, the United States began its intervention first with economic and later with military assistance. Similarly, the Soviet Union and Cuba provided military aid and advisers to Nicaragua and other "client" states. Another form of intervention is support for the opposition. For example, in the early 1970s, the United States channeled money to the opponents of Salvador Allende, the democratically elected president of Chile, and the Soviet Union at various times channeled money to peace groups in the Western European countries.

Toward the coercive end of the spectrum is limited military action. For example, in the 1980s, the United States bombed Libya in response to state-supported terrorism, and the Soviet Union helped one faction fighting a civil war in South Yemen.

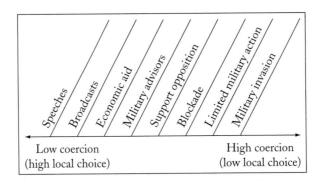

Figure 6.1

Full-scale military invasion or occupation is the upper end of the spectrum of coerciveness. Examples include U.S. actions in the Dominican Republic in 1965, Grenada in 1983, and Panama in 1989, and the Soviet Union's actions in Hungary in 1956, Czechoslovakia in 1968, and Afghanistan in 1979. Nor is it merely great powers that intervene with force. For example, in 1979 Tanzania sent troops into Uganda, and Vietnam invaded Cambodia.

The broad definition includes the whole range of behavior, from not very coercive to highly coercive. The degree of coercion involved in intervention is important because it relates to the degree of choice that the local people have, and thus the degree of outside curtailment of local autonomy.

Sovereignty

Sovereignty was a vital concept for the League of Nations. It is also at the heart of debates about the legitimacy of intervention. While sovereignty is absolute in the legal sense, de facto control by a government within its borders is often a question of degree.

For several reasons, governments rarely have full control over everything that happens within their borders. One is international economic interdependence. For example, when the Socialist Party came to power in France in 1981, it wanted to make major changes in French economic policies. But the Socialists found the French economy was so interdependent with the other European economies that when they tried to make changes unilaterally, capital fled abroad and the value of the French franc dropped. So eventually the French socialists came back to a common policy with the other European states. Interdependence did not limit French legal sovereignty, but it certainly limited de facto control. France was too economically interdependent to have a fully autonomous economic policy.

Economic interdependence is only one of several factors impinging on sovereignty. A massive influx of refugees can disrupt even stable states. Refugees from Haiti to the United States led to political problems in Washington in 1993 and 1994, while refugees from Rwanda into neighboring Burundi exacerbated ethnic conflict there. Drug and arms trafficking can also undermine sovereignty. The influx of arms into northern Pakistan from Afghanistan has limited the ability of the Karachi government to control its northern territory, while the illegal influx of drugs into the United States from abroad has created problems of law and order within the United States. States may be sovereign in the legal sense, but outside actors affect internal affairs.

Ironically, intervention may sometimes increase autonomy. Some poor states may have low de facto autonomy because they have very low capabilities. Some kinds of intervention may actually increase capabilities and thus real autonomy in the future. Economic or military assistance may help a state to become more independent in the long term. What looks like a loss of autonomy at one time may actually increase autonomy later. These are some of the complications in the relationship of sovereignty, autonomy, and intervention.

Judging Intervention

Realists, cosmopolitans, and *state moralists* have different views of intervention. For the realists, the key values in international politics are order and peace, and the key institution is the balance of power. Therefore, for the *realists,* intervention can be justified when it is necessary to maintain the balance of power and to maintain order. Examples are the spheres of influence during the Cold War (the American sphere of influence in the Western Hemisphere, the Soviet sphere of influence in Eastern Europe). In 1965, the United States intervened in the Dominican Republic on the grounds that there should be no more communist governments in the Western Hemisphere, and the Soviet Union intervened to preserve communist governments in Eastern Europe. Indeed, the Soviets proclaimed the Brezhnev Doctrine; that is, they had a right to intervene to preserve socialism in their sphere of influence. Realists might justify such interventions on the grounds that they preserved order and prevented the possibility of misunderstandings and miscalculations that might escalate to war, particularly nuclear war.

For the *cosmopolitans,* the key value is justice and the key international institution is a society of individuals. Therefore, intervention can be justified if it promotes justice. It is permissible to intervene on the side of the good. But how is "good" to be defined? During the Cold War, liberal cosmopolitans said that intervention was justified against right-wing regimes such as the Marcos dictatorship in the Philippines or the apartheid regime in South Africa, while conservative cosmopolitans said that intervention was justified against left-wing governments. In the 1980s, some Americans proclaimed a Reagan Doctrine; that is, that it was right to intervene against the Sandinista government in Nicaragua and against the communist governments in Angola and Mozambique because of their violation of democratic rights. In the 1990s, with the end of the Cold War, cosmopolitans urged humanitarian intervention in Somalia (1992) to halt widespread starvation, in Haiti (1994) to restore the democratically elected Jean-Bertrand Aristide to power, and in Zaire (1996) to help stop starvation and ethnic violence triggered by the influx of refugees from neighboring Rwanda. What cosmopolitans, left and right, had in common was the view that intervention is justified if it promotes justice.

For *state moralists,* the key value in international politics is the autonomy of the state and its people. The key institution is a society of states with certain rules and international law. The most important of these rules is nonintervention in the sovereign territory of another state. So for the state moralists, intervention is rarely justified. War is justified to defend a state's territorial integrity or to defend its sovereignty against external aggression. However, the real world is sometimes more complicated. External aggression is often ambiguous. For example, in June 1967, Israel crossed the border and attacked Egypt first. Yet, it is often argued that Israel was not the aggressor because it was engaged in a preemptive strike against an impending Egyptian attack. Who was the aggressor, the Egyptians who massed their forces on the border and appeared to be preparing an attack on Israel, or the Israelis who struck just before the Egyptians could attack?

Exceptions to the Rule

In *Just and Unjust Wars,* Michael Walzer discusses four situations that could morally justify war or military intervention in the absence of overt aggression. The first exception to a strict rule is preemptive intervention, exemplified by the Israeli attack in 1967. If there is a clear and sufficient threat to a state's territorial integrity and political sovereignty, it must act right away or it will have no chance to act later. But the threat must be imminent. Such an argument would not justify, for example, the

Soviet intervention in Afghanistan. There is a distinction between preemptive wars and preventive wars. A preemptive strike occurs when war is imminent. A preventive war occurs when statesmen believe merely that war now is better than later. As we have seen, such preventive war thinking influenced the German general staff in 1914. Many feared that if they waited until 1916, Russia would be too strong for the Schlieffen Plan to work. Walzer's first exception to nonintervention would not have allowed a preventive war because there was no clear and present danger to Germany. And as we saw earlier with our counterfactual examples, many other things might have changed the situation between 1914 and 1916.

The second exception to the strict rule occurs when intervention is needed to balance a prior intervention. This rule goes back to John Stuart Mill and the nineteenth-century liberal view that a people has the right to determine its own fate. If an intervention prevents local people from determining their own fate, a counter-intervention nullifying the first intervention can be justified because it restores the local people's own right to decide. The United States sometimes used this as a justification for its involvement in Vietnam. Mills's argument permits intervention only as far as it counterbalances a prior intervention; more than that is not justifiable. In 1979, China intervened in Vietnam by crossing the border, but China pulled its troops back within a few weeks. China argued that it was countering Vietnam's intervention in Cambodia. Intervention is allowed only to the extent that the first intervention is countered and no further, because the key principle is to allow the local people to solve their own problems.

The third exception to the rule against intervention is when it is necessary to rescue people who are threatened with massacre. If such people are not saved from total destruction, there is no point to nonintervention as a sign of respect for their autonomy or rights. Tanzania invaded Uganda when a dictatorial leader was slaughtering large numbers of people, and it justified its intervention as rescuing people threatened by massacre. Vietnam used a similar pretext for its invasion of Cambodia. Still, massacre or genocide do not necessarily lead states or the international community to intervene. Note the reluctance of the United States to send troops to Rwanda in 1994, to Bosnia between 1992 and 1995, or to Liberia in 1996.

The fourth exception to nonintervention is the right to assist secessionist movements when they have demonstrated their representative character. In other words, if there is a group of people within a country who have clearly demonstrated they want to be a separate country, it is legitimate to assist their secession because doing so helps them to pool their rights and develop their autonomy as a nation. But when does a secessionist movement become worthy of assistance? Is their success the way to judge their worthiness? Part of Mills's argument was that to become a legitimate nation, a people must be able to seek its own salvation and fight for its own freedom. Such a view is consistent, at least, with the principle of nonintervention and a society of states, but it is deficient as a moral principle because it suggests that might makes right.

Self-Determination

The problem of intervention on behalf of secessionist movements is defining *what* is a people? Who shares a common life? How do outsiders know whether a people really agreed to pool their rights in a single community or state? Self-determination is an important principle, but there is always the question of who determines: What is the self that will determine? Consider Somalia, whose people, unlike many other African states, had roughly the same linguistic and ethnic background. Neighboring Kenya was formed by colonial rule from dozens of different peoples or tribes, with different linguistic backgrounds and customs. Part of northern Kenya was inhabited by Somalis. Somalia said the principle of national self-determination should allow the Somalis in the northeastern part of Kenya and the Somalis in the southern part of Ethiopia to secede, because they were one Somali nation. Kenya and Ethiopia refused, saying they were still in the process of building a nation. The net result was a number of wars in northeast Africa over the Somali nationalist question.

Voting does not always solve such problems. First, there is the question of where one votes. Take the question of Ireland. If a vote is held within the political area of Northern Ireland, the two-thirds Protestant majority would rule. If a vote is held within the geographical area of the entire island, the two-thirds Catholic majority would rule. Who determines where the vote is held? Also, when does one vote? The Somalis wanted to vote right away; Kenya wanted to wait 40 or 50 years while it went about its nation-building.

Does secession harm those left behind? What about the resources the secessionists take with them, or the disruption they create in the country they leave? For example, after the dismantlement of the Austrian Empire in 1918, the Sudetenland was incorporated into Czechoslovakia even though the people spoke German. After the Munich Agreement in 1938, the Sudeten Germans seceded from Czechoslovakia and joined Germany, but that meant the mountainous frontier went under German control, which was a terrible loss for Czech defenses. Was it right to allow self-determination for the Sudeten Germans, even if it meant stripping Czechoslovakia of its military defenses? More recently, when eastern Nigeria decided it wanted to secede and form the state of Biafra in the 1960s, other Nigerians resisted in part because Biafra included most of Nigeria's oil. They argued that the oil belonged to all the people of Nigeria, not just the eastern area.

After 1989, the issue of self-determination became acute in Eastern Europe and the former Soviet Union. Czechoslovakia was once again divided along ethnic lines, this time peacefully between the western Czech Republic and the eastern state of Slovakia. Throughout the former Soviet Union, different ethnic groups claimed the right of self-determination, just as many of them had done between 1917 and 1920. In the Caucasus, Azerbeijanis, Armenians, Georgians, Abkhazians, and Chechens all demanded states on the basis of self-determination.

In the former state of Yugoslavia, different ethnic and religious groups seceded and claimed self-determination. The Slovenes, Serbs, and Croats managed to carve out independent republics, but the Muslims in Bosnia-Herzegovina were less successful. While both Serbia and Croatia had ethnic minorities, Bosnia was more ethnically mixed than either and included large minorities of Serbs and Croats. After 1992, Bosnian Muslims were subjected to a campaign of ethnic cleansing by both Croatian and Serb forces. The war in Bosnia was devastating for the civilian population, and war-crimes tribunals were convened in The Hague to convict those responsible for the massacres. Yet, for much of the conflict, the United Nations, the North Atlantic Treaty Organization (NATO), and the European Union were divided over how to respond. Part of what made the war in Bosnia so difficult for the international community was the problem of assessing how much the conflict was a civil war among Bosnian Croats, Serbs, and Muslims and how much it was intervention by Serbia. If it was not simple aggression, then the only grounds for intervention would be to prevent massacre. As with Rwanda, the international community was united in its condemnation but was unable to agree on joint action until late in the conflict in 1995.

Motives, Means, and Consequences

If consistency is impossible, what other principles can be used to judge interventions? There are three dimensions of judgment related to the just war tradition: motives, means, and consequences. All three are important because judging interventions by one dimension alone may obtain the wrong answer. For example, judging intervention by consequences alone is equivalent to saying "might makes right." Obviously, more than consequences must be considered.

On the other hand, neither do good intentions alone justify an intervention. For example, the writer Norman Podhoretz argued that the United States was right to intervene in Vietnam because the Americans were trying to save the South Vietnamese from totalitarian rule. Here is an analogy. Suppose a friend offers to drive your child home one night. It is a rainy night; your friend goes too fast and skids off the road and your daughter is killed. Your friend says, "My intentions were purely good. I wanted to get her home early for the SATs." If Podhoretz is right that the American action in Vietnam was what he called "imprudent but moral," do good intentions make it right? We have to consider more than the motivation; consequences must be considered as well.

In the Vietnam War, it was not enough that the United States tried to save South Vietnam from the horrors perpetrated by North Vietnam. Even if the cause was just, the means used are a different proposition. One question to ask is, were there alternatives? Was intervention a last resort? Were there efforts to protect innocent life? Was it proportional—did the punishment fit the crime, so to speak—or was it excessive? Were there procedures to ensure impartiality? To what extent was there attention to international multilateral procedures that might have checked the human tendency to weight these considerations in one's own favor? What about the consequences? What about the prospects for success? What about the danger of unintended consequences because a local situation was not well enough understood, because of the difficulty of differentiating between civilians and guerrillas? As obvious as it seems, it is still necessary to stress the need to be careful about situations where there is enormous complexity and very long causal chains. Motives, means, and consequences must all be considered before judgments can be made.

Consider how the policy of containment led to intervention in Vietnam. As we have seen, in the early stages just after World War II, the issue was whether the United States should step into Britain's place in the eastern Mediterranean to preserve Turkey and Greece from possible Soviet encroachment. The debate inside the United States was about how to explain it to the American people. Secretary of State George Marshall and others were quite cautious. Others such as Undersecretary Dean Acheson and Senator Arthur Vandenburg wanted a moral tone to make it a larger cause. So when President Truman explained his actions in the Truman Doctrine, he talked of protecting free people everywhere.

AMERICAN INTERVENTION IN VIETNAM

The U.S. sent its troops into Vietnam to reverse the verdict of a local struggle, which meant, in turn, imposing a ghastly cost in death and suffering upon the Vietnamese. As it turned out, the U.S. could not reverse that verdict finally; it could only delay its culmination.

Those of us who opposed American intervention yet did not want a communist victory were in the difficult position of having no happy ending to offer—for the sad reason that no happy ending was possible any longer, if ever it had been. And we were in the difficult position of urging a relatively complex argument at a moment when most Americans, pro- and antiwar, wanted blinding simplicities.

—Irving Howe and Michael Walzer, "Were We Wrong About Vietnam?"[1]

George Kennan, who had warned against Stalin's aggressive plans, became disillusioned as containment became highly ideological. He argued that the United States was trying to contain Soviet power; therefore, anything that balanced Soviet power without intervening directly with American troops was for the good. But those who took the more ideological view said the United States should contain communism directly. Over time, the argument for balancing Soviet power gave way to a broader view of containment as keeping the world free from communism. In Vietnam, this view led leaders to underestimate national differences among communist states. The United States began to feel it had to contain Chinese and Soviet power and the spread of communist ideology. By the time the doctrine of containment moved from the eastern Mediterranean in 1947 to Southeast Asia in the 1950s, it had become a justification for an overly ambitious and ill-fated intervention.

In conclusion, although the simple absolute principle of nonintervention is frequently breached in practice, the norm of nonintervention remains important. Exceptions to nonintervention must be judged on a case-by-case basis by looking at the motives, means, and consequences.

INTERNATIONAL LAW AND ORGANIZATION

Sovereignty and nonintervention are enshrined in international law and organization. People sometimes have problems in understanding international law and organization because they use a domestic analogy. But international organization is not like domestic government, and international law is not like domestic law. International organization is not an incipient world government for two reasons. First, the sovereignty of member states is protected in the charters of most international organizations. Article 2:7 of the Charter of the United Nations says, "Nothing in the Charter shall authorize the United Nations to intervene in matters within domestic jurisdiction." In other words, the organization is not an effort to replace the nation-states.

Domestic Analogies

The other reason that international organization is not incipient world government is because of its weakness. There is an international judiciary in the form of the International Court of Justice, which consists of 15 judges elected for 9-year terms by the United Nations, but the International Court of Justice is not a world supreme court. States may refuse its jurisdiction, and a state may refuse to accept its judgments, even if the state has accepted the court's jurisdiction. In the 1980s, for example, the Reagan administration refused to accept an International Court of Justice ruling that the United States had acted illegally in mining the harbors of Nicaragua.

If we imagine the UN General Assembly as the equivalent of Congress, it is a very strange kind of legislature. It is one based on the principle of one state, one vote, but that is not a principle which reflects either democracy or power relations in the world. Democracy rests on the principle of one person, one vote. In the UN General Assembly, the Maldive Islands with 100,000 people in the southern Indian Ocean has one vote and China, which is a country with over a billion people, has one vote. That means a Maldive Islander has 10,000 times the voting power of a Chinese in the UN General Assembly. So it does not fit well with the democratic criteria for legislatures. Nor is it a very good reflection of power, because the Maldive Islands has the same vote in the General Assembly as the United States or India or China. So there is an oddity about the General Assembly that makes states unwilling to have it pass binding legislation. UN General Assembly resolutions are just that: resolutions, not laws.

Finally, we might imagine that the secretary-general of the United Nations is the incipient new president of the world. But that is also misleading. The secretary-general is a weak executive. If the secretary-general has power, it is more like the power of a pope than of a president. Trying to understand international organizations by analogy to domestic government is a sure way to get the wrong set of answers.

Nor is international law like domestic law. Domestic law is the product of legislatures and customs, sometimes called common law. Domestic law involves provisions for enforcement, adjudication by individuals (you can go to a court yourself and bring suit), and orderly revision by legislation. Public international law is similar in the sense that it consists of treaties, which are agreements among states, and customs, which are the generally accepted practices of states. But it differs dramatically in enforcement and adjudication. On enforcement, there is no executive to make a state accept a court decision. International politics is a self-help system. In the classic ways of international law, enforcement was sometimes provided by the great powers. For example, in the law of the sea, a custom developed that a state could claim a 3-mile jurisdiction out into the oceans. When countries like Portugal and Uruguay in the seventeenth and eighteenth centuries claimed broader territorial seas to protect the fisheries off their coasts, Britain, the great naval power of the day, sent gunboats within 3 miles of their coast. So customary law was enforced by the great power. You might ask who enforced the law against Britain if Britain violated the law. The answer is that enforcement in self-help systems is a one-way street.

Adjudication in international law is by states, not by individuals. Instead of any of the world's billions of citizens bringing cases to the international court, only the states can bring cases, and they are unlikely to bring cases unless they want to get them off their docket or think they have a reasonable chance of winning. Thus, the court has had relatively few cases. In addition, there are problems about how customary rules should be interpreted even when a principle is agreed upon. Take the principle of expropriation. It is accepted that a state can nationalize a corporation from another country that operates on its territory, but it must pay compensation for what the corporation is worth. But who is to say what is just compensation? Many of the less developed countries have argued that low compensation is adequate; rich countries usually want higher levels.

Finally, even when the UN General Assembly has passed resolutions, there is a good deal of ambiguity about what they mean. They are not binding legislation. The only area in the UN Charter where a state must legally accept a decision is Chapter VII, which deals with threats to peace, breaches of the peace, and acts of aggression. If the Security Council (not the General Assembly) finds there has been an act of aggression or threats to peace warranting sanctions, then member states are bound to apply the sanctions. That is what happened in 1990 when Iraq invaded Kuwait.

The other way in which new law is sometimes created is through large intergovernmental conferences that negotiate draft treaties for governments to sign. Such conferences are often very large and unwieldy. For example, in the 1970s, the law of the sea conference involved over a hundred states participating, trying to draft principles for a 12-mile territorial sea, an exclusive economic zone for fisheries out to 200 miles, and designating the manganese nodules on the bottom of the ocean as the common heritage of all. The trouble was that some states agreed to only parts of the text, leaving the outcome unclear in international law.

International law basically reflects the fragmented nature of international politics. The weak sense of community means there is less willingness to obey or restrain oneself out of a sense of obligation or acceptance of authority. The absence of a common executive with a monopoly on the legitimate use of force means that sovereign states are in the realm of self-help and in the realm of force and survival. And when matters of survival come up, law usually takes second place.

Predictability and Legitimacy

Nonetheless, international law and organization are an important part of political reality because they affect the way states behave. States have an interest in international law for two reasons: predictability and legitimacy.

States are involved in conflicts with each other all the time. The vast range of international transactions, both public and private, includes trade, tourism, diplomatic missions, and contacts among peoples across national boundaries. As interdependence grows, those contacts grow and there are increasing opportunities for friction. International law allows governments to avoid conflict at a high level when such friction arises. For example, if a U.S. tourist is arrested for smuggling drugs in Mexico, or a British ship collides with a Norwegian ship in the North Sea, or a Japanese firm claims that an Indian company has infringed its patents, the governments may not want to spoil their other relations over these private collisions. Handling such issues by international law and agreed principles depoliticizes them and makes them predictable. Predictability is necessary for transactions to flourish and for the orderly handling of the conflicts that inevitably accompany them.

Legitimacy is a second reason why governments have an interest in international law. Politics is not merely a struggle for physical power, but also a contest over legitimacy. Power and legitimacy are not antithetical, but complementary. Humans are neither purely moral nor totally cynical. It is a political fact that the belief in right and wrong helps to move people to act, and therefore legitimacy is a source of power. If a state's acts are perceived as illegitimate, the costs of a policy will be higher. States appeal to international law and organization to legitimize their own policies or delegitimize others, and that often shapes their tactics and outcomes.

The Suez Canal

The Suez crisis of 1956 provides a good example. The Suez Canal was built by the British and French in the nineteenth century and became important for Britain's trade routes to India. In 1956, about a quarter of British imports came through the Suez Canal. In July 1956, President Gamal Nasser of Egypt nationalized the Suez Canal. Sir Anthony Eden, the British prime minister, saw this as a major threat to Britain. He regarded Nasser as a new Hitler, and he drew analogies to the 1930s and Britain's failure to take a stand when Hitler entered the Rhineland. Britain feared that Nasser's appeal to Arab nationalism would undercut Britain's position in the Middle East and worried about the fact that Nasser had accepted Soviet arms—this, of course, being at the height of the Cold War.

In August and early September of 1956, Britain and the United States proposed a Suez Canal users' association, saying Egypt could nationalize the canal, but the control would rest with those who used it for shipping. Nasser rejected that compromise. In the meantime, Britain had developed a secret plan with France and Israel. Israel, which had been suffering from cross-border guerrilla attacks that Nasser instigated, would invade Egypt. Britain and France would then intervene on the pretext there was a threat to the Suez Canal. Thus, Israel crossed into the Sinai region of Egypt, arguing it was acting out of self-defense. It appealed to Article 51 of the UN Charter that permits self-defense as the one legitimate use of force. As Israel advanced into the Sinai toward the Suez Canal, Britain and France said they had to intervene to prevent any damage to the canal. The UN Security Council discussed the crisis, rejected the pretext, and called for a cease-fire. Britain and France used their vetoes to prevent the cease-fire. They wanted the intervention to keep going until they could get rid of Nasser.

Dag Hammarskjöld, the UN secretary-general, working with Canadian foreign minister Lester Pearson, devised a plan to separate the Israelis and the Egyptians by inserting a UN peacekeeping force. Then the British and the French would no longer have a pretext for their intervention. A resolution in the General Assembly, where there was no veto, authorized a UN force in the Sinai region. The United States did not support its European allies, worrying that their intervention would antagonize Arab nationalists and increase the opportunities for the Soviet Union in the Middle East. Instead, the United States backed Pearson and Hammarskjold's plan. To add to the pressure on Britain, the United States refused to let the International Monetary Fund (another international organization) provide a backup loan to Britain, whose pound sterling was now under pressure. The British and the French caved in and agreed to a cease-fire. (The Soviets at this time were busy intervening in Hungary, which was trying to achieve its own freedom.)

A LETTER TO PRESIDENT DWIGHT EISENHOWER

In the nineteen-thirties Hitler established his position by a series of carefully planned movements. These began with occupation of the Rhineland and were followed by successive acts of aggression against Austria, Czechoslovakia, Poland and the West. His actions were tolerated and excused by the majority of the population of Western Europe. . . .

Similarly the seizure of the Suez Canal is, we are convinced, the opening gambit in a planned campaign designed by Nasser to expel all Western influence and interests from Arab countries. He believes that if he can get away with this, and if he can successfully defy eighteen nations, his prestige in Arabia will be so great that he will be able to mount revolutions of young officers in Saudi Arabia, Jordan, Syria and Iraq. (We know that he is already preparing a revolution in Iraq, which is most stable and progressive.) These new Governments will in effect be Egyptian satellites if not Russian ones. They will have to place their united oil resources under the control of a United Arabia led by Egypt and under Russian influence. When that moment comes Nasser can deny oil to Western Europe and we here shall be at his mercy.

—Prime Minister Anthony Eden, 1956[2]

The British and French had to accept the cease-fire partly because of American pressure, and partly because they had been caught on their own legal pretext. There was now another way of separating the Israelis and the Egyptians and preventing damage to the canal. On November 15, the first UN expeditionary force was inserted into the Sinai between the opposing forces, and later in December, the United Nations took on the task of clearing the ships that had been sunk in the canal. The use and abuse of international law and organizations played an essential part in the politics of the Suez crisis.

In major conflicts of interest, international law may not restrain states, but it often helps to shape the flow of policy. Law is part of the power struggle. Cynics may say these are just games that lawyers play; but the very fact that governments find it important to make legal arguments or to take the resolutions of international organizations into account shows they are not completely insignificant. To put it in an aphorism: "When claims to virtue are made by vice, then at least we know virtue has a price." Simply put, governments may be trapped by their own legal excuses.

Another example is UN Security Council Resolution 242. Passed at the end of the 1967 Middle East War, it called for a return to prewar boundaries. Over the years, it had the effect of denying the legitimacy of the Israeli occupation of the territories it captured during that war. That put Israel on the defensive in the United Nations. The Arab states lost the war, but were nonetheless able to put pressure on Israel. In 1976, when the Arab coalition tried to expel Israel from the United Nations, the United States spent a good deal of political capital lobbying before the General Assembly to prevent Israel's expulsion, another indication that symbols of legitimacy in international organizations are part of a power struggle.

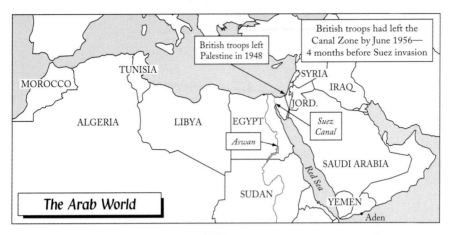

British troops left
Palestine in 1948

British troops had left the
Canal Zone by June 1956—
4 months before Suez invasion

TUNISIA

MOROCCO

SYRIA

IRAQ

JORD.

ALGERIA

LIBYA

EGYPT

*Suez
Canal*

Aswan

SAUDI ARABIA

Red Sea

SUDAN

YEMEN

Aden

The Arab World

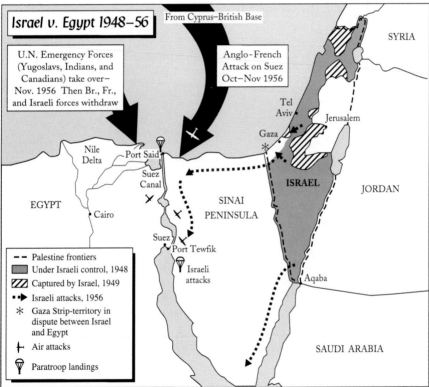

Israel v. Egypt 1948–56

From Cyprus–British Base

SYRIA

U.N. Emergency Forces
(Yugoslavs, Indians, and
Canadians) take over–
Nov. 1956 Then Br., Fr.,
and Israeli forces withdraw

Anglo-French
Attack on Suez
Oct–Nov 1956

Tel
Aviv

Jerusalem

Gaza

Nile
Delta

Port Said

Suez
Canal

ISRAEL

JORDAN

EGYPT

Cairo

SINAI
PENINSULA

Suez

Port Tewfik

Israeli
attacks

Aqaba

– – Palestine frontiers

Under Israeli control, 1948

Captured by Israel, 1949

Israeli attacks, 1956

* Gaza Strip-territory in
dispute between Israel
and Egypt

Air attacks

Paratroop landings

SAUDI ARABIA

Figure 6.2

When vital issues of survival are at stake, a state will use its most effective form of power, which is military force. And that may explain the limited success of efforts of international law and organization to deal with the use of force. It is one thing to handle drug smuggling or collision of ships at sea or patent infringement by international law; it is another to put the survival of one's country at risk by obeying international law. That was the problem with collective security in the 1930s, but a modified form of collective security was recreated in the UN Charter.

UN Peacekeeping and Collective Security

The classical balance of power did not make war illegal. The use of military force was accepted, and it often assured the stability of the system. During the nineteenth century, with changes in technology making war more destructive, and with the rise of democracy and peace movements, there were several efforts to organize states against war. Twenty-six states held a peace conference at The Hague in 1899. In 1907, another Hague conference was attended by 44 states. The approach taken in these conferences was very legalistic. The conferees tried to persuade all states to sign treaties of arbitration so that disputes would be handled by arbitration rather than force. They also tried to codify rules of war in case arbitration did not work.

As we have seen, after World War I, the League of Nations was an attempt to develop a coalition of states that would deter and punish aggressors. In the eyes of Woodrow Wilson and those who thought as he did, World War I had been largely an accidental and unnecessary war caused by the balance of power, and such wars could be prevented by an alliance of all states for collective security. If the League of Nations was designed to prevent World War I after the fact, the United Nations was designed in 1943–1945 to prevent World War II. Forty-nine states met in San Francisco in 1945 to sign a charter that included innovations to repair the deficiencies of the League. The threat or use of force was outlawed, except for self-defense or when it involved collective security. Unlike the balance of power system of the nineteenth century, the offensive use of force was now illegal for any state that signed the UN charter. Any use of force had to be either for self-defense, or collective self-defense, or collective security.

The UN designers also created a Security Council composed of five permanent members, and a rotating pool of nonpermanent members. The Security Council can be seen as a nineteenth-century balance of power concept integrated into the collective security framework of the UN. The Security Council is able to pass binding resolutions under Chapter VII of the Charter. If the five great power policemen did not agree, they each had the veto, which was like a fuse box in a house lighting system. Better a veto that made the lights go out than the house burn down in the form of a war against a great power.

During the Cold War, the UN collective security system did not work. In the Cold War ideological cleavage, there was little agreement on what was a legitimate use of force, and great problems arose in defining aggression. For example, how should one weigh covert infiltration against forces crossing a border first? As we have seen, in 1967, Israel had been suffering from Egyptian guerrilla attacks covertly, yet Israeli's conventional forces crossed the border first. Depending on your side in the

Cold War, you took different views on who was the initial aggressor. For two decades during the Cold War, UN committees tried to define aggression. They came up with a rule that did not do much: A list of acts of aggression was followed by the proviso that the Security Council could determine that other acts also constituted aggression. And even when armed force had been used, the Council could choose not to declare there had been any aggression. So as far as the UN was concerned, aggression was committed when the Security Council said so. Everything depended on a consensus in the Security Council, and that was rare during the Cold War.

The impasse over collective security gave rise to the concept of UN preventive diplomacy. Rather than identifying and punishing the aggressor, which is the basic concept of collective security, the UN would assemble independent forces and interpose them between the warring powers. The model developed by Dag Hammarskjöld and Lester Pearson in 1956 was used many times afterward. Even though the Cold War prevented the UN from implementing the revised doctrine of collective security, it did not prevent the innovation of using international forces to keep two sides apart. In collective security, if a state crosses a line, all the others are to unite against it and push it back. In preventive diplomacy, if a state crosses a line, the UN steps in and holds the parties apart without saying who was right or wrong. During the Cold War, one of the basic principles of UN peacekeeping was that the forces always came from small states, not from the Soviet Union or the United States, so that the great powers would be kept out of direct conflict. Preventive diplomacy and peacekeeping was an important innovation that still plays a significant role, but it was not collective security.

Iraq's 1990 invasion of Kuwait was the first crisis after the Cold War. Since the Soviet Union and China did not exercise their vetoes, UN collective security was used for the first time in 40 years. There were three reasons for this remarkable resurrection. First, Iraq committed an extraordinarily clear-cut aggression, very much like the 1930s, which reminded statesmen of that failure of collective security. The second reason was the feeling that if UN collective security failed in such a clear case, it would not be a principle for order in a post–Cold War world. Third, the small states in the UN supported the action because most of them were fragile and had disputable postcolonial boundaries. The arguments Saddam Hussein used to justify his invasion of Kuwait threatened most of the other small states as well. To paraphrase the Haitian delegate to the League of Nations quoted earlier, they did not want to become someone else's Kuwait.

Will UN collective security be a basis for a new world order? Only in part. There are important qualifications. First, the UN system works best when there is clear-cut aggression; it will be much more difficult to apply in civil wars. Second, collective security will work if there is no veto, but if the United States and Russia or the United States and China come to cross purposes again, collective security will be hamstrung once more. Moreover, in 1945, UN collective security was not designed to be applicable against the five great powers with vetoes in the Security Council. Third, collective security works when the member states provide the resources, but it is difficult to imagine collective security working if the states with large military forces do not provide resources. Collective security was a miserable failure in the 1930s, was put on ice during the Cold War, and then, like Lazarus, rose from the dead in the Persian Gulf in 1990. But it was only a minor miracle, for, as we see in Chapter 8, collective security is only part of what will be needed for world order after the Cold War.

The United Nations has political effects, even when collective security cannot be applied, because the presumption against force written into the UN charter places the burden of proof on those who want to use force. In addition, the Security Council discussion of international violence dramatizes the practice of collective concern and centralizes attention in times of crisis. It sometimes crystallizes viewpoints, raising the costs of aggressive uses of force, and acts as a safety valve for diplomacy. Finally, the role of the UN peacekeeping forces is limited but useful. These trip wires and buffer zones are devices that states have found in their interests again and again. With the end of the Cold War, there were more opportunities for the UN. The UN played a role in the decolonization of Namibia, in monitoring human rights in El Salvador, in the elections in Nicaragua, in the administration in Cambodia, as well as in overseeing peacekeeping forces. Even though the original doctrines of collective security do not fit as neatly as once thought, it would be a mistake to dismiss international law and organization. They are part of the political reality of the anarchic state system. It is a mistake to be too cynical or too naive about international organization and law. States do not live by law alone, but they do not live completely without it.

CONFLICTS IN THE MIDDLE EAST

Torn by strife, the Middle East is a good case to illustrate regional conflicts. Although it best fits the realist view of international politics, it is also an area where international law and organization have played some role. What is the cause of so much conflict? Nationalism, religion, and balance of power politics each provide part of the answer.

The Iran-Iraq War, which began in September 1980, provides a good example. Why did Iraq invade its larger neighbor? One reason was the Islamic revolution that overthrew the shah of Iran. Under the shah, Iran had claimed the whole waterway between Iran and Iraq. But after the 1979 Iranian Revolution deposed the shah, Iran was torn apart by domestic strife, and Iraq's president, Saddam Hussein, saw an opportune time to attack. Moreover, revolutionary Iran was causing problems inside Iraq. Iraqi Muslims were divided between Sunnis and Shi'ites, and Saddam Hussein was a secular head of state. The Shi'ite fundamentalists in Iran urged the Iraqi Shi'ites to rise up against Saddam Hussein. This transnational religious appeal failed when Saddam Hussein killed many Iraqi Shi'ite leaders. But Iraq also miscalculated. Iranians are not Arabs, and there was a large Arabic-speaking minority in the part of Iran adjacent to Iraq. Iraqis thought they would be welcomed as liberators in the Arabic-speaking part of Iran, but that was not the case. Instead, Iraq's attack helped to unite the Iranians.

After this pair of miscalculations, the war bogged down into a long drawn-out affair, instead of the short profitable war that Saddam Hussein had intended. Iraq decided it wanted to get out, but Iran refused to let go. Having been attacked, it was not going to let Iraq decide when to quit. The Ayatollah Khomeini, spiritual leader of Iran, said that Iran would not end the war until the downfall of Saddam Hussein. For most of the decade, the rest of the world looked on. Conservative Arab countries like Saudi Arabia and Jordan supported Iraq against Iran because they were more afraid of Iranian revolutionary power. But, as we have seen, Arab Syria, a secular and radical regime in many ways similar to Iraq, supported Iran for balance of power reasons. They were worried about the rising strength of their neighbor Iraq, rather than more distant Iran.

Outsiders also took sides. The United States, worried about the growth of Iranian power, provided covert assistance to Iraq. Israel secretly shipped U.S.-built weapons to Iran, even though fundamentalists in Iran were calling for the abolition of Israel. Israel's covert weapons assistance can be explained by balance of power considerations. Israel feared both Iraq and Iran, but Iraq was a closer threat, and on the principle of "the enemy of the enemy is my friend," Israel provided assistance to Iran. So a war that started from miscalculations rooted in religion, nationalism, and ambition was expanded by balance of power concerns into an intractable, nearly decade-long conflict.

The Questions of Nationalism

How does nationalism cause war? Indeed, what is nationalism and what is a nation? The dictionary defines a nation as a group claiming common identity and the right to be a state. But what kinds of groups does that encompass? What is the source of the common identity? One claim is ethnic similarity, but the United States is ethnically diverse and yet one nation. Another claim is linguistic similarity, but Switzerland is linguistically diverse and yet one nation. Others say religion can be the basis of a nation and some states, such as Israel and Pakistan, are largely based on religious identity. The point is that when a group of people with a common identity calls itself a nation, there can be various sources of that identity. As the French thinker Ernest Renan put it: "The essential element of a nation is that all its individuals must have many things in common, but they must also have forgotten many things."[3]

Nationalism is tricky because it is not merely a descriptive term, it is also prescriptive. When words are both descriptive and prescriptive, they become political words used in struggles for power. Nationalism has become a crucial source of state legitimacy in the modern world. Therefore, claims to nationhood become powerful instruments. If a people can get others to accept its claim to be a nation, it can claim national rights and use such claims as a weapon against its enemies. For example, in the 1970s, the Arab states successfully lobbied in the UN General Assembly to pass a resolution that labeled Zionism as racism. Their intent was to deprive Israel of the legitimacy of calling itself a nation. To be labeled as racist is bad; to be labeled as nationalist is generally good. To argue that Israel was not a nation was to use words as weapons.

The analytic problem with the argument was that religion can be a basis of national identity. It is also true that a religious basis can make it more difficult for minorities outside the religion to share the national identity. The world is harder for Muslims in Israel than for Jews, just as the world is harder for Hindus in Pakistan than for Muslims. But it does not follow that because a people use religion to call themselves a nation that the state is racist. The UN General Assembly finally annulled the resolution by a second vote in 1991.

In the eighteenth century, nationalism was not all that important. Why have claims to nationalism become so important now? After all, humans are capable of multiple loyalties—above and below the state level—and these loyalties can change. Loyalties tend to change when the usual patterns of life are disrupted. The idea of the nation often starts among the most disrupted, with people who are marginal figures in their own cultures and less certain about their identity. These are often people who are jolted out of normal patterns, starting to ask questions. National claims often start with intellectuals or with deviant religious groups. For example, the early Arab nationalists in the nineteenth century were often Christians rather than Muslims. Gradually, their concern about a new identity developed broader support as industry and urbanization disrupted the traditional patterns and loyalties of rural societies.

The disruptions that mobilize people for new identities can come from internal or from external forces. Modern nationalism was greatly stimulated by the French Revolution. The rise of the middle class disrupted traditional political and social patterns. Rising political groups no longer wanted the state of France to be defined by the king but to be defined in terms of the nation, all the people. And externally, as Napoleon's armies marched across Europe, they disrupted society and mobilized nationalist feelings among German-speaking peoples and others. By the middle of the century, there was widening support for the idea that each nation should have a state. This ideal culminated in the unification of Germany and Italy. Ironically, Bismarck was a conservative who did not try to unite all German speakers, only those he could control for the Prussian crown. Nonetheless, he turned nationalism to his purposes, and the unification of Germany and Italy became the model of success.

World War II weakened the European colonial empires, and decolonization was one of the major movements in Asia and Africa over the next three decades. The metropolitan societies had been weakened by the war itself, and elites in the colonized areas began to use the idea of nationalism against the European empires. But if the nineteenth-century model of states based on language and ethnicity had been used to organize the postcolonial world, it would have led to thousands of mini-states in Africa and many parts of Asia. Instead, the postcolonial elites asserted the right of the state to make a nation, just the opposite of the nineteenth-century pattern. The local leaders argued they needed to use the state machinery that the colonists had established—the budget, the police, the civil service—to shape a nation out of smaller tribal groups. The same ideology of nationalism came to be used to justify two things that are almost the opposite of each other—nation makes state or state makes nation—because nationalism is a political word with an instrumental use.

In the early romantic days of colonial liberation movements, there was often a successful blurring of these differences in "pan" movements. Europe in the nineteenth and early twentieth centuries saw the rise of pan-Slavism, claiming a common identity of all Slavic-speaking peoples. The modern Middle East saw pan-Arabism, and Africa, pan-Africanism. Early opponents of alien rule argued that since colonized people all suffered alike from the external colonizers, they should form pan-African or pan-Arab nations. But when it came to the actual business of governing, as opposed to liberating or resisting colonialism, the business of government required the instruments of state such as budgets, police, and civil service. And those instruments existed not on a pan basis, but on the basis of the artificial boundaries created by colonial rule. So, as the romanticism gradually wore away, identity based on the state began to replace that of the pan movements. Nonetheless, the romanticism of the pan movements often lingered on as a disruptive force.

The Middle East has seen constant appeals to pan-Arabism and odd situations where countries suddenly announce they are forming a union, as Egypt and Syria did in forming the United Arab Republic in 1958, or countries as disparate as Libya and Morocco did in 1989. Over time, however, the forces of the state have prevailed over these pan-nationalist movements. For example, Egyptian nationalism focused on the state gradually became stronger in public opinion than pan-Arabism. But the gradual process is far from complete. In much of the postcolonial world, there is enormous disruption of the normal patterns of life because of economic change and modern communications. Political leaders try to gain control of this postcolonial discontent. Some use national appeals, some use pan-Arab appeals, others use fundamentalist religious appeals, all contributing to the complexity of the forces that create conflict in regions like the Middle East.

The Arab-Israeli Conflicts

The Arab-Israeli conflict produced six wars between two groups of people asserting different national identities, but claiming the same small, postage-stamp-size piece of land. The Israeli claim dates to biblical times when the area was controlled by Jews before their expulsion and dispersal in A.D. 70. In modern historical times, Israelis appeal to the experience in World Wars I and II. During World War I, the British issued the Balfour Declaration, a letter written by the British government to Lord Rothschild of the British Zionist Federation promising that the British government would work for a Jewish homeland in Palestine. After World War II, Israelis argue, the horrors of Hitler's Holocaust proved the need for a Jewish state. In 1948, Jewish settlers were willing to accept a partition of Palestine, but the Arab people in the area were not. The UN recognized their state, but the Israelis had to fight to preserve it from Arab attack. This, the Israelis say, is the historical origin and justification of the state of Israel.

The Palestinian Arabs respond that they also have lived in the area for centuries. At the time of World War I, when the Balfour Declaration was issued, 90 percent of the people living in the area of Palestine were Arabs. Indeed, as late as 1932, 80 percent of the people were Arabs. They argue that Britain had no right to make a promise to the Jews at the Arabs' expense. What's more, the Arabs continue, the Holocaust may have been one of history's greatest sins, but it was committed by Europeans. Why should Arabs have to pay for it?

Both sides seem to have valid points. In World War I, the area that is now Palestine was ruled by the Turks, and the Ottoman Empire was allied with Germany. After defeat, the empire was dismembered, and its Arab territories became mandates under the League of Nations. France ruled Syria and Lebanon;

His Majesty's Government views with favour the establishment in Palestine of a national home for the Jewish people, and will use their best endeavours to facilitate the achievement of this object, it being clearly understood that nothing shall be done which may prejudice the civil and religious rights of existing, non-Jewish communities in Palestine, or the rights and political status enjoyed by Jews in any other country.

—The Balfour Declaration, November 2, 1917

Britain called the area it received between the Jordan River and the Mediterranean "Palestine," and the area it governed across the Jordan river, "Trans-Jordan."

In the 1920s, Jewish immigration to Palestine increased slowly, but in the 1930s, after the rise of Hitler and intensified anti-Semitism in Europe, it began to increase quite rapidly. By 1936, nearly 40 percent of Palestine was Jewish, and the influx led the Arab residents to riot. The British set up a royal commission, which recommended partition into two states. In May 1939, with the approach of World War II, Britain needed Arab support against Hitler's Germany, so Britain promised the Arabs it would restrict Jewish immigration. But restriction was hard to enforce after the war. Because of the Holocaust, many in Europe were sympathetic to the idea of a Jewish homeland, and there was a good deal of smuggling of Jewish refugees. In addition, some of the Jewish settlers in Palestine used terrorist acts against their British rulers. Britain, meanwhile, was so financially and politically exhausted from World War II and the decolonization of India that it announced in the fall of 1947 that come May of 1948, it would turn Palestine over to the United Nations.

In 1947, the UN recommended a partition of Palestine. Ironically, it would have been better for the Arabs if they had accepted the UN partition plan, but instead they rejected it. That led to outbreaks of local fighting. In May 1948, Israel declared itself independent, and Israel's Arab neighbors attacked to try to reverse the partition. The first war lasted for eight months of on-and-off fighting. Even though the Arabs outnumbered the Israelis 40 to 1, they were poorly organized and hampered by disunity. After a cease-fire and UN mediation, Jordan controlled the area called the West Bank and Egypt controlled Gaza, but most of the rest of the Palestinian mandate was controlled by the Israelis; in fact, more than they would have had if the Arabs had accepted the UN plan of 1947.

The war produced a flood of Palestinian refugees, a sense of humiliation among many Arabs, and a broad resistance to any idea of permanent peace. The Arabs did not want to accept the outcome of the war because they did not want to legitimize Israel. They believed time was on their side. Arab leaders fostered pan-Arab feelings and the belief they could destroy Israel in another war. In fact, when King Abdullah of Jordan tried to sign a separate peace treaty with Israel in 1951, he was assassinated.

The second war occurred in 1956. In 1952, Gamal Abdel Nasser and other young nationalist officers overthrew King Farouk of Egypt. They soon received arms from the Soviet Union and maneuvered to gain control of the Suez Canal. They harassed Israel with a series of guerrilla attacks. As we saw earlier, Britain and

France, angry about the canal and worried about Nasser dominating the Middle East, colluded with Israel to attack Egypt. However, the United States refused to help Britain, and the war was stopped by a UN resolution and peacekeeping force that was inserted to keep the sides apart. But there was still no peace treaty.

The third war, the Six-Day War of June 1967, was the most important because it gave shape to the subsequent territorial problems. Nasser and the Palestinians continued to harass the Israelis with guerrilla attacks, and Egypt closed the Straits of Tiran, which cut off Israeli shipping from the Red Sea. Nasser was not quite ready for war, but he saw the prospect of a Syrian-Israeli war looming and thought he would do well to join. Nasser asked the United Nations to remove its peacekeeping forces from his border. Israel, watching Nasser prepare for war, decided not to wait, but to preempt. The Israelis caught the Egyptian air force on the ground and went on to capture not only the whole Sinai Peninsula, but also the Golan Heights from Syria and the West Bank from Jordan.

At that point the superpowers stepped in to press the two sides to accept a cease-fire. In November 1967, the UN Security Council passed Resolution 242, which said that Israel should withdraw from occupied lands in exchange for peace and recognition. But there were some deliberate ambiguities in Resolution 242. It did not say all territories, it just said territories, implying that some might not have to be returned. It was also ambiguous about the status of the Palestinians, who were not recognized as a nation but were described as refugees. Again, the basic issue was not settled.

The fourth war, the War of Attrition, was a more modest affair. In 1969–1970, Nasser, with support from the Soviet Union, organized crossings of the Suez Canal and other harassments. These provoked an air war in which Israeli and Egyptian pilots fought a number of air battles. Eventually, the air war tapered off into a stalemate.

The fifth war was the Yom Kippur War of October 1973. After Nasser died, he was succeeded by Anwar Sadat, who realized that Egypt could not destroy Israel. But he felt that some psychological victory was necessary before he could make any conciliatory moves toward peace. Sadat decided to attack across the Suez Canal, but not to try to recapture all of the Sinai Peninsula. Sadat colluded with the Syrians and achieved an effective surprise. In the first stages, the war went well for the Egyptians, but the Israelis counterattacked.

Once again, the superpowers stepped in and called for a cease-fire. Secretary of State Henry Kissinger flew to Moscow, but while he was there, the Israelis surrounded the Egyptian armies. The Soviets felt they had been cheated. They mobilized their forces in the southern part of the Soviet Union and sent the United States a letter suggesting that the superpowers introduce their own forces directly. The United States responded by raising the nuclear alert level in the United States, and the Soviets dropped their demand. The Israelis also backed down under American pressure and released the noose around the Egyptian army.

The war was followed by a series of diplomatic maneuvers in which the United States negotiated a partial drawback by Israel. UN observers were placed in the Sinai and on the Golan Heights. The most interesting result of the war, however, was delayed. In 1977, Sadat went to Israel and announced that Egypt was ready to negotiate a separate peace. In 1978 and 1979, with President Jimmy Carter's media-tion, Israel and Egypt negotiated the Camp David Accords, which returned the Sinai to Egypt and provided for talks about local autonomy in the West Bank. The Camp David Accords meant that the largest Arab state had quit the coalition con-fronting Israel, and Egyptian nationalism had prevailed over pan-Arabism. Sadat broke the pan-Arab coalition, but a few years later, he was assassinated by religious fundamentalists who objected to his policy.

The sixth war was Israel's invasion of Lebanon in 1982. Initially, Lebanon had been delicately balanced between Christian and Muslim Arabs. The Muslims, in turn, were divided among Sunnis, Shi'ites, and Druzes. The Palestine Liberation Organization (PLO) was a major presence in Lebanon, and the Christians were also split into factions. Lebanon was once cited as a haven of stability in the Middle East, the one area of true pluralism and diversity, but as Lebanon began to break apart into civil war, it presented increasing opportunities for outside intervention. Syria began to impose order in the north, and in 1978 Israel went into southern Lebanon as far as the Litani River.

In June 1982, Israeli Defense Minister Ariel Sharon decided to go further. First he said that Israel would go only 25 miles into Lebanon to protect the northern parts of Israel, but in fact Israeli troops marched further north and besieged Beirut for ten weeks. The siege led to the evacuation of the PLO from Beirut, and a Lebanese Christian leader, Bashir Gemayel, signed a peace treaty with Israel. How-ever, Gemayel was soon assassinated, the treaty collapsed, and Lebanon fell further into chaos. Eventually, in 1985, the Israelis withdrew from most of Lebanon, but they continued to occupy a buffer zone in the south. Though they had succeeded in driving the PLO out of Beirut and out of Lebanon, the Israelis had little to show for their efforts, and Israel continued to be vulnerable to rocket attacks from various groups in southern Lebanon.

The experience of the Middle East shows that regional conflicts based on eth-nicity, religion, and nationalism tend to become embittered and difficult to resolve. Hard-liners reinforce each other. Arab governments were slow to make peace because they did not want to legitimize Israel, and in their rejection they reinforced the domestic position of those Israelis who did not want to make peace with the Arabs. The extremists formed a de facto transnational coalition that made it very difficult for moderates who wanted to find a compromise. In 1973 and 1977, Sadat took risks, but eventually paid for it with his life. In such a world of extremes, trust and cooperation are difficult, and Prisoner's Dilemma provides an accurate model of regional politics.

During the bipolar period, wars in the Middle East tended to be short, in part because the superpower role was so prominent. On the one hand, each superpower supported its clients, but when it looked like the clients might pull the superpowers toward the nuclear brink, it pulled its clients back. The pressures for cease-fires came from outside. In 1956, it was the United States via the UN; in 1967, the United States and the Soviet Union used their hotline to arrange a cease-fire; in 1973, the United States and the Soviet Union stepped in; and in 1982, the United States pressed Israel to draw back from Lebanon. While in many instances, the Cold War exacerbated regional conflicts, it also placed a safety net underneath them. With the end of the Cold War, the smaller states have increasingly looked to the UN to provide that safety net, but it remains to be seen how effective the UN safety net will be. In 1990–91, responding to Iraq's invasion of Kuwait, the United Nations passed its first post–Cold War test.

The 1991 Gulf War and Its Aftermath

The Gulf crisis started on August 2, 1990, when Saddam Hussein invaded Kuwait. Iraq had always claimed that Kuwait was an artificial creation of the colonists and should not be a separate state. In 1961, it had tried to take over Kuwait but was deterred by Britain. However, as we have seen, the idea that colonial boundaries are meaningless promised to create enormous havoc in other regions of the postcolonial world, which may explain why so many countries in the United Nations rejected the Iraqi reasoning.

In any case, there were deeper economic and political reasons. Iraq had been economically devastated by its eight-year war with Iran. It had an $80 billion debt, which was increasing at the rate of $10 billion every year. At the same time, Iraq sat next to a gold mine—Kuwait—with enormous oil surpluses and a small population. In addition, Iraq was angry with Kuwait over Kuwait's oil policy. Iraq argued that Kuwait cheated on the OPEC oil agreements and that every dollar reduction in the price of a barrel of oil cost Iraq $1 billion per year. Capturing Kuwait, therefore, looked like a solution to Iraq's economic problems.

Politically, Saddam Hussein was worried about the security of Iraq. He believed that everybody was out to undercut his country. After all, in 1981 the Israelis had bombed his nuclear research reactor, and with the decline of the Soviet Union, it looked as though the United States and Israel were becoming ever more powerful. In a speech in Amman, Jordan, in February 1990, Saddam said the Soviet Union was in decline and could no longer counter the Americans and the Israelis. Saddam believed he would have to do it himself. He undertook a number of actions designed to test the Americans. Ironically, the United States was trying to appease Saddam Hussein, to bring him back into the community of responsible nations, and to use Iraq as an effective balance to Iranian power in the region. The inconsistency of American policy misled Saddam Hussein, and he believed he could get away with the invasion of Kuwait without suffering serious reprisals.

Saddam was wrong. A series of UN resolutions applied the doctrine of collective security against Iraq. Why did the United States and others respond as they did? One argument is that it was all for oil. Certainly, oil exports made the gulf an abnormally important region, but there was more to the crisis than oil. For example, Britain was deeply involved in the war, but Britain did not import any oil. There was also concern about collective security and echoes of failure to stand up to aggression in the 1930s. There was also a third dimension: preventive war. Saddam Hussein was building weapons of mass destruction. He had a nuclear weapons program with covertly imported materials; he had chemical weapons and there were rumors of biological weapons. If he were to have, in addition to this, the revenues that came from Kuwait's oil, the world would face a larger, stronger, more devastating Iraq later in the decade. Some reasoned that if there were to be a war, better now than later.

But others argued the war was unnecessary because economic sanctions would have forced Iraq to evacuate its troops from Kuwait. The counterfactual is hard to prove. It is impossible to know that if the coalition in the United Nations would have held together for a year or more, it would have taken sanctions to work. Eventually, it took a month of war before Iraq quit Kuwait. By October 1990, the Bush administration concluded that sanctions would not work. In November, the United States doubled its troops in Saudi Arabia in the prelude to war. Why did Saddam Hussein not escape at the last minute by saying he would withdraw or find some other ruse? Partly, his miscalculation seemed to be, as he told the American ambassador in August 1990, that the United States had no stomach for high casualties. In that sense, he was a victim of the Vietnam analogy. And partly, it may have been pride, and not being able to back down after being at the center of the world stage.

What did the war solve? It revived the doctrine of UN collective security and it may deter other such incidents, but as we have seen, there are questions about how typical this regional conflict was. The war destroyed Iraq's capability for weapons of mass destruction before they became fully operational and the cease-fire set a precedent whereby UN inspectors visited Iraq and destroyed its nuclear and chemical facilities. But it left unsolved the conflicts that arose from fragmented national politics and the weak domestic societies of the Middle East.

Yet, in the aftermath of the Gulf War, the Israeli government and the Palestine Liberation Organization (PLO) made significant progress toward peace and normalized relations. Using the political leverage it accrued from the war, the Bush administration pressured the PLO and the government of Yitzhak Shamir to meet along with other Arab governments in Madrid in late 1991 and in Washington in 1992. While these talks stalled, back-channel negotiations between Israeli officials and PLO officials outside of Oslo, Norway, led to the Declaration of Principles signed in Washington, D.C., in September 1993 between the PLO and the government of Yitzhak Rabin. The Declaration was followed by a series of agreements for the withdrawal of Israeli troops from the Gaza Strip and from Palestinian towns and villages in the West Bank. The PLO was recognized by Israel as the legitimate voice of the Palestinian people, and the reins of local autonomy, including policing, were handed over to Yasir Arafat and the PLO in several stages after 1994.

At the same time, King Hussein of Jordan negotiated a peace treaty with the Rabin government, and the treaty was signed in Washington in 1994. During the Gulf War, Jordan had equivocated in its support for the U.S.-led coalition, and King Hussein calculated that normalizing relations with Israel would put him back into the good graces of the United States and the oil-producing states in the Middle East. The PLO had backed Saddam Hussein and Iraq during the Gulf War and, as a result, had seen its once generous donations from Kuwait, Saudi Arabia, and the other oil-states disappear. With its financial situation desperate, the PLO relaxed its opposition to a negotiated settlement.

Yet, the potential for conflict in the Middle East remains. In spite of the peace negotiations, the Israeli public was far from resolved about the policy of ceding occupied territory. Ultraconservative Israelis considered Rabin a traitor, and in late 1995, he was assassinated. The PLO government and Arafat were widely perceived by Palestinians as corrupt and authoritarian, thereby giving strength to opposition groups such as the fundamentalist Hamas, which sought to disrupt the peace process. Terrorist bombings by Arab groups opposed to the peace process affected the 1996 Israeli elections. Throughout the region, autocratic governments are faced with internal challenges to their authority, and many of these threaten to explode into civil war, as they have in Algeria and the Sudan.

The post–Gulf War developments illustrate the same dynamics of the individual, the state, and the international system that we have seen in other conflicts. At one level, individuals such as Arafat, Rabin, and King Hussein determined whether or not there would be peace accords. Yet, without the changes in the international system brought about by the Gulf War, it is unlikely such a process would have translated into tangible results. The internal pressures on state government, such as the economic crisis in Jordan, also contributed to the outcome.

The states of the region frequently act in a manner consonant with the realist model—seeking power and security in competition with other states—but international law and organizations have helped shape the political struggles, as have individual actors. At the same time, issues such as religion, ethnicity, economic underdevelopment, and population pressures continue to make Middle Eastern politics volatile.

NOTES

1. Irving Howe and Michael Walzer, "Were We Wrong About Vietnam?" *The New Republic,* August 18, 1979, p. 18.

2. Robert R. Bowie, *Suez 1956* (New York: Oxford University Press, 1974), p. 124.

3. Ernest Renan, quoted in Hans Kohn, *Nationalism: Its Meaning and History* (Princeton, NJ: Van Nostrand, 1955), p. 137.

SELECTED READINGS

1. Khong, Yuen F., "The Lessons of Korea and the Vietnam Decision of 1965," in George Breslauer and Philip Tetlock, eds., *Learning in U.S. and Soviet Foreign Policy* (Boulder, CO: Westview Press, 1989), pp. 302–349.

2. Finlayson, Jock, and Mark Zacher, "The United Nations and Collective Security," in Toby Gati, ed., *The U.S., the U.N., and the Management of Global Change* (New York: New York University Press, 1983), pp. 162–183.

3. Chipman, John, "Third World Politics and Security in the 1990s," in Aspen Strategy Group, *Facing the Future: American Strategy in the 1990s* (Lanham, MD: University Press of America, 1991), pp. 205–231.

4. Congressional Quarterly, *The Middle East*, 6th ed. (Washington, DC: Congressional Quarterly, 1986), pp. 1–31.

FURTHER READINGS

Ajami, Fouad, "The Summer of Arab Discontent," *Foreign Affairs*, Vol. 69, No. 1 (Winter 1990/91), pp. 1–20.

Bowie, Robert R., *Suez 1956* (New York: Oxford University Press, 1974).

Deutsch, Karl W., *Nationalism and Its Alternatives* (New York: Knopf, 1959).

Gause, F. Gregory, "Sovereignty, Statecraft, and Stability in the Middle East," *Journal of International Affairs,* Vol. 45, No. 2 (Winter 1992), pp. 441–469.

Goodrich, Leland M., Edvard Hambro, and Anne Patricia Simons, *Charter of the United Nations: Commentary and Comments* (New York: Columbia University Press, 1969).

Gordon, Michael, and Bernard Trainor, *The Generals' War: The Inside Story of the Conflict in the Gulf* (Boston: Little Brown, 1995).

Hehir, J. Bryan, "World of Faultlines: Sovereignty, Self-Determination, Intervention," *Commonwealth,* Vol. 119, No. 16 (September 25, 1992), pp. 8–10.

Jacobson, Harold K., *Networks of Interdependence: International Organizations and the Global Political System* (New York: Knopf, 1979).

Kohn, Hans, *Nationalism: Its Meaning and History* (Princeton, NJ: Van Nostrand, 1955).

Moynihan, Daniel P., *On the Law of Nations* (Cambridge, MA: Harvard University Press, 1990).

Podhoretz, Norman, *Why We Were in Vietnam* (New York: Simon & Schuster, 1982).

Quandt, William B., ed., *The Middle East: Ten Years After Camp David* (Washington, DC: Brookings Institution, 1988).

Safran, Nadav, *From War to War: A Study of the Arab-Israeli Confrontation 1948–1967* (New York: Pegasus, 1969).

Sifry, Micah L., and Christopher Cerf, *The Gulf War Reader: History, Documents, Opinions* (New York: New York Times Books, 1991).

Vincent, R. J., *Nonintervention and International Order* (Princeton, NJ: Princeton University Press, 1974).

Walzer, Michael, *Just and Unjust Wars: A Moral Argument with Historical Illustrations* (New York: Basic, 1977).

STUDY QUESTIONS

1. When is intervention justified? Is there a difference between international law and morality?

2. How does the United Nations differ from the League of Nations?

3. What are the respective claims of the Palestinians and the Israelis to the territory Israel now encompasses? Which group has a better argument, in your opinion, or are they equally valid?

4. What was the UN Palestine partition proposal? Why did the Arabs reject this plan?

5. What were the causes of the Middle East wars of 1956, 1967, 1973, and 1982? Were they inevitable? If so, when and why? Is another Arab-Israeli war inevitable?

6. The 1967 war yielded the present configuration of the Arab-Israeli dispute. What happened in that war? What was the famous Security Council Resolution 242?

7. Sadat claimed that he had to go to war in 1973 to go to peace with Israel afterward. Assess this argument. What parallels can you draw between Nasser's success in 1956 and Sadat's in 1973?

8. How successful have the UN peacekeeping operations in the region been? What have been their limitations?

9. How will the great powers and the United Nations deal with future regional conflicts?

CHRONOLOGY: THE ARAB-ISRAELI CONFLICT

1897	Publication of Herzl's *The Jewish State;* First World Zionist Congress meets
1915	MacMahon-Sharif Husain agreements leading to Arab revolt against Turks in return for British assurances on independent Arab state
1916	Sykes-Picot agreement secretly establishing Anglo-French spheres of influence in the Middle East
1917	Balfour Declaration stating that the British government favored "the establishment in Palestine of a national home for the Jewish people . . . it being understood that nothing shall be done which may prejudice the civil and religious rights of existing non-Jewish communities in Palestine."
1922	Great Britain given the Palestine mandate by the League of Nations
1936	Formation of Arab High Committee with aim of uniting all Arabs in opposition to Jewish claims
1937	Palestinian Arab revolt against British authority; Peel Commission report proposes partition into three states: one Arab, one Jewish, and a British-administered territory; scheme adopted by the World Zionist Congress and rejected by the Pan-Arab Congress
1939	British White Paper calls for independent Palestine in ten years
1945	Egypt, Iraq, Jordan, Lebanon, Saudi Arabia, and Yemen create the Arab League
1947	British government refers Palestine dispute to the United Nations; UN General Assembly votes for partition of Palestine into Jewish and Arab states with Jerusalem under UN trusteeship; UN partition plan accepted by Jews but rejected by Arabs
1948	Fighting between Arabs and Jews in Palestine; British mandate comes to end; Jewish provisional government under David Ben-Gurion proclaims the State of Israel; Israel recognized by the United States and the USSR
1948–1949	War between Israel and the Arab League
1949	Israel admitted to the United Nations
1952	Free Officer revolt led by Gamal Abdel Nasser in Egypt
1955	Soviet-Egyptian arms deal concluded; Baghdad Pact created with Great Britain, Iran, Iraq, Turkey, and Pakistan as members
1956	Suez Crisis: Israeli forces invade the Sinai; Britain and France bomb and land paratroopers in the Suez Canal zone
1957	Eisenhower Doctrine: President granted congressional authority for U.S. intervention in event of communist aggression in the Middle East
1958	Antimonarchical revolt in Iraq; crisis in Lebanon and Jordan; American Marines land in Beirut
1964	Formation of the Palestine Liberation Front (PLO)
1967	Six-Day War: Israel occupies the Sinai, Gaza Strip, West Bank, and the Golan Heights; adoption of UN Resolution 242 calling for Israeli withdrawal from occupied Arab lands in return for peace within negotiated permanent borders; Palestinian demands referred to only as the "refugee" problem
1969	War of Attrition

1970	"Black September" in Jordan: Jordanian army expels Palestinian commandos from Jordan; death of Nasser. Anwar Sadat becomes Egyptian president
1973	October 1973/Yom Kippur War: Egypt and Syria launch surprise attack against Israel
1973–1974	Arab oil embargo
1974	Military disengagement accords between Israel and Egypt and Syria
1975	Sinai Agreement between Israel and Egypt permitting reopening of Suez Canal
1977	Sadat becomes first Arab head of state to recognize Israel and to address Israeli Knesset in Jerusalem
1978	Camp David Summit with Carter, Begin, and Sadat
1979	Climax of Iranian Revolution; shah forced into exile; Ayatollah Khomeini returns to Tehran as new Iranian leader. Egyptian-Israeli peace treaty signed in Washington, D.C. American Embassy overrun by Iranians, and staff taken hostage; Soviet forces invade Afghanistan
1980	Carter Doctrine: United States will use force to counter Soviet aggression in the Persian Gulf region; Iraqi forces invade Iranian territory; beginning of Iran-Iraq War; Iraq invades Iran
1981	Sadat assassinated in Cairo
1982	Israeli forces invade Lebanon
1983	Multinational peacekeeping force arrives in Beirut; attacks against American embassy and Marine barracks
1987	Beginning of Palestinian uprising (*intifada*) in Gaza Strip and West Bank
1988	Jordan's King Hussein renounces Jordanian sovereignty over West Bank; PLO declares independent Palestinian states on West Bank and Gaza
1990	Iraq invades Kuwait; UN Security Council votes sanctions
1991	Iraq expelled from Kuwait in Gulf War
1991–1992	Arab-Israeli peace talks in Madrid and Washington, D.C.
1993	Oslo negotiations and Declaration of Principles between Israel and the PLO
1994	Jordanian-Israeli peace treaty signed in Washington, D.C.
1995	Rabin assassinated in Tel Aviv.

INTERDEPENDENCE AND POWER

Oil wells in the Middle East

Economic interdependence increased rapidly in the postwar period, but it was the 1973 oil crisis that brought economic conflict to center stage. Some people think that interdependence means peace and cooperation, but unfortunately it is not that simple. Conflict goes on, even in a world of interdependence. Because the coalitions are more complex and different forms of power are used, the conflicts are often like playing chess on several boards at the same time. Conflicts in the late twentieth century involve *both* guns and butter. China's Chairman Mao Tse-tung said that power grows out of the barrel of a gun. After the oil crisis of 1973, the world was reminded that power can also grow out of a barrel of oil. Some realists overreacted to the oil crisis of 1973, likening it to events in 1914 and 1939. Hans Morgenthau, a great thinker in the realist tradition, said that 1973 was historically unprecedented because it divorced military power from economic power based on raw materials.

The 1973 oil crisis presents an important question: Why did the most powerful countries in the world allow the transfer of hundreds of billions of dollars to weak states and not use force? Such an event would have been unthinkable in the eighteenth century. Or in the nineteenth century, the rich countries would have used their superior military power, colonized the troublesome area, and settled the situation on their own terms. What changed in 1973? It was neither a new era of power based on raw materials and cartels nor a total divorce of military and economic power. Rather, all these factors became intertwined in complex relationships. To understand the changes in world politics, we must consider how interdependence can be a source of power.

THE CONCEPT OF INTERDEPENDENCE

Interdependence is a fuzzy term used in a variety of conflicting ways like other political words such as nationalism or imperialism. Statesmen and analysts have different motives when they use political words. The statesman wants as many people marching behind his or her banner as possible. Political leaders blur meanings and try to create a connotation of a common good: "We are all in the same boat together, therefore we must cooperate, therefore follow me." The analyst, on the other hand, makes distinctions to understand the world better. She distinguishes questions of good and bad from more and less. The analyst may point out the boat we are all in may be heading for one person's port but not another's, or that one person is doing all the rowing while another steers or has a free ride. In other words, interdependence can be used both ideologically as well as analytically, and we should be aware of such different usage. As a political verb, interdependence is conjugated "I depend; you depend; we depend; they rule."

As an analytical word, interdependence refers to situations in which actors or events in different parts of a system affect each other. Simply put, interdependence means mutual dependence. Such a situation is neither good nor bad in itself, and there can be more or less of it. In personal relations, interdependence is summed up by the marriage vow in which each partner is interdependent with another "for richer, for poorer, for better, or for worse." And interdependence among nations sometimes means richer, sometimes poorer, sometimes for better, sometimes for worse. In the eighteenth century, Jean-Jacques Rousseau pointed out that along with interdependence comes friction and conflict. His "solution" was isolation and separation. But this is seldom possible in the modern world. When countries try isolation, like Albania or Myanmar (formerly Burma), it comes at enormous economic cost. It is not easy for nations to divorce the rest of the world.

Sources of Interdependence

Four distinctions illuminate the dimensions of interdependence: its sources, benefits, relative costs, and symmetry. Interdependence can originate in physical (i.e., in nature) or social (economic, political, or perceptual) phenomena. Both are usually present at the same time. The distinction helps to make clear the degree of choice in situations of reciprocal or mutual dependence.

Military interdependence is the mutual dependence that arises from military competition. There is a physical aspect in the weaponry, especially dramatic since the development of nuclear weapons and the resulting possibility of mutually assured destruction. However, there is also an important element of perception involved in interdependence, and a change in perception or policy can reduce the intensity of the military interdependence. Americans lost little sleep over the existence of British or French nuclear weapons because there was no perception that those weapons would ever land on American soil. Similarly, Westerners slept a bit easier in the late 1980s after Gorbachev announced his "new thinking" in Soviet foreign policy. It was not so much the number of Soviet weapons that made the difference, but the change in the perception of Soviet hostility or intent.

Generally speaking, economic interdependence is similar to military interdependence in that it is the stuff of traditional international politics and has a high degree of social, especially perceptual, origin. Economic interdependence involves policy choices about values and costs. For example, in the early 1970s, there was concern the world's population was outstripping global food supplies. Many countries were buying American grain, which in turn drove up the price of food in American supermarkets. A loaf of bread cost more in the United States because the Indian monsoons failed and because the Soviet Union had mishandled its harvest. In 1973, the United States, in an effort to prevent price rises at home, decided to stop exporting soybeans to Japan. As a result, Japan invested in soybean production in Brazil. A few years later, when supply and demand were better equilibrated, U.S. farmers greatly regretted that embargo because the Japanese were buying their soybeans from a cheaper source in Brazil. Social choices as well as physical shortages affect economic interdependence in the long run. It is always worth considering the long-term perspective when making short-term choices.

Benefits of Interdependence

The benefits of interdependence are sometimes expressed as zero sum and non–zero sum. In a zero sum situation, your loss is my gain and vice versa. In a positive sum situation, we both gain; in a negative sum situation, we both lose. Dividing a pie is zero sum, baking a larger pie is positive sum, and dropping it on the floor is negative sum. Both zero sum and non–zero sum aspects are present in mutual dependence.

Some liberal economists tend to think of interdependence only in terms of joint gain, that is, positive sum situations in which everyone benefits and everyone is better off. Failure to pay attention to the inequality of benefits and the conflicts that arise over the distribution of relative gains causes such analysts to miss the political aspects of interdependence. It is true that both sides can gain from trade, for example, if Japan and Korea trade textiles and television sets, but how will the gains from trade be divided? Even if Japan and Korea are both better off, is Japan a lot better off and Korea only a little better off, or vice versa? The distribution of benefits—who gets how much of the joint gain—is a zero sum situation in which one side's gain is the other's loss. The result is that there is almost always some political conflict in economic interdependence. Even when there is a larger pie, people can fight over who gets the biggest slices. Even if interdependent countries enjoy a joint gain, there may be conflict over who gets more or less of the joint gain.

Some political analysts make the mistake of thinking that as the world becomes more interdependent, cooperation will replace competition. Their reason is that interdependence creates joint benefits, and those joint benefits encourage cooperation. But economic interdependence can also be used as a weapon—witness the oil crisis of 1973. Indeed, economic interdependence is more effective than force in some cases because it may have more subtle gradations and fewer collateral costs. And in some circumstances, states are less interested in their absolute gain from interdependence than how the relatively greater gains of their rivals might be used to hurt them.

Even ecological interdependence can be used as a weapon, as it was in 1991 when Iraq set fire to Kuwait's oil fields and released oil into the Persian Gulf. There can also be conflicts over global ecological issues. For example, if global warming occurs, who will win and who will lose? If the temperature of the earth rises on average two degrees centigrade, Maldive Islanders at sea level or Africans who live at the edge of the Sahara would suffer terribly if the islands were submerged or the desert moved southward. But some Siberians or Canadians might be better off. If so, will Siberians or Canadians pay to slow global warming?

Some analysts believe that traditional world politics was always zero sum. But that is misleading about the past. Traditional international politics could be positive sum, depending on the actors' intentions. It made a difference whether Bismarck or Hitler was in charge of Germany. If one party sought aggrandizement, as Hitler did, then indeed politics was zero sum—one side's gain was another's loss. But if all parties wanted stability, there could be joint gain in the balance of power. Conversely, the new politics of economic interdependence has competitive zero sum aspects as well as cooperative positive sum aspects.

In the politics of interdependence, the distinction about what is domestic and what is foreign becomes blurred. For example, the soybean situation mentioned earlier involved the domestic issue of controlling inflation at home, as well as American relations with Japan and Brazil. Or to take another example, after Iran's 1979 revolution curtailed oil production, the American government urged citizens to cut their energy consumption by driving 55 mph and turning down thermostats. Was that a domestic or a foreign policy issue? Should the United States allow strip mining of coal if the coal is to be exported? Do those who import that coal pay the additional costs that accompany the destruction of the countryside in West Virginia? Interdependence thoroughly mixes domestic and foreign issues, which gives rise to much more complex coalitions, more intricate patterns of conflict, and a different way of distribution of benefits than in the past.

Interdependence also affects domestic politics in a different way. In 1890, a French politician concerned with relative gains needed a policy of holding Germany back. Today a policy of slowing economic growth in Germany is not good for France. Economic interdependence between France and Germany means that the best predictor of whether France is better off economically is when Germany is growing economically. Now it is in the self-interest of the French politicians that Germany do well economically. The classical balance of power theory, which predicts that one country will act only to keep the other down lest the other gain preponderance, does not fit well. In economic interdependence, states are interested in absolute gains as well as gains relative to other states.

ECOLOGICAL AND ECONOMIC INTERDEPENDENCE

"For the first time in more than a decade, the developing countries have an issue where they have some real leverage," said an official from a Caribbean nation. "They had none during the debt negotiations. But they are part of the environment, so they have leverage now. And they are using it. It's their negotiating strategy."

Poor nations, he said, see leverage because the north, the main polluter, wants them to cut emissions, stop deforesting and make other changes. But to adapt to those changes, they argue, they need funding and technology.

—*New York Times*, March 17, 1992[1]

Costs of Interdependence

The costs of interdependence can involve short-run sensitivity or long-term vulnerability. *Sensitivity* refers to the amount and rapidity of the effects of dependence; that is, how quickly does change in one part of the system bring about change in another part? For example, in the 1970s, a rumor about a possible change in exchange rates led to $2 billion flooding into Germany in one day. In 1987, the New York stock market crashed suddenly because of foreigners' anxieties about U.S. interest rates and what might happen to the price of bonds and stocks. It all happened very quickly; the market was very sensitive to the withdrawal of foreign funds.

A high level of sensitivity, however, is not the same as a high level of vulnerability. *Vulnerability* refers to the relative costs of changing the structure of a system of interdependence. It is the cost of escaping from the system or of changing the rules of the game. The less vulnerable of two countries is not necessarily the less sensitive, but rather the one that would incur lower costs from altering the situation. During the 1973 oil crisis, the United States depended on imported energy for only about 16 percent of its total energy uses. On the other hand, in 1973, Japan depended about 95 percent on imported energy. The United States was sensitive to the Arab oil boycott insofar as prices shot up in 1973, but it was not as vulnerable as Japan was.

Vulnerability involves degree. When the shah of Iran was overthrown in 1979, Iranian oil production was disrupted at a time when demand was high and markets were already tight. The loss of Iran's oil caused the total amount of oil on the world markets to drop by about five percent, but that led to a very large increase in oil prices. Markets were sensitive, and shortages of supply were rapidly transformed into higher prices. But Americans could save five percent of their energy use simply by turning down their thermostats and driving 55 mph. It appears that the United States was sensitive but not very vulnerable if it could avoid damage by such simple actions.

Vulnerability, however, depends on more than aggregate measures. It also depends on whether a society is capable of responding quickly to change. For example, the United States was less adept at responding to changes in the oil markets than Japan. Furthermore, private actors, large corporations, and speculators in the market may each look at a market situation and decide to hoard supplies because they think shortages are going to grow worse. Their actions will drive the price even higher, because it will make the shortages greater and put more demand on the market. Thus degrees of vulnerability are not quite so simple as they first look.

SENSITIVITY INTERDEPENDENCE

. . . The Bank of Japan is under pressure to raise interest rates—for the fourth time since last May—to bolster the sagging yen. Fear of inflation are [sic] also lingering, due to a severe shortage of labor, soaring land prices and rapid growth in the nations's money supply.

The adjustment to higher short-term interest rates in Tokyo last week took place in the American financial markets a few weeks ago, as United States rates bobbed upward and stock prices slid under similar pressures.

"Tokyo's markets rode the Shinkansen to catch up with Amtrak," said Mr. Okumura, referring to Japan's famous bullet train and the well-known American railroad. "Tokyo has only caught up with movements that took place in New York several weeks ago, and now everyone is watching the situation in Germany."

—*New York Times*, February 26, 1990[2]

Vulnerability also depends on whether or not substitutes are available and whether there are diverse sources of supply. In 1970, Lester Brown of the World Watch Institute expressed alarm about the increasing dependence of the United States, and therefore its vulnerability, on imported raw materials. Of 13 basic industrial raw materials, the United States was dependent on imports for nearly 90 percent of aluminum, chromium, manganese, and nickel. By 1985, he predicted the United States would be dependent on imports in 10 of the basic 13.[3] He felt this would lead to a dramatic increase in U.S. vulnerability as well as a drastic increase in strength for the less developed countries that produced those raw materials.

But in the 1980s, raw materials prices went down, not up. What happened to his prediction? In judging vulnerability, Brown failed to consider the alternative sources of raw materials and the diversity of sources of supply that prevented producers from jacking up prices artificially. Moreover, technology develops. Yesterday's waste may become a new resource. Companies now mine discarded tailings because new technology has made it possible to extract copper from ore that was considered depleted years ago. Today's reduced use of copper is also due to the introduction of fiber optic cables made from silicon, whose basic origin is sand. Thus projections of U.S. vulnerability to shortages of raw materials went wrong because technology and alternatives were not adequately considered.

Symmetry of Interdependence

Symmetry refers to situations of relatively balanced versus unbalanced dependence. Being less dependent can be a source of power. If two parties are interdependent but one is less dependent than the other, the less dependent party has a source of power as long as both value the interdependent relationship. Manipulating the asymmetries of interdependence can be a source of power in international politics. Analysts who say that interdependence occurs only in situations of equal dependence define away the most interesting political behavior. Such perfect symmetry is quite rare; so are cases of complete imbalance in which one side is totally dependent and the other is not dependent at all. Asymmetry is at the heart of the politics of interdependence (See Figure 7.1).

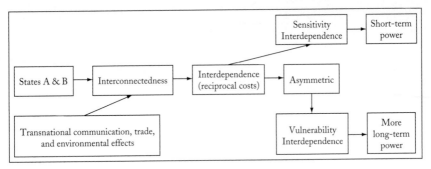

Figure 7.1

Asymmetry often varies according to different issues. In the 1980s, when the United States cut taxes and raised expenditures, it became dependent on imported Japanese capital to balance its federal government budget. Some argued that this gave Japan tremendous power over the United States. But the other side of the coin was that Japan would hurt itself as well as the United States if it stopped lending to the United States. In addition, Japanese investors who already had large stakes in the United States would have found their investments devalued by the damage done to the American economy if Japan suddenly stopped lending to the United States. Japan's economy was a little over half the size of the American economy, and that meant the Japanese needed the American market for their exports more than vice versa, although both needed each other and both benefited from the interdependence.

Moreover, security was often linked to other issues in the U.S.-Japanese relationship. After World War II, Japan followed the policy of a trading state and did not develop a large military capability or gain nuclear weapons. It relied on the American security guarantee to balance the power of the Soviet Union and China in the East Asian region. Thus when a dispute seemed to be developing between the United States and Japan over trade in 1990, the Japanese made concessions to prevent weakening the overall security relationship.

When there is asymmetry of interdependence in different issue areas, a state may try to link or unlink issues. If each issue could be thought of as a poker game, and all poker games were played simultaneously, one state might have most of the chips at one table and another state might have most of the chips at another table. Depending on a state's interests and position, it might want to keep the games separate or create linkages between the tables. Therefore, much of the politics of interdependence involves the creation or prevention of linkage. States want to manipulate interdependence in areas where they are strong and avoid being manipulated in areas where they are relatively weak.

By setting agendas and defining issue areas, international institutions often set the rules for the trade-offs in interdependent relationships. States try to use international institutions to set the rules that affect the transfer of chips among tables. Ironically, international institutions can benefit the weaker players by keeping some of the issues where the poorer states are relatively better endowed separated from the military table where strong states dominate. The danger remains, however, that some players will be strong enough to overturn one or more of the tables. With separate institutions for money, shipping, pollution, and trade, if the militarily strong players are beaten too badly, there is a danger they may try to kick over the other tables. Yet, when the United States and Europe were beaten at the oil table in 1973, they did not use their preponderant military force to kick over the oil table because, as we see later, a complex web of linkages held them back.

The largest state does not always win in the manipulation of economic interdependence. If a smaller or weaker state has a greater concern about an issue, it may do quite well. For instance, because the United States accounts for nearly three-quarters of Canada's foreign trade while Canada accounts for about one-quarter of the U.S. foreign trade, Canada is more dependent on the United States than vice versa. Nonetheless, Canada often prevailed in a number of disputes with the United States because Canada was willing to threaten retaliatory actions, such as tariffs and restrictions, that deterred the United States. The Canadians would have suffered much more than the United States if their actions had led to a full dispute, but Canada felt it was better to risk occasional retaliation than to agree to rules that would *always* make them lose. Deterrence via manipulation of economic interdependence is somewhat like nuclear deterrence in that it rests on a capability for effective damage and credible intentions. Small states can often use their greater intensity and greater credibility to overcome their relative vulnerability in asymmetrical interdependence.

A natural outgrowth of rising interdependence is the proliferation of trade pacts. The European Union is the most sophisticated of these agreements and requires the member states not just to forfeit some economic sovereignty, but political sovereignty as well. By early 1994, the United States, Mexico, and Canada had ratified the North American Free Trade Agreement (NAFTA). For Mexico and Canada, NAFTA was appealing because it bound their economies more tightly to the larger U.S. economy and, in so doing, increased their access to U.S. markets and their ability to export their products to the United States. For the United States, NAFTA expanded the realm of U.S. exports and made it easier for U.S. companies to do business in Canada and Mexico.

Pacts such as NAFTA may increase interdependence and lessen the asymmetry in a relationship. By agreeing to intertwine its economy with that of Mexico, the United States assumed some of the liabilities of the Mexican economy along with the benefits of easier access. When the value of the Mexican peso plummeted in 1994, the Clinton administration rushed in early 1995 to shore up the flagging currency and assembled a multibillion dollar aid package. At a time when the U.S. Congress was deadlocked over increased domestic spending for services such as health care, the administration saw little choice but to rescue the peso. With greater interdependence, even strong countries can find themselves sensitive to economic developments beyond their borders.

Leadership in the World Economy

By and large, the rules of international economy are set by the largest states. In the nineteenth century, Great Britain was the strongest of the major world economies. In the monetary area, the Bank of England adhered to the gold standard, which set a stable framework for world money. Britain also enforced freedom of the seas for navigation and commerce, and provided a large open market for world trade until 1932. After World War I, Britain was severely weakened by its fight against the kaiser's Germany. The United States became the world's largest economy, but it turned away from international affairs. The largest player in the world economy behaved as if it could still take a free ride rather than provide the leadership its size implied. Some economists believe that the Great Depression of the 1930s was aggravated by bad monetary policy and lack of American leadership. Britain was too weak to maintain an open international economy and the United States was not living up to its new responsibilities.

After World War II, the lessons of the 1930s were on the minds of American statesmen and they set up institutions to maintain an open, international economy. The International Monetary Fund (IMF) lends money, usually to developing countries, to help when they have difficulties with their balance of payments or with paying interest on their debts. The IMF generally conditions its loans on the recipient country reforming its economic policies, for example reducing budget deficits and price subsidies. The International Bank for Reconstruction and Development (the World Bank) lends money to poorer countries for development projects. (There are also regional development banks for Asia, Latin America, Africa, and Eastern Europe.) The General Agreement on Tariffs and Trade (GATT) established rules for liberal trade and has served as the locus for a series of rounds of multilateral negotiations that have lowered trade barriers. The Organization for Economic Cooperation and Development (OECD) serves as a forum for two dozen of the most developed countries to coordinate their international economic policies. Since the mid-1970s, the leaders of the seven largest economies that account for two-thirds of world production have met at annual summit conferences (the Group of Seven) to discuss conditions of the world economy. These institutions helped reinforce government policies that allow rapid growth of private transnational interactions. The result has been a rapid increase in economic interdependence. In most of the period after 1945, trade grew between 3 and 9 percent a year, faster even than the growth of the world product. International trade, which represented 4 percent of the U.S. GNP in 1950, tripled to 13 percent of the U.S. GNP by 1990. Large multinational corporations with global strategies became more significant as international investments increased by nearly 10 percent per year.

Nonetheless, there are still problems in managing a transnational economy in a world of separate states. In the 1980s, the United States became a net debtor when it refused to tax itself to pay its bills at home and instead borrowed money from abroad. Some analysts believed that this was setting the scene for a repeat of the 1930s, that the United States would experience decline as Britain did while Japan became the new world economic superpower. They feared the Japanese in the 1990s would have the same free-rider mentality that the Americans had in the 1930s, unwilling to open their markets or maintain international stability. But this need not be the case. The United States need not decline and turn inward. Much will depend on what happens in the relationships of the large economies and the willingness of their governments to cooperate to maintain stability in the international economic system. In any case, the international political and economic system is more complicated and complex. There will be more sectors, more states, more issues, and more private actors involved in the complexity of interdependent relationships.

Realism and Complex Interdependence

What would the world look like if the three key assumptions of realism were reversed? These assumptions are that states are the only significant actors, military force is the dominant instrument, and security is the dominant goal. Reversed, we postulate a different world politics: (1) States are not the only significant actors—transnational actors working across state boundaries are also major actors; (2) force is not the only significant instrument—economic manipulation and the use of international institutions are the dominant instruments; (3) security is not the dominant goal—welfare is the dominant goal. We can label this antirealist world *complex interdependence.* Social scientists call complex interdependence an "ideal type." It is an imaginary concept that does not exist in the real world, but neither does realism perfectly fit the real world. Complex interdependence is a thought experiment that allows us to imagine a different type of world politics.

Both realism and complex interdependence are simple models or ideal types. The real world lies somewhere between the two. We can ask where certain country relationships fit on a spectrum between realism and complex interdependence. The Middle East is closer to the realist end of the spectrum, but relations between the United States and Canada or relations between France and Germany today come much closer to the complex interdependence end of the spectrum. Different politics and different forms of the struggle for power occur depending on where on the spectrum a particular relationship between a set of countries is located. In fact, countries can change their position on the spectrum. In the Cold War the U.S.-Soviet relationship was clearly near the realist end of the spectrum, but with Gorbachev's changes the Soviet-U.S. relationship moved closer to the center between realism and complex interdependence (see Figure 7.2).

A prime example of the interaction in the real world between complex interdependence and realism is the U.S. relationship with the People's Republic of China. As with Japan, U.S. imports from China far outstrip U.S. exports. The result is a significant trade deficit of billions of dollars. While the bilateral trade relationship between the United States and China is asymmetrical in China's favor, the United States is not particularly vulnerable to Chinese trade practices because it could compensate for the potential loss of Chinese goods by purchasing them elsewhere. Still, the potential size of the Chinese market for American goods and the domestic demand for Chinese goods in the United States mean that the ability of the U.S. government to act against China is somewhat constrained by transnational actors, including U.S. multinational corporations that have pressured the U.S. government not to implement sanctions against China for unfair trade practices and human rights violations.

| Realism | Israel/Syria United States/Russia United States/Canada India/Pakistan France/Germany | Complex Interdependence |

Figure 7.2

THE TRANSNATIONAL POLITICS OF OIL

Different issues also vary in how closely they fit the assumptions of the two ideal types. Oil is an issue that highlights both realism and complex interdependence. Interdependence in a given area often occurs within a framework of rules, norms, and institutions that are called a *regime.* The international oil regime changed dramatically over the last 30 years. In 1960, the oil regime was a private oligopoly with close ties to the governments of the major consuming countries. Oil at that time sold for about two dollars a barrel, and seven large transnational oil companies, sometimes called the seven sisters, determined the amount of oil that would be produced. The price of oil depended on how much the large companies produced and on the demand in the rich countries where most of the oil was sold. Transnational companies set the rate of production and prices were determined by conditions in rich countries. The strongest powers in the international system in traditional military terms occasionally intervened to keep the system going. For example, in 1953 when a nationalist movement tried to overthrow the shah of Iran, Britain and the United States covertly intervened to return the shah to his throne. The oil regime was then largely unchanged.

After 1973, however, there was a major change in the international regime governing oil. The producing countries set the rate of production and therefore had a strong effect on price, rather than price being determined solely by the market in the rich countries. There was an enormous shift of power and wealth from rich to relatively poor countries. How could such a dramatic change be explained?

A frequently offered explanation is that the oil-producing countries banded together and formed the Organization of Petroleum Exporting Countries (OPEC). The trouble with this explanation is that OPEC was formed in 1960 and the dramatic change did not occur until 1973. Oil prices fell despite OPEC, so there is more to the story. There are three ways to explain these changes in the international oil regime: the overall balance of power, the balance of power in the oil issue, and international institutions.

Realists look at changes in the balance of power resting primarily on military force, particularly in regard to the Persian Gulf, the major oil-exporting region of the world. Two changes affected that balance: the rise of nationalism and decolonization. In 1960, half of the OPEC countries were colonies of Europe; by 1973, they were all independent. Along with the rise in nationalism went a rise in the costliness of military intervention. It is much more expensive to use force against a nationalistically awakened and decolonized people. When the British and Americans intervened in Iran in 1953, it was not very costly, but if the Americans had tried to keep the shah on his throne in 1979, the costs would have been prohibitive. One reason why the rich countries did not go in and colonize the oil-producing countries in 1973 had to do with the costliness of using force against nationalistically awakened peoples.

The change in U.S. and British power also affected the balance of power in the Persian Gulf. When OPEC was formed and earlier, Britain was to a large extent the policeman of the Persian Gulf. In 1961, it prevented an earlier Iraqi effort to annex Kuwait. But by 1971, Britain was economically weakened and the British government was trying to cut back on its international defense commitments. In 1971, Britain ended what used to be called its role "east of Suez." That may sound a bit like 1947 when Britain was unable to maintain its role as a power in the eastern Mediterranean. At that time, the United States stepped in to help Greece and Turkey, and formulated the Truman Doctrine. But in 1971, the United States was not well placed to step in to replace Britain as it did in 1947. The United States was deeply embroiled in Vietnam and unwilling to add a major military role in the Persian Gulf. As a result, President Nixon and Secretary of State Kissinger designed an American strategy that relied heavily on regional powers. Their chosen instrument was Iran. By using Iran as the regional hegemon, they thought they could replace the British policeman, if you will, on the cheap. So a realist would point to these changes in the overall structure of power, particularly the balance of power in the Persian Gulf region to explain the change in the oil regime.

A second way of explaining the change is a modified form of realism that focuses solely on the distribution of power within the issue of oil itself, rather than the overall military structure. There were important changes in the issue structure of power. The United States used to be the largest oil producer in the world, but American production peaked in 1971. American imports began to grow thereafter and the United States no longer had any surplus oil. During the two Middle East wars of 1956 and 1967, the Arab countries tried an oil embargo, but their efforts were easily defeated because the United States was producing enough oil to supply Europe when it was cut off by the Arab countries. Once American production peaked in 1971 and the United States began to import oil, the power to balance the oil market switched to countries like Saudi Arabia and Iran. No longer was the United States the supplier of last resort that could make up any missing oil.

A third way to explain the difference in the oil regime after 1973 relies less on realism than on changes in the role of international institutions, particularly the multinational corporations and OPEC. The seven sisters gradually lost power over this period. One reason was their obsolescing bargains with the producer countries. When a multinational corporation goes into a resource-rich country with a new investment, it can strike a bargain in which the multinational gets a large part of the joint gains. From the point of view of the poor country, having a multinational come in to develop its resources will make it better off. Even if it only gets 20 percent of the revenues and the multinational gets 80 percent, the poor country has more than it had before. So at the early stages when multinationals have a monopoly on capital, technology, and access to international markets, they strike a bargain with the poor countries in which the multinationals get the lion's share. But over time, the multinationals inadvertently transfer resources to the poor countries, not out of charity but in the normal course of business. They train locals. Saudis learn how to run oil fields, pumping stations, and loading docks. Locals develop expertise in marketing and so forth.

Eventually the poor countries want a better division of the profits. The multinational could threaten to pull out, but now the poor country can threaten to run the operation by itself. So over time, the power of the multinational company, particularly in raw materials, diminishes in terms of its bargaining with the host country. That is the "obsolescing bargain." Over the course of the period from the 1960s to 1973, the multinationals inadvertently transferred technology and skills that developed the poor countries' capacity to run oil operations themselves.

There were other developments. The seven sisters were joined by "little cousins" when new transnational corporations entered the oil market. Although they were not as large as the seven sisters, they were still big, and they began to strike their own deals with the oil-producing countries. Thus, when an oil-producing country wanted to get out of the hands of the seven sisters, it could strike a deal with smaller independent multinationals. That again reduced the bargaining power of the largest multinationals.

Institutionally, there was a modest increase in the effectiveness of OPEC as a cartel. Cartels restricting supply had long been typical in the oil industry, but in the past, they had been private arrangements of the seven sisters. Cartels generally have a problem because there is a tendency to cheat on production quotas when markets are soft and the price drops. Cartels work best when there is a shortage of oil, but when there is a surplus, people want to sell their oil and tend to cut the price in order to get a bigger share of the market. With time, market forces tend to erode cartels. OPEC represented an effort to shift from a private to a governmental cartel of the oil-producing countries. In its early years, OPEC had trouble exercising power because there was plenty of oil. As long as oil was in surplus, the OPEC countries had incentives to cheat to get a larger share of the market. OPEC was unable to enforce price discipline from the year it was founded, 1960, until the early 1970s. But after oil became short, OPEC's role in coordinating the bargaining power of the producers increased.

The Middle East War of 1973 gave OPEC a boost, a signal that now it could use its power. The Arab countries cut oil supply in the 1973 war for political reasons, but that created a situation where OPEC could become effective. Iran, which is not an Arab country, was allegedly the American instrument for policing the Persian Gulf, but the shah of Iran quadrupled oil prices and the other OPEC countries followed suit. Over the long term, OPEC was not able to keep oil prices up permanently because of market forces, but there was a stickiness on the downside that was an effect of the OPEC coalition.

A more important institutional factor was the role the oil companies played in "smoothing the pain" in the crisis itself. At one point in the crisis, Secretary of State Henry Kissinger said that if the United States faced "strangulation," force might have to be used. Fifteen percent of traded oil was cut, and the Arab embargo reduced oil exports to the United States by 25 percent. However, oil companies made sure that no one country suffered much more than any other. They redistributed the world's traded oil. When the United States lost 25 percent of its Arab oil imports, the companies shipped it more Venezuelan or Indonesian oil. They smoothed the pain of the embargo so that the rich countries all lost about 7 to 9 percent of their oil, well below the strangulation point.

Why did they do this? It was not out of charity. Transnational companies are long-run profit maximizers; that is, they want to maximize their profit in the long term. To do this, they want stability and market access. The multinational companies feared situations where they would be nationalized in a country if they refused to sell to that country. For example, Prime Minister Edward Heath of Britain demanded that the head of British Petroleum sell only to Britain and not to other countries. The head of British Petroleum replied that if he followed such an order, the company would be nationalized by those other countries, which would destroy British Petroleum. The British prime minister backed down. Essentially, because the oil companies were long-run profit maximizers, they tried to stabilize the market rather than have the pain strike any one country strongly. By reducing the threat of strangulation, they reduced the probability that force would be used.

In short, oil is an illustration of an issue that falls between the ideal types of realism and complex interdependence. Changes in three dimensions—the overall balance of power, the issue structure of power, and the institutions within the oil issue area—help to explain this dramatic difference between the oil regime of 1960 and the oil regime after 1973.

Oil as a Power Resource

How powerful was the oil weapon in 1973? By cutting production and embargoing sales to countries friendly to Israel, Arab states were able to bring their issues to the forefront of the U.S. agenda. They also created temporary disarray in the alliances between Japan, Europe, and the United States. In order to protect their oil supplies, France and Japan took independent positions. The oil weapon encouraged the United States to play a more conciliatory role in arranging the settlement of the Arab-Israeli dispute in the aftermath of the Yom Kippur War. On the other hand, the oil weapon did not change the basic policy of the United States in the Middle East. The Americans did not suddenly switch from their alliance with Israel to support of the Arab cause. Oil was a power resource that had an effect, but not a strong enough effect to reverse American policy.

Why was the oil weapon not more effective? Part of the answer is reciprocity in interdependence. Saudi Arabia, which became the key country in oil markets, had large investments in the United States. If the Saudis damaged the U.S. economy too much, they would also hurt their own economic interests. In addition, Saudi Arabia was dependent on the United States in the security area. In the long run, the United States was the only country able to keep a stable balance of power in the Persian Gulf region, and the Saudis realized this. So they were careful about how far they pushed the oil weapon.

What was the role of force as a power resource in the oil crisis of 1973? There was no overt use of force. There was no military intervention because strangulation never occurred. Moreover, the Saudis were benefiting from the long-run security guarantee provided by the United States. Thus force played a background role. There was an indirect linkage between the security interdependence and the oil interdependence. Force was too costly to use overtly, but it played a role as a power resource in the background.

OPEC'S PROBLEMS

Another major development that has curbed OPEC's role as the arbiter of prices is the advent of news and telecommunications systems—the thousands of instant market-monitoring, computerized devices that tell bankers, oil traders and commodity market speculators what the price of oil is at any moment. They also relay news that affects those prices.

That development has encouraged wild growth in the trading of oil futures, placing hundreds of new investors in the oil markets whose role is limited to trading "paper barrels" for the sake of betting on oil's price.

Such trading on the New York Mercantile Exchange alone reached 40 million barrels a day in 1987. By comparison, world oil consumption that year was 49 million barrels a day.

This means the speculators' ability to influence oil prices approaches the power of OPEC and non-OPEC producers combined.

. . . OPEC, however, is a consistent, and sore, loser in this game. When prices drift too low, it is obligated to promise meetings or curbs on output that prop up its image as the protector of oil prices, a role it can no longer veritably perform.

The organization has not helped itself by its constant failure to meet the goals of the ceilings on production that it sets. OPEC members consistently either produce above their quotas or discount their oil to stimulate sales, or both.

—*International Herald Tribune*, April 9, 1988[4]

TRANSNATIONAL ACTORS

A characteristic of economic conflicts is the role of transnational actors—nonstate actors acting across international borders. Traditional international politics is discussed in terms of states. We use shorthand expressions like "Germany wanted Alsace" or "France feared Britain." That shorthand is a useful simplification, especially in the classical period of international politics. In the eighteenth century, the monarch spoke for the state. If Frederick the Great wanted something for Prussia, Frederick was Prussia. In the nineteenth century, a broader elite class controlled foreign policy decisions, but even on the eve of World War I, European diplomacy was a relatively narrowly held cabinet diplomacy. In addition, in the classical period of international politics the agenda was more limited. Military security issues dominated the agenda, and they were handled primarily by the foreign office.

Qualitatively, transnational actors have played a role for centuries, but the quantitative shift in the last half of the twentieth century marks a significant change in the international system. In a world of greater interdependence, the agenda of international politics is broader, and everyone seems to want to get into the act. In the United States, for example, almost every domestic agency has some international role. The Department of Agriculture is interested in international

---

NAVAL COOPERATION IN THE 1982 FALKLAND (MALVINAS) ISLANDS WAR

From day one of the task force, pleas for everything from missiles to aviation fuel flooded the Pentagon from the British military mission on Massachusetts Avenue. There were also many telephone calls from British fleet headquarters in Northwood direct to friends in the United States Navy. Many of these requests were not known about by senior officials. To those intimately involved, it seemed at times as if the two navies were working as one—with the Americans delighted to see a friendly navy called on to do a real job of work. They hoped that lessons would not be lost on their own masters.

—*The Economist*, March 3, 1984[5]

---

food issues; the Environmental Protection Agency is interested in acid rain and global warming; the Coast Guard is interested in ocean dumping; the Department of Commerce is interested in trade; the Treasury Department in exchange rates. The State Department does not control all these issues. Every bureau of the U.S. government has its own little foreign ministry. In fact, if we look at the representation of the United States abroad, only a minority of the Americans in most embassies are from the State Department.

In complex interdependence, societies interact at many points. There is too much traffic for one intersection or for one cop at one intersection. These interactions across state borders outside the central control of the foreign policy organs are called transnational relations. They include but are not limited to migration of populations, the rapid transfer of capital from one country to another that occurs daily in the world stock and money markets, illicit trafficking in weapons and drugs, and certain forms of terrorism. Governments can try to control these activities, and in the case of terrorism or smuggling, they need to, but control often comes at a very high price. For example, the Soviet Union closely controlled transnational relations, and the Soviet economy suffered for it. Myanmar closed itself off from world markets and saw its economy deteriorate as a result. In circumstances with high degrees of interdependence and a great number of transnational actors, we can be led astray by the shorthand that was so useful in the classical period. We say things like "Japan agreed to import more" or "America opposed broad claims to the continental shelf," but looking more carefully, we notice that Japanese firms acted transnationally to export more or that some U.S. citizens lobbied internationally to promote a broad definition of the continental shelf.

This complexity of interests has always existed but it is greater in economic and social issues than in the traditional military security issues. Security issues are often more collectively shared. The survival of a people as a whole is obviously a collective good. Social and economic issues are often less broadly shared; there are more differences of interest. Thus with the rise of economic interdependence, and the rise of economic issues on the agenda of international politics, we find that our traditional shorthand less adequately describes the political process.

Frustrated by the oil industry's battered condition in Texas, the first Republican ever appointed to the Texas Railroad Commission plans to urge OPEC members in Vienna this week to adopt production limits with non-OPEC nations to keep prices above $18 a barrel.

"These people have more effect on our economy in Texas than any other people in the world," Kent Hance said. "If we could get stable prices around $18, it would be good for the producer and good for the consumer."

—*New York Times*, April 25, 1985[6]

Let us look again at the case of oil. We say that the consumer nations wanted low prices and the producer nations wanted high prices in 1973. But the politics was a lot more complex than that. Producing interests inside the consumer countries wanted high oil prices. Small Texas oil producers were not at all unhappy that OPEC raised oil prices, for they had the same interests as the Arabs, not the same interests as the consumers freezing in New England. Producers of nuclear energy were not unhappy to see oil prices rise because that might help nuclear energy become a more competitive energy source. The declining coal industry in Europe and unemployed coal miners were not unhappy about the rise of oil prices either. Nor were ecologists who believed that higher prices would curtail consumption and pollution. So inside the consumer countries there were enormous differences in the interests over oil prices. In a situation of interdependence, politics looks different if we lift the veil of national interest and national security. One of the reasons why consumer countries did not use more extreme measures such as force was the sensitivity interdependence that led to high energy prices was regarded as good by important political actors inside the consumer countries. There was a de facto transnational coalition that was not unhappy with higher oil prices.

Of course, the existence of contradictory interests inside nations is not new. In the nineteenth-century United States, politics was marked by differences between Southern farmers and Northern industrialists over tariffs. So it is nothing new to have different interests within a country. Domestic politics has always been important to foreign policy, but with the expansion of participation in domestic politics, it becomes more so. Moreover, as some of those domestic interests develop the capability to communicate and interact directly with other interests in other countries, they develop a different type of world politics.

Two forms of world politics are illustrated by Figure 7.3. The traditional form of international politics is the outside shell in the left-hand diagram of the figure. Traditional international politics follows the regular solid lines. If people in society 1 want to put pressure on government 2, they ask government 1 to talk to government 2. But in transnational relations, people in society 1 will put pressure on government 2 directly, or people in society 1 may put pressure on people in society 2 directly. The dotted lines in the right-hand diagram are individual actors going across national boundaries. When we talk about the politics of interdependence,

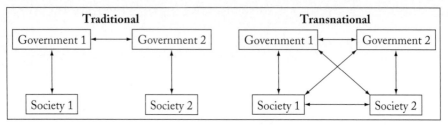

Figure 7.3

we must not assume that everything is captured by the traditional model of government-to-government relations. One of the distinguishing characteristics of complex interdependence is the significance of other actors in addition to the states.

The traditional shorthand is not wrong. It remains the best first approximation even for the politics of interdependence. States usually are the major actors. But if you restrict your attention to states alone, you may be misled about the politics of interdependence. States may look invulnerable in the aggregate, but a more careful look shows that parts of states are highly vulnerable while other parts are not. And those parts may act transnationally to remedy their situation. In short, states remain the most important actors in international politics, but when you have said that, you have not said everything that is important to know about political conflicts in the midst of twentieth-century interdependence.

NOTES

1. "North-South Divide Is Marring Environmental Talks," *New York Times*, March 17, 1992, p. 8.
2. "German Shift Felt in Japan," *New York Times*, February 26, 1990, p. D1.
3. Lester Brown, *World Without Borders* (New York: Random House, 1972), p. 194.
4. "OPEC: Cartel Facing the Fact That Some Producers Are Beyond Its Reach," *International Herald Tribune*, April 9, 1988.
5. "America's Falklands War," *The Economist*, March 3, 1984, p. 30.
6. "Texan to Urge Limits in Non-OPEC Output," *New York Times*, April 25, 1988, p. 3.

SELECTED READINGS

1. Keohane, Robert O., and Joseph S. Nye, Jr., *Power and Interdependence*, 2nd ed. (Glenview, IL: Scott Foresman, 1989), Chapters 1–3.
2. Yergin, Daniel, *The Prize: The Epic Quest for Oil, Money, and Power* (New York: Simon & Schuster, 1991), pp. 588–632.
3. Stobaugh, Robert, "Oil Companies in Crisis," *Daedalus*, Vol. 104, No. 4 (Fall 1975), pp. 179–202.

4. Gilpin, Robert, *The Political Economy of International Relations* (Princeton, NJ: Princeton University Press, 1987), pp. 263–305.

FURTHER READINGS

Baldwin, David A., *Economic Statecraft* (Princeton, NJ: Princeton University Press, 1985).

Bergsten, C. Fred, et al., *The United States and Japan in the 1990s* (Washington, DC: International Institute of Economics, 1991).

Castaneda, Jorge, "Can NAFTA Change Mexico?" *Foreign Affairs*, Vol. 72, No. 4 (October 1993), pp. 66–80.

Cohen, Benjamin J., *The Question of Imperialism: The Political Economy of Dominance and Dependence* (New York: Basic, 1973).

Doyle, Michael, *Empires* (Ithaca, NY: Cornell University Press, 1986).

Galtung, Johan, "A Structural Theory of Imperialism," *Journal of Peace Research*, Vol. 18, No. 2 (1971), pp. 81–118.

Graham, Edward, and Paul Krugman, *Foreign Direct Investment in the United States* (Washington, DC: IIEE, 1991).

Grieco, Joseph, "Anarchy and the Limits of Cooperation," *International Organization*, Vol. 42, No. 2 (Summer 1988), pp. 485–508.

Haggard, Stephan, *Pathways from the Periphery* (Ithaca, NY: Cornell University Press, 1990).

Keohane, Robert O., *After Hegemony* (Princeton, NJ: Princeton University Press, 1984).

Keohane, Robert O., and Joseph S. Nye, Jr., *Transnational Relations and World Politics* (Cambridge, MA: Harvard University Press, 1972).

Kindleberger, Charles P., *The World in Depression, 1929–1939* (Berkeley: University of California Press, 1973).

Krasner, Stephen D., ed., *International Regimes* (Ithaca, NY: Cornell University Press, 1983).

Reich, Robert B., *The Work of Nations: Preparing Ourselves for 21st-Century Capitalism* (New York: Knopf, 1991).

Spero, Joan E., *The Politics of International Economic Relations* (New York: St. Martin's Press, 1977).

Strange, Susan, *States and Markets* (London: Pinter, 1988).

Vernon, Raymond, *Sovereignty at Bay: The Multinational Spread of U.S. Enterprises* (New York: Basic, 1971).

STUDY QUESTIONS

1. What is *complex interdependence*? Is it a descriptive model? Where do we find complex interdependence most developed today?

2. What makes economic power powerful?

3. What were the underlying and immediate causes of the 1973 oil crisis? Why didn't it occur earlier—say, in 1967? Was it a unique event or the beginning of a revolution in international politics?

4. Liberal theory was optimistic that increasing international commerce would seriously decrease the attractiveness of military force as a tool in international politics. What does the international oil regime indicate either to support or falsify this thesis?

5. Under classical realist assumptions, we would not expect to see cooperation among states under conditions of anarchy. How can you explain the high degree of cooperation achieved by the oil-producing states in 1973?

6. Did the embargo achieve its objectives? How did it succeed? How did it fail?

7. Will ecological interdependence produce cooperation?

8. What is the role of large states in the governance of the international economy? What is the role of institutions?

8   A NEW WORLD ORDER?

ALTERNATIVE DESIGNS FOR THE FUTURE: THE NATION-STATE AND THE FUTURE OF INTERNATIONAL CONFLICT

We have defined international politics as politics in the absence of a common sovereign. As a result, international politics is a realm of self-help where states face security dilemmas and force plays a considerable role. There are mitigating devices like the balance of power and international law and organization, but they have not prevented all wars. The logic of international conflict as described by Thucydides still applies in parts of the world today.

With the end of the Cold War, there was a good deal of talk about the prospects for a new world order. As we see later, there was far less clarity about what that meant. There was a new world order in the sense that the bipolar system established after World War II had broken down. But that was order within the anarchic state system, and it was not necessarily a just order. Others thought a new world order meant escaping from the problems of the anarchic state system. Is such a world possible? Arnold Toynbee, the British historian, wrote at the beginning of the Cold War that the nation-state and the split atom could not coexist on the same planet. In a world of sovereign states, where war is the ultimate form of defense and nuclear bombs are the ultimate weapon, he believed that something had to go.

The territorial state has not always existed in the past, so it need not exist in the future. Fragmented units and state systems have existed since the days of Thucydides, but the large territorial state as the prime basis of international politics developed only after the Renaissance. The Thirty Years' War of the seventeenth century still had some features of a feudal war and was thus both the last of the wars of feudalism and the first of the wars of the territorial state. The large territorial state as we know it today has been the dominant institution of modern world politics for only three or four centuries. A number of futurists have predicted the decline of the territorial state. Their new world order involves structures that overcome the anarchic dilemma. Since World War II, there have been four major efforts to develop alternatives that go beyond the nation-state as the model for world politics.

(1) *World Federalism.* One of the oldest traditions of European thought, federalism posits a solution for the problem of anarchy by way of an international federation: States would agree to give up their national armaments and accept some degree of central government. Federalists often draw analogies to the way the 13 American colonies came together in the eighteenth century. Some believe that history is a

record of progress toward larger units. But federalism has not proven to be a very successful design in the twentieth century. Peace is not the only thing people value. As Immanuel Kant pointed out, perpetual peace is available only in the grave. People also want justice, welfare, and autonomy, and they do not trust world government to protect them. In addition, few people are convinced that the federal remedy would work, that it would be a cure for the problem of war. Even if the anarchic system of states is part of the cause of war, getting rid of independent states would not necessarily be the end of war. The majority of wars in recent years have been *internal* to states.

(2) *Functionalism.* Because of the inadequacies of federalism, the idea of international functionalism was developed. Popular in the 1940s, functionalism suggested that economic and social cooperation could create communities that cut across national boundaries and thus eliminate war. Sovereignty would then become less relevant, and though the formal shell of the state would still exist, its hostile content would be drained away. At the end of World War II, functionalist thinking gave rise to some of the specialized UN agencies, such as the Food and Agricultural Organization, the World Health Organization, and others. To some extent, functionalism exists today, with a world full of transnational interests, nongovernmental organizations, multinational corporations, and so on. But functionalism has not proven a sufficient design for *world* order, and most states are reluctant to allow themselves to become so interdependent that they become highly vulnerable to others.

(3) *Regionalism.* Regional integration became very popular in the 1950s and 1960s. Jean Monnet, head of the French Planning Commission, thought that the functional approach at a regional level might lock Germany and France together and thereby prevent a resurgence of the conflicts that had led to World Wars I and II. In 1950, Europe started the process with the Schumann Plan, integrating Western European coal and steel industries. After 1957, the Treaty of Rome established the European Common Market, which provided a step-by-step reduction of trade barriers and harmonization of a whole range of agricultural and economic policies that culminated with the creation of the European Union in 1992. As we have seen, other regions have tried to emulate European regionalism, with NAFTA the most significant example in the Western Hemisphere.

Yet, in 1965, General de Gaulle, then president of France, and later, in the 1980s, Margaret Thatcher, then prime minister of Great Britain, set limits on how far regional integration could go. By the mid-1990s, there was widespread ambivalence in the countries of the European Union over just how much sovereignty to cede to a regional government. But even though the drive toward federation was slowed, Europe had changed. In today's Europe, everybody may not be in the same boat, but the boats are lashed together in a variety of ways that are very different from earlier periods.

(4) *Ecologism.* In the 1970s, ecologism provided a new brand of hope for a different type of world order. Richard Falk's *This Endangered Planet* argued that two things could provide the basis of a new world order: the growing importance of transnational, nonterritorial actors and growing interdependence under conditions of scarcity. Falk argued there would be a gradual evolution of grassroots, populist values that would transcend the nation-state. Anticolonialism, antiracialism, greater equal-

ity, and ecological balance would lead not only to strengthening of majorities in the UN, but to the creation of new regimes for handling the world's dwindling resources. The end result would be international norms of peace, justice, and ecological balance and a new form of world order.

Yet, Falk overestimated how scarce resources would become and underestimated how much new technologies can compensate for the scarcity there is. Furthermore, grassroots populist movements do not easily lend themselves to transnational cooperation. The very localism that gives them strength mitigates against international coordination.

Contrary to the predictions of these four models, the nation-state has not yet become obsolete. Those who believe it has often use a simple analogy. They say that the nation-state today is penetrable by rockets that can cross its borders in no time. Just as gunpowder and infantry penetrated and destroyed the medieval castle, so nuclear missilery has made the nation-state obsolete. But people want three things from their political institutions: physical security, economic well-being, and communal identity. The nation-state has provided more of those than any other institution. Multinational corporations and international organizations lack the force to provide for security and the legitimacy to provide a focus for communal identity. So, despite the long tradition of efforts to design alternatives, the territorial state and its problems remain central to world politics.

NATIONALISM AND TRANSNATIONALISM

Nationalism and transnationalism will be the contending forces in the post–Cold War world. The world is experiencing revolutionary changes in technology, especially in communication and transportation. In one sense, the world is getting smaller. Large international institutions such as the multinational corporations organize economic production on a global basis and pursue global strategies. Yet, at the same time, many people are reacting to rapid change with nationalistic responses.

Communications are changing the world. Diplomacy is carried out in real time. In the Gulf War, both Saddam Hussein and George Bush were watching CNN for the latest news. Human rights problems and mass suffering in distant parts of the globe are brought to our living rooms by television. Even before the World Wide Web, the Canadian thinker Marshall McLuhan argued that modern communications was producing what he called a "global village." But the metaphor of a global village can be misleading because global political identity remains weak. In most of the world, nationalism seems to be getting stronger, not weaker. Instead of a global village, we have villages around the globe that are more aware of each other.

The End of History?

Some analysts argued that large ideological cleavages had driven international conflict over the last century. Large ideological movements such as fascism and communism were responses to the disruption of traditional life by modernization. Industrialization tore people from their villages or small communities and made them available for mobilization by the large ideological movements. Over time, however, liberal capitalism proved more successful in producing a higher level of welfare and citizen participation. The end of the Cold War suggests that liberal capitalism has prevailed, and there is no longer one single competitor to liberal capitalism as an overarching ideology. For authors like Francis Fukuyama who believe that ideas drive history, then history might well seem to be over. But rather than the "end of history," the post–Cold War world could be described as the *return* of history.

The return of history means more normal circumstances where a single ideological cleavage does not drive the larger conflicts in international politics. Liberal capitalism has many competitors, albeit fragmented ones. China allows for capitalism in its southwestern provinces, particularly Guandong and Hong Kong. Yet, China in its politics and ideology is neither liberal nor fully capitalist. In other areas, religious fundamentalism challenges the norms and practices of liberal capitalism. We sometimes lump all religious fundamentalisms together, but there are many Islamic fundamentalisms and great differences between the Algerian and the Saudi variants. What they have in common is a reaction against and a resistance to secular liberal capitalism.

The major response and competitor to liberal capitalism after the Cold War is ethnic nationalism. As we saw earlier, nationalism tends to rise when identities are challenged by major social changes. People with similar ethnic characteristics asserting their common identity is a very powerful idea. But it makes a difference what form nationalism takes. As we saw earlier, many things are grouped together under the label of nationalism. It is instructive to look at the difference between Eastern and Western Europe. Under communist rule in the East, nationalistic and ethnic conflicts were frozen for a half century. The end of the Cold War and the removal of Soviet hegemony thawed many of these tensions. For example, with the end of the Cold War and the demise of its communist government, ancient hatreds between Serbs and Croats came to the fore again in Yugoslavia. Throughout Eastern Europe and the former Soviet Union, many ethnic groups spill across borders, stirring up more potential for further ethnic conflict and revivals of nationalism.

Contrast that with Western Europe, where countries that had previously held strong nationalist passions and great animosities have formed a larger European community. Even reluctant Britain went along with the major lines of the agreements. In Western Europe, countries are overcoming their ancient animosities and unifying while many Eastern European countries are rediscovering their ancient animosities. What can explain it?

Part of the explanation may be the role of economic growth. When people are better off, the animosities may be less tense. Part of it may be democracy, for when people have a chance to work out their procedures openly, passions can be overcome. Some of the ancient animosities were exorcised through democratic processes— witness the debate that went on in West Germany at the end of World War II that led to changes in the textbooks and the new understanding of Germany history. And part of the answer lies in the regional institutions that pulled West Europeans together in a larger framework in which the more extreme nationalist views were discouraged.

But even in Western Europe, nationalism is far from dead and gone. Many Europeans do not want their national identity submerged completely in a European identity. There are still residual fears between French and Germans. One reason why the French support European integration is to tie the Germans down. In addition, many West Europeans worry and react against immigrants. They fear migration from the north of Africa as well as from Eastern Europe. The invading armies from the south and east will be poor and come as individuals. Right-wing parties in Western Europe appeal to xenophobia and provide a warning signal that the problems of nationalism are not totally banished from Western Europe. Sovereignty still protects the rich minority from the poor majority of the world. Nonetheless, the comparison between Western and Eastern Europe is remarkable.

Transnationalism

What about the other side of the coin? Because of transnational communications, there is much more awareness of what is going on in other parts of the globe and groups are better able to organize on a global basis. The most impressive, of course, is the multinational corporation. By spreading investments around the world and making profits in different parts of the global market, the transnational corporation is producing a different type of world economy. Governments compete to attract international investments. A large part of international trade is trade within multinational corporations. Honda now produces more automobiles in the United States than it does in Japan, and it transports American-made automobiles back to Japan. The U.S. government pressed the European Union to accept Honda vehicles made in the United States. In other words, the United States defined the export of Japanese cars made in the United States to Europe as an American national interest. Similarly, IBM is the largest producer of mainframe computers in Japan. IBM/Japan does its research in Japan and hires Japanese employees.

This has led the political economist Robert Reich to ask, "Who is us?" Should Americans focus on the identity of the headquarters of a company or on where it does its research and production? He argues that in terms of what is good for the people living within the borders of the United States, a foreign company working inside the United States may be more important than an American company working in Japan. Critics have responded to Reich by saying that he is looking further into the future than is currently justified. Most multinational corporations have a predominant national identity, and three-quarters of American production is done by companies with headquarters in the United States. Nonetheless, it is an interesting way of thinking about the future. Transnational investment is helping to confuse identities, to confuse the question of "who's us," and along with ecological interdependence, that might affect long-run views of global problems.

Technological change and economic growth accentuate ecological problems and put pressure on resources such as the oceans, atmosphere, Antarctica, and biological diversity that have been treated as global commons. Over the last century, governments have signed more than 170 environmental treaties concerning subjects of shared concern, including fisheries, acid rain, ozone depletion, endangered species protection, Antarctica, and ocean pollution. Two-thirds have been signed since the first UN environmental conference in Stockholm in 1972. Another major UN conference on environment and development was held in Brazil in 1992. Environmental issues have also spawned numerous nongovernmental organizations that lobby transnationally. The domestic politics of most developed countries show a strong growth of environmental concern.

But what happens if there are asymmetries in the ways different countries react? Japan, for example, has far more restrictive attitudes than the United States. There is four times more Japanese direct investment in the United States than American direct investment in Japan. If the United States responds by excluding Japan from American markets, it may simply create inefficient firms that are no longer able to compete on a global basis. The trouble with protectionist responses is that they may hurt the protector as much as they hurt the other side. So in the 1990s, the Americans and the Japanese negotiated over domestic impediments to trade. The United States pressed Japan over something strictly within Japanese domestic jurisdiction. Japan had laws restricting the size of supermarkets and other practices restricting access of foreign firms to the distribution system. A number of Japanese politicians and consumers were delighted to have this American pressure because it benefited the Japanese consumer. In a sense, there was a transnational coalition between U.S. producers and Japanese consumers. The Japanese government in turn pressed the United States to change its budget deficit, arguing correctly that the U.S. trade deficit was related to the government budget deficit. In other words, Americans and the Japanese officials were dealing with each other not at water's edge, but on matters that were deep within the sovereign jurisdiction of each country.

Some observers worried about the effects of such practices. They argued that the more the two sides pressed each other on sensitive domestic issues, the more the other side was going to resent it. Interdependence meant more friction. In other words, every time the United States pressed Japan to open some segment of its market, it pleased some Japanese, but it stimulated others to react nationalistically. Liberals responded that protectionism would not stem the rise of nationalism and would mean forgoing the gains from interdependence as well as the efficiency that comes from competition.

In short, technology is creating a market in which transnational corporations can invest globally, but parts of domestic populations respond nationalistically. The interplay between transnationalism and nationalism will be a major feature of global politics.

Proliferation

Another transnational process is the spread of technology. Companies spread technologies. We saw that in the oil case where companies inadvertently transferred skills to poorer countries. Technology also can spread through trade or through smuggling. The basic truth is that, with time, technology spreads across borders. What will this spread of technology do to security? Already there are 20 countries with the potential to make weapons of mass destruction. The technology of chemical weaponry is nearly a century old; nuclear weaponry and ballistic missiles are half-century-old technologies. To some extent, policies of nonproliferation have slowed the rate of spread of nuclear weapons. But the problem of proliferation was exacerbated when the collapse of the Soviet Union made it less able to control its former client states and less able to control the outflow of technology.

Before the Soviet collapse, eight countries had nuclear weapons. Five were formally declared nuclear weapons states in the 1968 Nuclear Non-Proliferation Treaty (NPT): the United States, the Soviet Union, Britain, France, China. Three states were widely reputed to have developed nuclear weapons covertly: Israel, India, and Pakistan. Interestingly, there were 30 more that could have produced nuclear weapons but did not; that is, there were three or four times more states able to have nuclear weapons than actually had them. That is quite a contrast to President Kennedy's fears when signing the Limited Test Ban Treaty in 1963 that there would be 25 countries with nuclear weapons by the 1970s.

Why wasn't there more proliferation? After all, in an anarchic world of sovereign states, nuclear weapons are the ultimate form of self-help. There are three major answers. One was the alliances that arose during the Cold War in which each super-(1)power gave security guarantees to its allies. For example, Germany and Japan did not develop nuclear weapons because they had American security guarantees. American promises to prevent any country from using nuclear blackmail against these allies reassured the Japanese and the Germans that they did not have to develop nuclear weapons. Alliances also made a difference to some of the smaller states. For example, South Korea and Taiwan each began to develop nuclear weapons when it looked as if the United States might withdraw from Asia in the 1970s in the aftermath of Vietnam, but they stopped when the United States protested and promised continued protection. Similarly, the Soviet Union constrained its East European allies and Third World client states from developing nuclear weapons.

Another cause was superpower cooperation. In the early stages of the nuclear (2)era, the superpower attitude on nuclear weaponry was highly competitive. The superpowers tried to use nuclear technology to earn points in the ideological competition. In 1953, President Eisenhower announced with great fanfare the "Atoms for Peace" program to help other countries develop nuclear technology for peaceful purposes, emphasizing the benign face of the atom to win more points for the United States. Similarly, the Soviet Union extended nuclear assistance to China. But by 1968, the United States and the Soviet Union were able to cooperate to the point that they could agree on a nonproliferation treaty. In 1977, the United States, the Soviet Union, and 13 other countries that supplied nuclear technology set up the Nuclear Suppliers Group to set guidelines on what sorts of nuclear technology could be exported.

A third reason was the existence of treaties and institutions. More than 170 (3)states have signed the Non-Proliferation Treaty, in which they agreed not to develop or to transfer nuclear weapons. The nonnuclear states agreed to have inspectors from the International Atomic Energy Agency in Vienna visit their peaceful nuclear facilities to assure they were not being misused. Israel, India, Pakistan, and some other significant states have not signed the treaty. Some signatories cheated. Iraq, for instance, signed the Non-Proliferation Treaty but had a massive nuclear program and was able to hide much of it.

After the Cold War, some of the things that slowed the spread of nuclear weapons changed. Soviet alliance guarantees collapsed and questions were raised about the longevity of NATO. Two of the open questions for the post–Cold War world were the future of alliances and security guarantees, and whether nuclear technology would flow from the former Soviet Union to would-be proliferators. Kenneth Waltz has argued that the spread of nuclear weapons may be stabilizing because deterrence will work. If nuclear weapons helped prevent the Cold War from becoming hot, why wouldn't their crystal ball effect produce prudence and order in other parts of the world such as the Middle East and South Asia? The trouble with this view is that it rests almost entirely on a rational model of deterrence. But if the real danger of nuclear weapons in the post–Cold War period is likely to be loss of control, then these rational models that provide the basis for confident predictions may be largely irrelevant. Many of the countries that will next develop nuclear weapons have an unstable record caused by coups and by armies splitting.

Nuclear weapons in the United States and the Soviet Union were equipped with elaborate technological devices that required a code from a higher authority in order to get access to the weapon. But many of the countries newly developing nuclear weapons will not have these elaborate technological devices. The end of the Cold War and the transnational spread of technology may produce a larger prospect of nuclear weapons being used in some of the new countries trying to enter the nuclear race than was true in the last half century. And one of the greatest threats in the future will be transnational terrorists getting hold of weapons of mass destruction.

A NEW WORLD ORDER?

Given the contradictory forces at work, what will be the shape of the world order at the end of the twentieth century? In 1991, President Bush said the Gulf War was about "more than one small country; it is a big idea; a new world order." It was "new ways of working with other nations . . . peaceful settlement of disputes, solidarity against aggression, reduced and controlled arsenals, and just treatment of all peoples."

Like Woodrow Wilson's fourteen points or Franklin Roosevelt's four freedoms, George Bush's rhetoric expressed goals designed to rally public support when a liberal democracy goes to war. But after the war, when reality intruded, people were led to compare the imperfect outcome of the war with an impossible ideal.

Different Concepts of Order

The end of the Cold War certainly altered the international system, but claims that the 1990s were the dawning of "a new world order" were undermined by the profoundly different ways people interpret the word *order*. Realists argue that wars arise from the effort of states to acquire power and security in an anarchic world, or one in which there is no ultimate arbiter of order other than self-help and the force of arms. In this view, *order* refers primarily to the structure or distribution of power among states. Liberals argue that conflicts and their prevention are determined not only by the balance of power, but by the domestic structure of states, their values, identities, and cultures, and by international institutions for conflict resolution. In contrast to realists, liberals argue that institutions such as the United Nations can help prevent conflict and establish order by stabilizing expectations, creating a sense of continuity and a feeling that current cooperation will be reciprocated in the future. Order for liberals, then, is tied to values such as democracy and human rights, as well as to institutions.

For others, order has more sinister connotations. In the view of nativist or nationalist groups such as that led by Pat Robertson in the United States, or by Jean-Marie Le Pen in France, "new world order" suggests a conspiracy among financial and political elites to dominate the world. In this view, multinational corporations, in league with the financial markets of Wall Street, London, and Tokyo, enrich themselves at the expense of the rest. In the view of certain Islamic fundamentalists, order is a purely Western concept designed to dominate the non-Western world.

These differing conceptions of order mean that the "new world order" is tricky to define. None of these schools of thought are adequate by themselves in understanding the causes of conflict in the current world. The realist emphasis on the balance of power is necessary but not sufficient when long-term societal changes are eroding the norms of state sovereignty. The view that peace has broken out among the major liberal democracies is accurate, but it is not a panacea when many states, including great powers, are not liberal democracies.

The old, bipolar Cold War order provided a stability of sorts. The Cold War exacerbated a number of Third World conflicts, but economic conflicts among the United States, Europe, and Japan were dampened by common concerns about the Soviet military threat, and bitter ethnic divisions were kept under the tight lid of the Soviet presence in Eastern Europe. With the passing of that bipolar order, conflict has not ended. It does, however, have different sources.

Future Configurations of Power

As historians and political observers since Thucydides have noted, rapid power transitions are one of the leading causes of great power conflict. Such power transitions were a deep structural cause of historically recent great power conflicts, including Germany's rise before each world war and the relative rise and resulting rivalry of the United States and the Soviet Union after World War II. There is a strong consensus that the period after the Cold War is one of rapid power transitions. There is considerable debate over the direction and magnitude of the transitions, however, and these debates are indicative of the unpredictability that makes such transitions a potential source of conflict.

One alternative is *multipolarity*. If the term multipolarity implies an historical analogy with the nineteenth century, it is highly misleading. That order rested on a balance of power of roughly five equal powers, whereas the great powers after the Cold War are far from equal. Russia has declined faster and farther since 1990 than almost anyone expected, though it retains an immense nuclear arsenal. China has risen faster than most anticipated, with a long period of double-digit economic growth. Japan and Germany have not become the full-fledged superpowers that some wrongly predicted in 1990. The United States is the only true superpower, with global assets in all dimensions of power.

This leads some to posit that the world is now ordered by *unipolar hegemony*. Some observers believe the Gulf War marked the beginning of a *Pax Americana* in which the world will acquiesce in a benign American hegemony. While the United States may be the only superpower, the hegemonic conclusion does not follow. There are many important security, economic, and political goals that the United States cannot achieve by itself. Military power is largely unipolar, with the United States the only country possessing both intercontinental nuclear weapons and large modern air, naval, and ground forces capable of deploying around the globe. But economic power is tripolar, with the United States, Japan, and Europe representing two-thirds of the world's products. China's growth may make economic power quadripolar early in the next millennium.

At the level of transnational relations that cross borders outside the control of government, and that includes actors as diverse as bankers and terrorists, power is widely dispersed. To take a few examples, private actors in global capital markets constrain the way interest rates can be used to manage the American economy; the transnational spread of technology increases the destructive capabilities of otherwise poor and weak states; and a number of issues on the international agenda—drug trade, AIDS, migration, global warming—have deep societal roots in more than one country and flow across borders largely outside of governmental control. Since neither military nor traditional economic means are very effective in coping with such problems, no great power will be able to solve them alone.

Others posit that the world will be organized around *three economic blocs*—Europe, Asia, and North America. Yet, even here, global technological changes and the increase of nonbloc, nonstate actors such as multinational corporations and ethnic groups will resist the capacity of these three blocs to constrain their activities. While some liberals argue that economic power has replaced military power as the central medium of international politics, this is greatly overstated. Security is like oxygen. It is often taken for granted when it is present, but you will think about nothing else once you begin to miss it. Realists rightly argue that economic instruments still cannot compete with military forces in their coercive and deterrent effects. Economic sanctions by the United Nations compelled neither Iraq to withdraw from Kuwait in 1990, nor the Haitian military junta to step down in 1993 and 1994.

The current distribution of power represents a combination of these different configurations into *multilevel interdependence*. No single hierarchy adequately describes a world politics that is like a three-dimensional chess game. Power on the military board is largely unipolar, with the United States strongest. The economic middle board has a tripolar distribution of power, while the bottom board of transnational interdependence shows a diffusion of power.

None of this complexity would matter if military power were as fungible as money and could determine the outcomes in all areas. But military prowess is a poor predictor of the outcomes on the economic and transnational boards of current world politics. The United States is better placed with a more diversified portfolio of power resources than any other country, but the current world order is not an era of American hegemony.

These predictions assume that the state will remain the primary determinant of international relations. That assumption may be wrong. Some believe that over the next decades, the contours of global politics will be increasingly defined by large global civilizations. They predict a *clash among civilizations,* with the Muslim world rejecting and at times fighting the Western Christian world, the Chinese world, and the Hindu world. The Hindu world in turn exists in an uneasy standoff with its Muslim Pakistani and Bangladeshi neighbors, while China and the West are often at odds over normative issues such as human rights and strategic issues. Thus far, however, more communal conflicts have occurred within these large civilizations than between them. In many parts of the world, particularly Africa, the Middle East, and Central Asia, communal conflicts are increasing because the state is collapsing. Conflicts arise as people attempt to staunch the chaos through ethnic nationalism and religious fundamentalism, and their weak states collapse under the pressure.

Many people point to the unpredictable effects of the *computer and information revolution* and hypothesize that these will erode state sovereignty and nationalism to such extent that the state will wither away. As people are able to access international information, individual cultures and governments will no longer command the primary loyalty of its members. People will form allegiances based on shared interests rather than ethnicity, language, or nationality. Already, the Internet means that a scientist in Osaka, Japan, may communicate as easily with another scientist in Cairo, Egypt, than either may with their physical neighbors. In this respect, the communications revolution is a boon to functionalism. However, it is very rarely the case that these "virtual" communities have acted in direct conflict with the state, and it is unclear if such shared interests will ever outweigh national, ethnic, or religious loyalties.

It is unquestionable that new technologies are changing the nature of power. More than ever, knowledge is power. The country that is best placed to lead the information revolution will be more powerful than any other. For the foreseeable future, that country is the United States. Important communications and information processing technologies, such as space-based surveillance, direct broadcasting, and high-speed computers make easier the tasks of containing conflict before it erupts, stemming proliferation of conventional and unconventional weapons, and maintaining communication between potential adversaries. It is also true, however, that these technologies increase the ability of nonstate actors, be they terrorists or corporations, to disrupt international politics and promulgate their agendas.

The Prison of Old Concepts

The world after the Cold War is *sui generis,* and we overly constrain our understanding by trying to force it into the procrustean bed of traditional metaphors with their mechanical polarities. Power is becoming more multidimensional, structures more complex, and states themselves more permeable. This added complexity means that world order must rest on more than the traditional military balance of power alone.

The realist view of world order is necessary but not sufficient because it does not take into account the long-term societal changes that have been slowly moving the world away from the Westphalian system. In 1648, after 30 years of tearing each other apart over religion, the European states agreed in the Peace of Westphalia that the ruler, in effect, would determine the religion of a state regardless of popular preferences. Order was based on the sovereignty of states, not the sovereignty of peoples. The mechanical balancing of states treated as empty billiard balls was slowly eroded over the ensuing centuries by the growth of nationalism and democratic participation, but the norms of state sovereignty persisted. Now the rapid growth in transnational communications, migration, and economic interdependence is accelerating the erosion of the classical conception and increasing the gap between norm and reality.

This evolution makes more relevant the liberal conception of a world society of peoples as well as of states, and of order resting on values and institutions as well as military power. Liberal views that were once regarded as hopelessly utopian, such as Immanuel Kant's plea for a peaceful league of democracies, seem less far-fetched now that political scientists report there are virtually no cases of liberal democracies going to war with each other. Debates over the effects of German reunification, for example, pitted against each other realists who saw Europe going back to the future and liberals who faulted such analysis for neglecting the fact that the new Germany is democratic and deeply enmeshed with its Western neighbors through the institutions of the European Union.

Of course these liberal conceptions of order are not entirely new. The Cold War order had norms and institutions, but they played a limited role. During World War II, Roosevelt, Stalin, and Churchill had agreed to a United Nations that assumed a multipolar distribution of power. The UN Security Council would enforce the doctrine of collective security and nonaggression against smaller states while the five great powers were protected by their vetoes.

Even this abbreviated version of Woodrow Wilson's institutional approach to order was hobbled, however, by the unforeseen rise of bipolarity. The superpowers vetoed each other's initiatives, and the organization was reduced to the more modest role of stationing peacekeepers to observe cease-fires rather than repelling aggressors. When the decline of Soviet power led to their new policy of cooperation with the United States in applying the UN doctrine of collective security against Iraq, it was less the arrival of a new world order than the reappearance of an aspect of the liberal institutional order that was supposed to have come into effect in 1945.

But just as the Gulf War resurrected one aspect of the liberal approach to world order, it also exposed an important weakness in the liberal conception. The doctrine of collective security enshrined in the UN Charter is state-centric, applicable when borders are crossed, but not when force is used among peoples within a state. Liberals try to escape this problem by appealing to the principles of democracy and self-determination: Let peoples within states vote on whether they want to be protected behind borders of their own. But, as we have seen, self-determination is not as simple as it sounds. Who decides what self will determine? Less than 10 percent of the states in today's world are ethnically homogeneous. Only half have one ethnic group that accounts for as much as 75 percent of their population. Most of the states of the former Soviet Union have significant minorities, and many have disputed borders. Africa might be considered a continent of roughly a thousand peoples squeezed within and across fifty-some states. In Canada, the French-speaking majority of Quebec demands special status and agitates for independence from the rest of Canada. Once such multiethnic, multilingual states are called into question, it is difficult to see where the process ends. In such a world, local autonomy and international surveillance of minority rights hold some promise, but a policy of unqualified support for national self-determination could turn into a principle of enormous world disorder.

The Evolution of a Hybrid World Order

How then is it possible to preserve some order in traditional terms of the distribution of power among sovereign states while also moving toward institutions that are based on "justice among peoples?" International institutions are gradually evolving in such a post-Westphalian direction. Already in 1945, Articles 55 and 56 of the UN Charter pledged states to collective responsibility for observance of human rights and fundamental freedoms. Even before the 1991 Security Council resolutions authorizing postwar interventions in Iraq, UN recommendations of sanctions against apartheid in South Africa set a precedent of not being strictly limited by the Charter's statements about sovereignty. In Europe, the 1975 Helsinki Accords codified minority rights, and violations could be referred to the European Conference on Security and Cooperation and the Council of Europe. International law is gradually evolving. In 1965, the American Law Institute defined international law as "rules and principles. . . dealing with conduct of states and international organizations." Two decades later, the institute's lawyers added, "as well as some of their relations with persons." Individual and minority rights are increasingly treated as more than just national concerns.

Of course, in many, perhaps most, parts of the world, such principles are flouted and violations go unpunished. To mount an armed multilateral intervention to right all such wrongs would be another enormous principle of disorder. But, as we have seen, intervention is a matter of degree, with actions ranging from statements and limited economic measures at the low end of the spectrum to full-fledged invasions at the high end. Limited interventions and multilateral infringements of sovereignty may gradually increase without suddenly disrupting the distribution of power among states.

On a larger scale, the Security Council may act under Chapter VII of the UN Charter if it determines that internal violence or development of weapons of mass destruction are likely to spill over into a more general threat to the peace in a region. Such definitions are somewhat elastic and may gradually expand over time. In other instances, groups of states may act on a regional basis as Nigeria and others did in 1990 by sending troops to Liberia under the framework of the Economic Community of West African States.

Such imperfect principles and institutions will leave lots of room for domestic violence and injustice among peoples. But the moral horrors will be less than would be the case if policymakers were to try either to right all wrongs by force or, alternatively, to return to the unmodified Westphalian system. Liberals must realize that the evolution of a new world order beyond the Westphalian system is a matter of decades and centuries; realists must recognize that the traditional definitions of power and structure in purely military terms miss the changes that are occurring in a world of global communications and growing transnational relations.

THINKING ABOUT THE FUTURE

What kind of world would you like to live in? You will live in a world that will be anarchic in the terms stated at the beginning of the book. Order will be provided both by the realists' balance of power among states and by the liberals' evolving international institutions. That order will not always be just. Justice and order are often at odds with each other, even in issues of self-determination. Is it more important to keep borders intact or to pursue humanitarian causes that violate territorial integrity? What do these choices do to principles of order? These debates are not easily reconciled.

But change is occurring. Robert Gilpin argues that international politics has not changed over two millennia, and that Thucydides would have little trouble understanding our world today. If Thucydides were plopped down in the Middle East, he would probably recognize the situation quite quickly. But if he were set down in Western Europe, he would probably have a more difficult time understanding the relations between France and Germany. Globally, there has been a technological revolution in the development of nuclear weaponry, an enormous growth in economic interdependence, and an emerging global society in which there is increased consciousness of certain values that cross national frontiers. Interestingly, similar changes were anticipated by Immanuel Kant in his eighteenth-century liberal view of international politics. Kant predicted that over the long run, humans would evolve beyond war for three reasons: the greater destructiveness of war, the growth of economic interdependence, and the development of what he called republican governments and we call today liberal democracies.

To understand the current world, we must understand both the realist and liberal views of world politics. We need to be able to think about both ideal types at the same time. Neither realism nor complex interdependence exists; both are ideals. The realist sees a world of states using force to pursue security. Reversing that produces complex interdependence, in which nonstate actors, economic instruments, and welfare goals are more important than security. Those two views are at the opposite ends of a conceptual continuum on which we can locate different real world relationships. Both sets of theories are helpful and necessary to understand international politics in a changing world.

That leads to some final questions. How much will the future resemble the past? To what extent will Europe go back to the future? Will there be a war between the United States and China? Between civilizations? The bipolar world is over, but it is not going to be replaced by a unipolar world of American hegemony. The world is economically multipolar, and there will be a diffusion of power as nationalism grows, interdependence increases, and transnational actors become more important. The new world will not be neat, and you will live with that.

SELECTED READINGS

1. Fukuyama, Francis, "The End of History," *The National Interest,* No. 16 (Summer 1989), pp. 3–18; and Huntington, Samuel, "No Exit: The Errors of Endism," *The National Interest,* No. 17 (Fall 1989), pp. 3–11.

2. Mearsheimer, John, "Back to the Future," *International Security,* Vol. 15, No. 1 (Summer 1990), pp. 5–56; and Hoffmann, Stanley, Robert Keohane, and John Mearsheimer, "Back to the Future: Part II," *International Security,* Vol. 15, No. 2 (Fall 1990), pp. 191–199.

3. Deutsch, Karl, *Nationalism and Its Alternatives* (New York: Knopf, 1969), Chapter 1.

4. Carnesale, Albert, et al., *Living with Nuclear Weapons* (Cambridge, MA: Harvard University Press, 1983), Chapter 10.

5. Rosecrance, Richard, *The Rise of the Trading State: Commerce and Conquest in the Modern World* (New York: Basic, 1986), Chapter 2.

6. Reich, Robert, "Who Is Us?" *Harvard Business Review,* Vol. 68, No. 1 (Jan.–Feb. 1990), pp. 53–64.

FURTHER READINGS

Barnet, Richard J., and John Cavanagh, *Global Dreams: Imperial Corporations and the New World Order* (New York: Simon & Schuster, 1994).

Brown, Michael, Sean Lynn-Jones, and Steven Miller, eds., *Debating the Democratic Peace* (Cambridge, MA: MIT Press, 1996).

Clark, Grenville, and Louis Sohn, *Introduction to World Peace Through World Law* (Chicago: World Without War Publications, 1973).

Falk, Richard A., *This Endangered Planet: Prospects and Proposals for Human Survival* (New York: Random House, 1971).

Gaddis, John L., "Towards the Post–Cold War World," *Foreign Affairs,* Vol. 70, No. 2 (Spring 1991), pp. 102–122.

Haas, Ernst B., *Beyond the Nation-State: Functionalism and International Organization* (Stanford, CA: Stanford University Press, 1964).

Huntington, Samuel, "The Clash of Civilizations?" *Foreign Affairs,* Vol. 72, No. 3 (Summer 1993), pp. 22–49.

Huntington, Samuel P., *The Third Wave: Democratization in the Late Twentieth Century* (Norman: University of Oklahoma Press, 1991).

Kaplan, Robert, *The Ends of the Earth: A Journey at the Dawn of the 21th Century* (New York: Random House, 1996).

Kennedy, Paul M., *The Rise and Fall of the Great Powers: Economic Change and Military Conflict from 1500 to 2000* (New York: Random House, 1987).

Mathews, Jessica A., *Preserving the Global Environment: The Challenge of Shared Leadership* (New York: Norton, 1991).

Mitrany, David, *A Working Peace System* (Chicago: Quadrangle, 1966).

Neustadt, Richard E., and Ernest R. May, *Thinking in Time: The Uses of History for Decisionmakers* (New York: Free Press, 1986).

Nye, Joseph S., Jr., *Bound to Lead: The Changing Nature of American Power* (New York: Basic, 1990).

Nye, Joseph, Jr., and William A. Owens, "America's Information Edge," *Foreign Affairs,* Vol. 75, No. 2 (March/April 1996), pp. 20–36.

Russett, Bruce, and James S. Sutterlin, "The U.N. in a New World Order," *Foreign Affairs,* Vol. 70, No. 2 (Spring 1991), pp. 69–83.

Wallace, William, *The Transformation of Western Europe* (London: Royal Institute for International Affairs, Pinter, 1990).

Weiss, Thomas George, David P. Forsythe, and Roger A. Coate, eds., *The United Nations and Changing World Politics* (Boulder, CO: Westview Press, 1994).

STUDY QUESTIONS

1. What does Fukuyama mean by the "end of history?"
2. Is there a new world order distinct from that which came to be after World War II? Can we characterize it as multipolar? Bipolar? Unipolar? Does it matter?
3. Is nationalism fading in importance in world politics, or is it stronger than ever? Cite examples.
4. Is the threat of nuclear war a thing of the past?

5. Why does Reich believe corporate nationality is irrelevant? Do you agree?

6. What kind of power is important and will be important in coming decades? How will this affect America's role in the world? What does the 1991 Gulf War imply about the answers to these questions?

7. What does realist theory predict about the future of Europe? What other factors might affect events?

8. What would realist and liberal theories predict will be the nature of U.S.-Japanese relations in the coming years? U.S.-European? U.S.-Russian? Does the spread of liberal democracy affect world peace?

9. Are conflicts more likely to occur between large civilizations or within them?

10. If the Internet strengthens transnational groups, how will that affect world politics?

CREDITS

Page 1 (photo): Alinari/Art Resource NY.

Page 5, "1910: The Unseen Vampire of War" (box): Excerpted from "From Our December 13 Pages, 75 Years Ago," *International Herald Tribune,* December 13, 1985. Copyright 1985 *International Herald Tribune* and The New York Times Syndicate. Reprinted by permission.

Page 27 (photo): Reuters/Corbis-Bettmann.

Page 50 (photo): Corbis-Bettmann.

Page 62 (map): Reprinted with permission from Brian Catchpole, *A Map History of the Modern World* (Oxford, England: Heinemann Publishers Ltd., 1982), p. 13.

Page 67 (map): Reprinted with permission from Brian Catchpole, *A Map History of the Modern World* (Oxford, England: Heinemann Publishers Ltd., 1982), p. 15.

Page 74 (photo): UPI/Corbis-Bettmann.

Page 79 (map): Reprinted with permission from Brian Catchpole, *A Map History of the Modern World* (Oxford, England: Heinemann Publishers Ltd., 1982), p. 27.

Page 87 (map): Reprinted with permission from Brian Catchpole, *A Map History of the Modern World* (Oxford, England: Heinemann Publishers Ltd., 1982), p. 69.

Page 92 (map): Reprinted with permission from Brian Catchpole, *A Map History of the Modern World* (Oxford, England: Heinemann Publishers Ltd., 1982), p. 73.

Page 98 (photo): Corbis-Bettmann.

Page 105 (map): Reprinted with permission from Brian Catchpole, *A Map History of the Modern World* (Oxford, England: Heinemann Publishers Ltd., 1982), p. 83.

Page 109 (map): Reprinted with permission from Brian Catchpole, *A Map History of the Modern World* (Oxford, England: Heinemann Publishers Ltd., 1982), p. 123.

Page 114 (box): Excerpted from George Kennan, "The Sources of Soviet Conduct," *Foreign Affairs,* Vol. 25, No. 4 (July 1947), p. 581. Reprinted by permission of *Foreign Affairs,* July 1947. Copyright 1947 by the Council on Foreign Relations, Inc.

Page 133 (photo): E. Kanalstein/United Nations.

INDEX

Note: Index entries found in figures are indicated with f after the page number.

A

Abdullah, king of Jordan, 152
Abkhazians, 138
Absolutism, 111
Acheson, Dean, 91, 108, 129, 139
Acquired Immune Deficiency Syndrome (AIDS), 190
Actors
    in international politics, 6, 8, 33, 170, 175–178, 190
    transnational, 170, 175–178, 190, 194
Adjudication, of international law, 141–142
Afghanistan, 8, 22, 115, 116, 117, 122, 124–125, 127, 135, 137, 160
Africa, 6, 82, 115, 164, 169, 185, 191, 192
    balance of power in, 28
    colonial system in, 59, 63, 69, 138, 150
    pan-Africanism, 29, 150
Agadir, Morocco, 69, 73
Ajami, Fouad, 157
Albania, 7, 67f, 73, 97, 105f, 162
Albrecht-Carrie, René, 46
Aleutians, 92f
Alexander II, czar of Russia, 48
Algeciras conference, 73
Algeria, 145f, 157, 184
Allan, Charles T., 129
Allende, Salvador, 134
Alliances, 99, 146
    African, 28
    balance of power and, 33, 55–57, 58–59, 75, 77–78, 123

bipolarity and, 29, 31, 34, 65, 66f, 111f, 120
    Cold War era, 187
    collective security and, 75, 77
    ideology and, 59
    effect of oil crisis on, 174
    World War I and, 60
    World War II and, 86
Allies, 80, 82, 94, 128
Allison, Graham T., 129
Alsace-Lorraine, 35, 58, 78, 79f
Ambrose, Stephen E., 129
American Law Institute, 193
American Revolution, 48
Amnesty International, 6
Analogies, 16, 70, 95, 108, 110, 140–141, 156, 183, 189
Anarchic system of states, 3–6, 12, 24, 41–42, 51, 55, 74–75, 76, 101. See also States
    international system and, 28, 29, 120, 121, 133, 148
    order and, 181, 182, 187, 188
Anarchy, 19–20, 39, 111
Angell, Norman, 36
Angola, 115, 116, 136
Anti-Comintern Pact, 84, 97
Anti-Semitism, 86, 152
Apartheid, 136, 193
Appeasement, 78, 83, 89, 106
Arab High Committee, 159
Arab League, 6, 159
Arab-Israeli conflict, 1, 136, 143–144, 145f, 146, 151–154, 156–157, 174
Arabs and Arab countries, 55, 94, 143–144, 145f, 148–149, 150–152, 154, 156–157, 159–160, 172, 173, 174
Arafat, Yasir, 156, 157
Arbitration, 146
Ardennes Forest, 85

Aristide, Jean-Bertrand, 136
Aristotle, 43
Armenians, 6, 138
Arms control, 115, 116, 122, 127
Arms Control and Disarmament Agency, 40
Arms race, World War I and, 70
Arms trafficking, 135, 176
Asia, 48, 93, 131, 169
    as economic bloc, 190
    Cold War and, 104–106, 107–108, 109f, 114, 115, 187
    colonial system in, 150
    conflict in, 191
Athens, 1, 9–12, 13–15, 16–17, 18, 19, 21, 26, 30, 31, 40, 54, 56, I94, 123
Atomic bomb. See Nuclear weapons
Atoms for Peace, 187
Attlee, Clement, 105f, 131
Australia, 92f, 109f
Austria, 32, 34, 35, 42, 48, 51, 58, 59
    in Cold War era, 114, 132
    after World War I, 78, 79f
    World War II and, 83, 84, 97, 105f, 144
Austro-Hungarian Empire (Austria-Hungary), 36, 48, 59, 60, 61, 63, 66f, 67f, 68, 73, 138
    origins of World War I, 56, 62f, 63–64, 66, 68, 70, 73, 127
Authoritarian states, 30
Autonomy, 182. See also Self-determination
Axelrod, Robert, 14, 25
Axis Pact, 84, 97, 128
Ayatollah, Khomeini, 148–149
Azerbeijanis, 138

B

Ba'ath party, 55
Baker, Ray S., 95
Balance of power, 2, 11, 20, 41,
    44–45, 164. *See also*
    Bipolarity; Multipolarity;
    Unipolarity
  in Asia, 167
  classical, 57, 146, 164
  Cold War and, 99, 101, 107,
    111, 113, 115, 123–124,
    136, 143
  vs. collective security
    approach, 74–75, 82
  containment and, 113–114
  democracy and, 74, 75
  distribution of power and,
    8–9, 31, 54, 71, 172, 187,
    192, 193. *See also*
    Resources
  in eighteenth century, 32
  European, 31, 32–35, 51, 52,
    54–55, 56, 57–58, 59,
    77–78, 81–82, 88, 89
  as multipolar system, 57–59,
    60–61
  in Middle East, 148–149
  in nineteenth century, 52,
    57–58, 59, 61, 77, 123
  nuclear weapons and,
    123–124
  oil regime and, 171–172, 174
  in Persian Gulf, 171–172
  as policy, 54–57, 60, 94
  to preserve order, 21, 181,
    188–189, 191
  purpose of, 51
  realist view of, 41, 54, 110,
    135–136, 189, 192
  resources and, 51–54
  World War I and, 50, 54–55,
    57, 59–65, 71, 74
Balance of terror, 123–124
Baldwin, David A., 179
Balfour Declaration, 151,
    152, 159
Balkan states, 48, 58, 62f, 63,
    67f, 68, 103, 127, 131
Balkan Wars, 61, 64, 70, 73
Baltic states, 21, 51
Bandwagoning, 55
Bangladesh, 18–19, 190
Bank of England, 97, 168–169
Bank of Japan, 166
Barkin, J. Samuel, 96

Barnet, Richard J., 195
Barnhart, Michael A., 96
Bartlett, C. J., 46
Baruch Plan, 106, 120
Battle of Britain, 82, 87f
Battle of Waterloo, 48
Bay of Pigs, 132
Beitz, Charles R., 25
Belgium, 6, 66, 69, 73, 78, 79f,
    85, 97, 109f
Belgrade, 73
Bell, P. M. H., 95, 96
Ben-Gurion, David, 159
Bentham, Jeremy, 17
Berchtold, Count, 64
Bergsten, C. Fred, 179
Berlin, 32
Berlin blockade, 100, 107, 131
Berlin crisis, 115, 122, 123,
    124, 132
Berlin Wall, 116, 117, 132
Biafra, 138
Biological weapons, 128, 155
Bipolarity, 29, 31, 32, 34, 35,
    44, 61, 65, 82, 113
  Cold War and, 31, 100,
    101, 108–110, 111f, 113,
    120, 123–124, 154, 181,
    189, 192
Bismarck, Otto von, 29, 33–35,
    43, 48, 52, 58, 59, 61, 63,
    78, 127, 150
Blight, James, 129
Blitzkrieg, 83, 85–86, 87f
Blocking coalitions, 33
Blum, Leon, 88
Boer War, 48, 60
Bohemia, 48, 84
Bolsheviks, 28, 78, 84, 85. *See
    also* Russian Revolution
Borneo, 92f
Bosnia, 16, 41
  conflict with Serbia, 137,
    138–139
  crisis of 1908, 61, 68, 69,
    71, 73
Bosnia-Herzegovina, 138
Boundaries, national, 22, 23, 37
Bowie, Robert R., 157
Brazil, 163, 185
Breslauer, George W., 129, 157
Bretton Woods Conference, 131
Brezhnev Doctrine, 136
Britain, 39, 94, 106, 109f, 141,
    155, 171, 174, 182, 187

  balance of power and, 56, 58,
    77–78, 81–82, 172
  British Empire, 2, 8, 48
  European Community
    and, 184
  imperialism of, 63
  in Falkland Islands War, 176
  in nineteenth century,
    47–48, 53, 54, 113, 143,
    168–169
  in Palestine, 151–152, 159
  in Persian Gulf, 155
  Suez Canal and, 143–144,
    145f, 152–153
  in world economy
  World War I and, 34, 52, 56,
    59, 60, 62f, 63, 65, 67f,
    68, 69, 70, 115, 151
  World War II and, 51, 82,
    85–86, 87f, 88, 89–90, 91,
    97, 104, 105f, 112
British Petroleum, 6, 174
British Zionist Federation, 151
Brown, Lester, 166, 178
Brown, Michael, 195
Bueno de Mesquita, Bruce, 46
Bulgaria, 67f, 73, 79f, 80, 105f
Bull, Hedley, 25
Bullock, Alan, 95, 96
Bülow, Prince Bernhand von,
    59–60, 64, 71
Bundy, McGeorge, 129
Bureaucracy, 42, 112, 117
Burma. *See* Myanmar
Burundi, 6, 135
Bush, George, 40, 134, 156,
    183, 188
Byrnes, James, 104

C

Calleo, David, 94, 95
Cambodia, 22, 28, 30, 57, 90,
    135, 137, 148
Camp David Accords, 154, 160
Canada, 7, 39, 48, 109f, 143, 145f,
    164, 168, 170, 171f, 192
Capital, 167, 176, 190
Capitalism, 88, 103, 106,
    118–119
  in post–Cold War era, 184
  U.S. hegemony and,
    100–101, 189–190
  war and, 36–37, 61, 63
Carnegie Endowment for
    International Peace, 37

Carnegie, Andrew, 37
Carnesale, Albert E., 194
Carr, E. H., 96
Cartel, 173
Carter Doctrine, 160
Carter, Jimmy, 115, 154, 160
Castaneda, Jorge, 179
Castro, Fidel, 126, 132, 134
Catholic Church, 99
Caucasus, 6, 138
Causation, 18–19, 29–30, 43,
    44, 65, 88–89, 93–94, 99
Cavanagh, John, 195
Celebes, 92f
Central America, 77
Cerf, Christopher, 158
Chamberlain, Neville, 85, 94,
    95, 97
Charles I, king of England, 47
Charles II, king of England, 47
Chechnya, 17, 138
Chemical weapons, 128, 155,
    186
Chile, 134
China, 2, 3, 7, 17, 22, 30, 57, 92f,
    125, 141, 167, 184, 187
    Communism in, 59, 100,
        103, 107, 131, 140, 161
    economy of, 189, 190
    in international system, 28, 37
    in Korean War, 108, 109f,
        114, 123, 132
    Manchurian crisis and,
        80–81, 97
    Nationalists in, 59, 80, 93, 125
    trade with United States, 170
    in United Nations, 147
    Vietnam intervention by,
        115, 137
    World War II and, 90, 91,
        93, 94
Chipman, John, 157
Choices, effect on interdepen-
    dence, 163
    human behavior and, 55
    intervention and, 135
    policy, 2, 12, 15, 19, 21, 24,
        34, 69
Christians, 154, 190
Churchill, Winston, 55, 71,
    100, 103, 104, 105f,
    112–113, 131, 192
City-states, 3
Civil War, U.S., 2
Clark, Grenville, 195

Class conflict, 88, 89f
Claude, Inis L., 95, 96
Clausewitz, Karl von, 121
Cleopatra, 44
Clifford, Clark, 104
Clinton administration, 168
CNN, 183
Coal industry, 177
Coalition of Rye and Iron, 64
Coast Guard, 176
Coate, Roger A., 195
Cobden, Richard, 36, 45, 50, 71
Cohen, Benjamin J., 179
Cold War, 16, 35, 170
    balance of power and, 99,
        113, 136, 143
    bipolarity and, 31, 100, 101,
        108–110, 111f, 113, 120,
        123–124, 154, 181, 189,
        192
    causes of, 44, 99–112
    collective security and,
        146–147, 192
    containment policy and,
        113–115
    defined, 98
    détente and, 115–116
    end of, 116–119, 181, 184,
        187, 188, 189
    nuclear deterrence and, 99,
        120–128, 187–188
    phases of, 103–108,
        114–116, 131–132
    states' goals in, 112–114
Collective security, 37
    vs. balance of power
        approach, 74–76, 82
    Ethiopian invasion and,
        81–82
    League of Nations and,
        75–82, 93, 146
    Manchurian crisis and,
        80–81
    problems with, 146
    United Nations and, 100,
        146–148, 154–155, 192
Colombia, 109f
Cominform, 131
Common Market, 39, 182
Communications, 2, 8, 13, 20,
    41, 88, 110, 111f, 118,
    122, 123, 127, 150, 177,
    183, 185, 191, 193
Communism, 28, 30, 36, 54, 56,
    59, 79f, 88

Cold War and, 99, 100, 103,
    105f, 106, 107, 108,
    110–112, 113–115, 116,
    117, 118, 122, 131, 136,
    140, 159, 184
Communist International
    (Comintern), 84
Communist Manifesto, 48
Community, sense of, 19
Concert of Europe, 33, 57–58, 78
Concessions. See Appeasement
Congress of Berlin, 48
Congress of Vienna, 9, 33, 34,
    35, 48, 52, 57, 78
Conrad, General, 64
Consequences, 139–140
Conservative Party (Britain),
    68, 88
Conservative Party (France), 88
Containment policy, 94, 99,
    107, 113–114, 115, 116,
    139–140
Cooperation, in international
    politics, 14, 15, 20, 32,
    34, 117, 121, 182, 183
    interdependence and,
        161, 164
    on nuclear technology, 187
Corcyra, 11, 13–14, 15, 16, 26, 94
Corinth, 11, 13–14, 15, 16, 94
Cosmopolitan view
    of ethics, 19, 23–24
    of intervention, 135, 136
Cotenability, 43. See also
    Plausibility
Council of Europe, 193
Council of Ministers, 39
Counter-Reformation, 99
Counterfactuals, 42–45, 65–69,
    89–90, 99, 124, 128, 156
Craig, Gordon A., 46, 95
Credibility, of deterrence,
    124–125, 126, 168
Credit-Anstalt, 97
Crimean War, 48, 58
Croatia, 40, 138–139, 184
Cromwell, Oliver, 47
Cronin, Bruce, 96
Crowe, Sir Eyre, 60, 61, 63, 134
Cuba, 115, 122, 132
Cuba, missile crisis, 18, 29, 115,
    122, 123, 125–126, 127,
    128, 132
Culture, 53, 54, 188
Customs, 141

Czech Republic, 138
Czechoslovakia, 42
 in Cold War era, 100, 103,
  105f, 107, 118, 131, 135
 World War I and, 78, 79f, 138
 World War II and, 80, 83,
  84–85, 97, 144

D
Dahl, Robert, 51
Daimler-Benz, 7
Dangerfield, George, 68
Danzig, 79f, 85
Darwin, Charles, 63
Dawes Plan, 97
de Gaulle, Charles, 182
Declaration of Principles, 156,
 160
Deep causes, 65, 89, 93, 118, 189
Delian League, 9, 16, 26
Democracy, 36, 41–42, 188
 balance of power and, 74, 75
 Cold War and, 118, 119
 in Germany, 78, 89
 public opinion in, 8, 38, 112
 rise of, 34, 57, 118, 146,
  184, 191
 states' goals and, 34
 war and, 18, 30, 37, 40–41,
  69, 18, 119, 192, 194
 World War II and, 83, 84,
  86, 88, 89
Democratic Party (U.S.), 100,
 116
Denmark, 47, 58, 79, 87f
Department of Agriculture,
 175–176
Department of Commerce, 176
Détente, 115–116
Deterrence, 11, 52, 75, 94, 95,
 122, 125, 168, 190
 nuclear, 8, 71, 99, 120–128,
  188
Detwiler, Donald, 46
Deutsch, Karl, 39, 158, 194
Dillon, Douglas, 126
Diplomacy, 28, 34, 61–63, 80,
 84, 85, 94, 100, 113, 148,
 153, 175, 183
 preventive, 147
Disarmament, under League of
 Nations, 80, 84
Distribution of power, 8–9, 28,
 31, 54, 71, 172, 187,
 192, 193

dispersed, 31
Distributive justice, 23
Djilas, Milovan, 101, 129
Dodd, William E., 95
Domestic law, 3, 141
Domestic politics, 186
 causes of war in, 36–37, 38,
  63–64, 65, 90, 93–94
 Cold War and, 102, 103,
  110, 111–112, 114,
  115–116, 117
 interdependence and,
  164, 177
 vs. international politics, 3, 4,
  16, 18, 55
 and international system, 34,
  36–38, 40, 42, 57–58
 intervention in, 134, 135
 in Middle East, 156, 157
 stability of, 51, 53, 78
 World War II and, 88–89,
  90, 93
Dominican Republic, 22,
 135, 136
Doyle, Michael, 40, 46, 119,
 179
Dresden, Germany, 120–121
Drug trafficking, 135, 176, 190
Druzes, 154
Dual Entente, 49, 69
Dulles, John Foster, 131
Dumbarton Oaks Conference,
 131
Dunkirk, 85–86
Dupont, E. I., 7
Dutch East Indies. *See*
 Indonesia
Dynastic territorial state, 3

E
East Asia, 37–38, 57, 167
Eastern Europe, 39–40, 84,
 169, 185
 ethnic nationalism in,
  138–139, 184
 pan-Slavism in, 61, 64, 150
 Soviet Union in, 42–43, 51,
  99, 100, 101, 102, 103,
  104, 106, 107, 114–115,
  117, 118, 119, 122, 136,
  184, 187
Ecological goals, 6
Ecologism, 182–183
Economic assistance, 21, 102,
 103, 104, 107, 134, 135

Economic Community of West
 African States, 193
Economic goals, 6–8, 83
Economic growth, 184, 185
Economic sanctions, 76, 81,
 99, 128, 142, 156, 160,
 170, 190
Economy
 alliances and, 58–59
 international, 101, 102, 113,
  119, 168–170, 185–186,
  190
 as power resource, 51, 53,
  162, 190
 war and, 36–37, 54, 80, 88,
  90, 93, 110, 157
Ecuador, 41
Eden, Anthony, 103, 143, 144
Edict of Nantes, 47
Edison, Thomas, 65
Edward VII, king of England, 65
Egypt, 63, 113, 151
 in Arab-Israeli conflict, 136,
  152–154, 159–160
 Camp David Accords,
  154, 160
 in Suez crisis, 143–145
Einstein, Albert, 120
Eisenhower Doctrine, 159
Eisenhower, Dwight, 114, 125,
 131, 187
El Salvador, 134, 148
Elba, 48
Elf Aquitaine, 7
Enabling Act, 97
Enforcement, of international
 law, 141
England, 47. *See also* Britain
Environment, 182–183, 185–186
Environmental Protection
 Agency, 176
Epidamnus, 11, 13, 26, 36
Eritrea, 81
Estonia, 51, 87f, 105f
Ethics
 in international politics, 3,
  17–24
 nuclear weapons and,
  122–123, 125, 127–128
Ethiopia, 80, 81–82, 84, 97,
 109f, 115, 116, 138
Ethnic groups, 78, 149, 192
 conflict and, 135, 136, 138,
  154, 157, 189, 191
 as transnational actors, 6, 190

Europe, 3, 63, 124, 127, 152, 190, 191
  balance of power in, 31, 32–35, 51, 52, 54–55, 56, 57–58, 59, 77–78, 81–82, 88, 89, 111, 114, 121, 125
  chronology of events in, 47–49, 73, 97
  Cold War and, 103, 104, 108, 110, 116, 189
  in eighteenth century, 47–48, 52, 57, 99
  1993 oil crisis and, 171, 174, 177
  in nineteenth century, 48, 52, 57, 150
  regionalism in, 182
  transnational society in, 38
European Commission, 39
European Conference on Security and Cooperation, 193
European Union, 35–36, 39–40, 138, 168, 182, 184, 185, 192
Exchange rates, 165, 176
Expansionism
  Soviet, 100, 104, 106, 108, 112–113, 114, 116, 117, 120
  U.S., 101, 120
Expropriation, 142

F
Facts, in counterfactuals, 43, 45
Falk, Richard, 5, 182–183, 195
Falkland (Malvinas) Islands War, 176
Farouk, king of Egypt, 152
Fascism, 78, 81, 84, 88, 118
Fashoda, 63
Fearon, James D., 46
Federal Republic of Germany, 131. See also Germany
Federalism, world, 181–182
Feudal system, 2, 181
Finland, 56, 87f, 100, 105f
Finlayson, Jock, 157
Fischer, Fritz, 64, 72
Food and Agricultural Organization , 182
Food supply, 18–19, 163
Force, use of, 3, 8, 18, 52, 146, 171, 174, 181, 194. See also War

Ford, Gerald, 115
Formosa, 92f
Forrestal, James, 100
Forsythe, David P., 195
France, 2, 8, 35, 37, 49, 79f, 83, 94, 128, 174, 187. See also Napoleonic Wars
  balance of power and, 57–58, 59, 60, 77–78, 81–82
  in Cold War era, 109f, 113
  collective security and, 80
  Communism in, 105f
  economy of, 135
  in eighteenth century, 47–48, 52, 53
  interdependence of, 164, 170, 171f, 182, 184–185, 194
  Suez Canal and, 143–144, 145f, 152–153, 159
  World War I and, 56, 62f, 63, 66, 68, 69, 73, 79f, 151
  World War II and, 51, 55, 85, 86, 87f, 88, 89–90, 97, 104, 112
Francis II, Holy Roman Emperor, 48
Franco, Francisco, 84
Franz Ferdinand, archduke of Austria, 43, 61, 64, 70, 73, 127
Franz Josef, emperor of Austria, 48, 64
Frederick the Great of Prussia, 33, 40
French Congo, 69
French Planning Commission, 182
French Revolution, 32, 33, 42, 48, 99, 150
Fukuyama, Francis, 184, 194
Fulton, Missouri, 104
Functionalism, 182, 191

G
Gaddis, John L., 101, 129, 130, 195
Galtung, Johan, 179
Garibaldi, 48
Gati, Tobi, 157
Gause, F. Gregory, 158
Gaza, 145f, 152, 156, 159, 160
Gemayel, Bashir, 154
General Agreement on Tariffs and Trade (GATT), 169
General Motors, 6, 7

Geneva Protocol, 97
Geneva summit, 115
Geopolitics, 28, 33
German People's Republic, 131. See also Germany
Germany, 42, 47
  balance of power and, 40, 54–55, 58–59, 60–61
  Cold War and, 104, 107, 112–113, 116, 117, 131, 132, 187
  democracy in, 78, 89
  Empire, 48
  in European Community, 35–36
  GDP, 7
  interdependence of, 164, 165, 170, 171f, 182, 184–185, 194
  in international system, 28
  League of Nations and, 84
  in nineteenth century, 48, 52, 54
  reunification of, 35, 38, 192
  Treaty of Locarno and, 78–80, 82, 84, 89
  Treaty of Versailles and, 78, 79f, 84, 85, 86, 88, 89
  unification of, 33, 48, 57, 58, 150
  World War I and, 33–35, 43, 54–55, 56, 59–70, 73, 77–78, 84, 110, 137, 151, 189
  World War II and, 82–90, 91, 93, 94, 97, 103, 104, 105f, 106, 120, 131, 138, 152, 189
Gershman, Carl, 40
Ghana, 28
Gilpin, Robert, 9, 24, 25, 179, 194
Ginn, Edward, 37
Glasnost, 117
Global society, 4, 9, 38, 183, 194
Global warming, 164, 176, 190
Goals, in international politics, 6–8, 32, 34, 101, 112, 170, 189
Golan Heights, 153, 159
Gold standard, 168–169
Gooch, G. P., 71
Goodrich, Leland M., 158
Gorbachev, Mikhail, 98, 117, 118, 119, 163, 170

Gordon, Michael, 158
Graham, Edward, 179
Gray, Colin S., 130
Great Britain, 47. *See also*
    Britain
Great Depression, 88, 89f, 169
Great Northern War, 47
Greater East Asia Co-
    Prosperity Sphere, 37, 90
Greece, 3, 6, 40, 67f, 73, 80. *See*
    also Peloponnesian War
    in Cold War era, 97, 100,
    105f, 106–107, 109f, 113,
    131, 139, 172
Grenada, 17, 22, 135
Grey, Sir Edward, 54, 63, 69, 73
Grieco, Joseph, 179
Gross domestic product, of
    selected countries, 6, 7
Group of Seven, 169
Guam, 92f
Guandong, 184
Guatemala, 7
Guinea, 28
Gulick, Edward, 57, 71
Guns of August, The
    (Tuchman), 127

H

Haas, Ernst B., 195
Haggard, Stephan, 179
Hague peace conferences, 146
Haiti, 82, 135, 136, 190
Haldane, Lord, 70
Hamas, 156–157
Hambro, Edvard, 158
Hammarskjold, Dâg, 143, 147
Hance, Kent, 177
Harriman, Averell, 100
Havel, Vaclav, 42, 45
Heath, Edward, 174
Hegemonic state, 8–9, 31, 38,
    54, 61, 83, 90, 99, 172,
    189, 190, 194
Hegemonic theory, 54
Hegemonic war. *See* World war
Hehir, J. Bryan, 158
Heinrichs, Jr., Waldo, 96
Helsinki Accords, 193
Herring, George C., 130
Herzegovina, 73
Herzl, Theodor, 159
Hilderbrand, Klaus, 96
Hinduism, 149, 190
Hinsley, F. H., 25

Hirohito, emperor of Japan, 91
Hiroshima, 106, 120–121,
    122, 131
History
    analogies of, 16, 70, 95, 108,
    110, 156, 189
    counterfactuals. *See*
        Counterfactuals
    nature of, 69
    "return" of, 183–184
Hitler, Adolf, 124, 142, 164
    before World War II, 82, 97
    pact with Stalin, 28, 51,
    56–57, 85, 102, 112, 113
    World War II and, 18, 29,
    35, 55, 83–88, 89–90,
    91, 93, 94–95, 97, 108,
    144, 152
Hoare, Sir Samuel, 82
Hoare-Laval Pact, 82, 97
Hobbes, Thomas, 3, 4, 20,
    24, 39
Hoffmann, Stanley, 8, 25, 30,
    46, 194
Holland, 48, 79f, 85, 109f
Hollweg, Bethmann, 59–60, 69
Holocaust, 151, 152
Holsti, K. J., 25
Holy Roman Empire, 48
Honda, 185
Hong Kong, 184
Hope, Ronald R., 129
Hopf, Ted, 46
Hopkins, Harry, 103
Hossbach memorandum, 83
Hossbach, Colonel, 83
Hotzendorff, Baron Conrad
    von, 71
Howe, Irving, 140, 157
Hughes, Jeffrey, 96
Hull, Cordell, 102
Human nature, as cause of
    war, 29
Human rights, 21, 23, 115, 170,
    183, 188, 190, 193
Hume, David, 50
Hungary, 48, 79f, 87f. *See also*
    Austria-Hungary
    in Cold War era, 100, 103,
    105f, 114–115, 117, 118,
    122, 132, 135, 143
Hungtington, Samuel P.,
    194, 195
Hussein, king of Jordan, 156,
    157, 160

Hussein, Saddam, 5, 20, 29, 40,
    55, 134, 147, 148–149,
    155, 183
Hydrogen bomb, 121, 131, 132

I

IBM, 6, 185
Identity, communal, 183
Ideology, 42, 45, 53, 58–59,
    81, 99
    in Middle East, 55
    in Cold War, 44, 101, 103,
    106, 107, 108, 111–112,
    113, 114, 116, 118, 122,
    123, 140, 146, 187
    in post–Cold War system,
    184
    of war, 71
    in World War I, 34–35
    in World War II, 56–57, 86,
    88, 89, 103
Il Sung, Kim, 108
Impartiality, 17
Imperial overstretch, 116, 118
Imperialism, 12, 63, 80, 81, 83,
    90, 112, 113
Independence, 51, 55, 75
India, 3, 7, 28, 48, 65, 113, 143,
    145f, 152, 171f, 187
Individuals
    cosmopolitan view of, 23, 136
    rights of, 193. *See also*
        Human rights
    role in Cold War, 110,
    111, 117
    role in Middle East, 157
    role in World War I, 64–65
    role in World War II, 86–88,
    89f, 93
    in system level analysis, 29
    as transnational actors,
    177–178
Indochina, 97
Indonesia (Dutch East Indies),
    91, 92f, 93
Inflation, 164, 166
Information, 39, 53, 118–119,
    191. *See also*
        Communication
Institute of Peace, 40
Institutions, 53
Instruments, of international
    politics, 6, 8, 32–33, 34, 35
Interdependence
    benefits of, 163–164

complex, 170–171, 174, 176, 178, 194
costs of, 142, 165–166
defined, 162
ecological, 5, 164
economic, 4–5, 8, 9, 23, 32, 37, 53, 56, 135, 161, 163–164, 168–169, 177, 186, 191, 194
international politics and, 164, 167–168, 175, 177–178
military, 163
multilevel, 190
realist view of, 170–174
reciprocity in, 174
security, 117, 174
sensitivity, 165, 167f, 177
social, 5
sources of, 162–163
symmetry of, 166–168
vulnerability, 165–166, 167f, 168, 182
Interest rates, 165, 166, 190
Intermediate causes, 65, 89, 93–94, 118
International Atomic Energy Agency, 187
International Bank for Reconstruction and Development (World Bank), 119, 131, 169
International Court of Justice (The Hague), 39, 97, 138, 141
International federation, 181–182
International functionalism, 182, 190
International institutions. See also League of Nations; United Nations
anarchic international politics and, 4, 8, 20, 24, 75
interdependence and, 167–168, 169, 170, 171, 172–174
intervention by, 133
post–Cold War, 183
in process of international system, 32, 38–39, 41–42, 188, 192–193
International law, 33, 144, 148, 181
defined, 193
vs. domestic, 3, 141

intervention and, 133, 136
nature of, 141–142, 157
reasons for, 20–21, 76, 142–143
success of, 146
International Monetary Fund (IMF), 131, 143, 169
International organizations, 140–141, 142, 144, 146, 148, 157, 181, 183, 193
International politics, 119. See also Cold War; International system; Security dilemma
actors in, 6
anarchy and, 2–6, 12, 15. See also Anarchic system of states
counterfactuals in, See Counterfactuals
defined, 2–3, 181
ethical concerns in, 16–24, 127–128
goals in, 6–8, 32, 34, 101, 112
instruments of, 6, 8
interdependence and, 164, 167–168, 175, 177–178
milieu goals in, 101, 112
military force in. See War
post–Cold War, 181–186, 188–194
realist vs. liberal approach to. See Liberalism; Realism
values in, 135
International system, 171
analysis of, 29–35, 36, 57–58, 60–65, 71, 88–89, 93–94, 108–111, 157
causation in, 27–30, 65–66
defined, 27
domestic politics and, 36–38, 42, 64
in eighteenth century, 32–33, 57
national interest and, 41–42
national interests in, 41–42
in nineteenth century, 33–35, 36, 57–58
post–Cold War, 188–191
process of, 31–35, 57–58, 61–64, 71, 88, 110, 157
structure of, 31–32, 33–34, 55, 57, 60–61, 65, 71, 88, 108–110, 119, 188
in twentieth century, 35–40

Intervention, 174, 193
defined, 134–135
ethical issues in, 22–23, 133–134
justification of, 22–23, 135–140
by United Nations, 143–144
Intifada, 160
Iran, 6, 22, 42, 100, 106, 128, 159
oil production in, 165, 171, 172, 173
Iran-Iraq War, 55, 148–149, 155, 160
Iranian Revolution, 148, 160, 164
Iraq, 6, 42, 128, 144, 145f, 159, 187, 192, 193
domestic politics of, 134
invasion of Kuwait, 5, 7, 17, 20, 22, 23, 142, 147, 155, 160, 172, 190
Persian Gulf War, 29, 40, 51, 155–156, 164
war with Iran. See Iran-Iraq War
Ireland, 68, 138
Iriye, Akira, 96
Iron curtain, 104, 105f, 131
Islam, 6, 55, 65, 138–139, 148–151, 154, 184, 189, 190
Isolationism, 77, 88, 89f, 93, 102, 103, 107, 111f, 162
Israel, 171f, 174, 187
-Arab conflict. See Arab-Israeli conflict
Camp David Accords, 154, 160
in Lebanon, 22
Iran-Iraq War and, 149
national claim of, 149, 151
Italy, 3, 34, 84
city-states, 28
invasion of Ethiopia, 80, 81–82, 84
in League of Nations, 78, 81–82
unification of, 48, 57, 58, 150
World War I and, 67f, 78
World War II and, 55, 97, 105f
Ivory Coast, 28

J

Jackson, Henry, 115
Jacobson, Harold K., 158

Jagow, Foreign Secretary, 66
Jamaica, 7
James, Robert Rhodes, 71
Japan, 36, 56, 80
    balance of power and, 47,
        59, 111
    in Cold War era, 187, 189
    economic interdependence
        of, 165
    economy, 5, 7, 8, 37–38, 83,
        167, 169, 190
    imperialism of, 37
    Manchurian crisis and, 80–81
    post–Cold War, 189
    trade relations, 37–38, 80,
        90, 93, 163, 167, 170,
        174, 185, 186
    World War II and, 5, 51,
        82, 83, 84, 86, 88,
        90–95, 97, 104–106,
        109f, 131
Java, 92f
Jervis, Robert, 25, 46, 96, 129
Jewish State, The (Herzl), 159
Jews, 149, 151–152, 159. See
    also Israel
Johnson, Hiram, 93
Joll, James, 71
Jordan, 144, 145f, 149, 152,
    153, 155, 157, 159, 160
Jordan, David Starr, 5
Just and Unjust Wars (Walzer),
    136–137
Just war doctrine, 20–21,
    127–128, 136–137, 139
Justice
    distributive, 23
    in international politics, 3,
        19, 20, 21, 23, 181, 182,
        183, 193
    intervention and,
        133–134, 136

K
Kagan, Donald, 15, 24, 25
Kant, Immanuel, 4, 17, 40, 182,
    192, 194
Kaplan, Robert, 195
Karachi government, 135
Kautilya, 28
Kellogg-Briand Pact, 80, 81, 97
Kennan, George, 98, 103, 104,
    106, 107, 110, 111,
    113–114, 116, 118, 129,
    130, 140

Kennedy, John F., 18, 29, 123,
    125–128, 132, 187
Kennedy, Paul M., 4, 72, 116,
    118, 195
Kenya, 113
Keohane, Robert O., 25, 46,
    178, 179, 194
Keynes, John Maynard, 9
Khomeini, Ayatollah, 55, 160
Khong, Yuen Foong, 25, 129
Khrushchev, Nikita, 29, 108,
    110, 114–115, 117, 123,
    125, 132
Kiel, Germany, 70
Kindleberger, Charles P., 179
Kissinger, Henry, 4, 25, 46, 153,
    172, 173
Kohn, Hans, 157–158
Kolko, Gabriel, 100, 130
Kolko, Joyce, 130
Korea, 80
Korean War, 59, 108, 109f,
    114, 122, 123, 125,
    131, 132
Krasner, Stephen D., 179
Krugman, Paul, 179
Kugler, Jacek, 72
Kupchan, Charles, 72
Kurds, 6
Kuwait, 7, 17, 20, 22, 23, 40,
    142, 147, 155–156, 160,
    164, 172, 190

L
Lafeber, Walter, 130
Lalman, David, 46
Larson, Deborah W., 130
Latin America, 169
Latvia, 51, 87f, 105f
Lausanne Conference, 97
Laval, Pierre, 82
Law, domestic vs. international ,
    3, 141
Law of the sea, 141, 142
Le Pen, Jean-Marie, 189
League of Nations, 135, 151
    collective security and,
        75–82, 93, 97, 146
    Ethiopian invasion and,
        81–82
    Germany and, 84
    Manchurian crisis and, 80–81
    Middle East mandates
        created by, 151–152, 159
    United States and, 75–77

Lebanon, 19, 22, 154, 159, 160
Lebow, Richard Ned, 71, 72,
    96, 130
Legitimacy
    as reason for international
        law, 142, 143
    of state, 149, 183
Legvold, Robert, 130
Lend-lease, 88, 100, 104
Lenin, V. I., 36, 45, 63
Levering, Ralph B., 129
Levy, Jack S., 25, 46
Liberal Party (Britain), 68, 69
Liberalism
    collective security and, 74,
        75, 77
    end of Cold War and, 118
    justification for interven-
        tion, 137
    neoliberalism, 37–41
    view of ethics, 19–20
    view of interdependence,
        163, 186
    view of international politics,
        4–6, 19–20, 24, 54, 190,
        191–192, 193, 194
    World War I and, 36–37
Liberia, 137, 193
Libya, 128, 134, 145f, 151
Limited Test Ban Treaty, 115,
    122, 187
Lithuania, 51, 87f, 105f
Little Entente, 78
Litvinov, Maxim, 106
Location, in geopolitics, 28
Locke, John, 4
Lodge, Henry Cabot, 77
Louis XIV, 8, 34, 47
Luther, Martin, 99
Luxembourg, 73, 109f
Lynn-Jones, Sean, 72, 195
Lytton, Lord, 81

M
Maastricht Treaty, 39
Machiavelli, Niccolò, 3, 28
MacMahon-Sharif Husain
    agreements, 159
MacPherson, C. B., 24
Maginot line, 85, 87f
Maier, Charles S., 72
Malaya, 92f
Maldive Islands, 141, 164
Mali, 28
Manchukuo, 81

Manchuria, 80–81, 90–91, 97, 104, 109f
Mandelbaum, Michael, 130
Mao Tse-tung, 17, 100, 161
Marc Antony, 44
Marcos, Ferdinand, 136
Maria Theresa of Austria, 32
Marshall Plan, 101, 107, 131
Marshall, George, 107, 139
Marx, Karl, 15, 48
Marxism, 28, 30, 36–37, 48, 116
Mastny, Vojtech, 130
Mathews, Jessica A., 195
May, Ernest R., 195
McCarthy, Joseph, 108
McCarthyism, 108
McKinley, William, 40
McLuhan, Marshall, 183
McNamara, Robert, 126, 127, 129
Means, 139–140
Mearsheimer, John, 35, 40, 46, 119, 194
Mediterranean, 105f, 106–107, 139, 140, 172
Megara, 11, 15, 16
Mein Kampf (Hitler), 83
Melos, 17, 18, 19, 22, 26
Metternich, Prince, 34
Mexico, 39, 69, 77, 168
Middle East, 6, 42, 55, 170, 174, 194
    Cold War and, 106, 122, 124
    conflicts in, 148–149, 150–157, 159–160, 172, 191. See also Arab-Israeli conflict; Persian Gulf War; Suez crisis
Middle East War of 1967, 144
Middle East War of 1973, 115, 173
Middlemas, Keith, 96
Migration, 176, 185, 190, 191
Milieu goals, 101, 112
Military assistance, 134, 135
Military force
    under collective security, 75, 146
    as resource, 51, 52, 53, 71, 161, 162, 168, 171
Military security, 6–8, 170, 176, 183, 186, 187, 188, 190, 194
Mill, John Stuart, 4, 137
Miller, Steven, 72 , 195

Mitrany, David, 195
Mitsubishi, 7
Mobil, 6
Moltke, Gerneral von, 66, 68
Monarchy, 32, 34, 61, 175
Money, 168–169
Monnet, Jean, 182
Monroe Doctrine, 77
Montenegro, 67f
Montesquieu, Baron de, 4
Morality. See Ethics
Morgenthau, Hans, 24, 161
Morocco, 61, 63, 69, 73, 141
Motives, 139–140
Moynihan, Daniel P., 158
Mozambique, 115, 136
Mueller, John, 124, 129
Multinational corporations, 6, 7, 169, 170, 171, 172–174, 182, 183, 185–186, 189, 190
Multipolarity, 31, 33, 56–58, 101, 123, 189, 192, 194
Munich Agreement, 138
Mussolini, Benito, 55, 78, 81–82, 97
Myanmar (Burma), 42, 92f, 162, 176

N

Nagasaki, 106, 131
Namibia, 148
Napoleon Bonaparte, 32, 33, 34, 48, 150
Napoleon III, 48
Napoleonic Wars, 32, 33, 34, 48, 52, 78
Nasser, Gamal Abdel, 143, 144, 152–153, 159, 160
National Academy of Sciences, 120
National Endowment for Democracy, 40
National interest, 41–42, 177
National Security Council, 126, 127
National Security Council Document 68 (NSC–68), 107–108, 114, 131
National Socialist Party (Germany), 80
Nationalism
    in Africa, 138
    Arab, 143, 148–149
    in Asia, 114

ethnic, 191
    in international politics, 2, 8, 34–35, 183–185, 186, 189, 194
    in Middle East, 154, 171
    in nineteenth century, 34–35, 72, 57–58
    pan-Africanism, 150
    pan-Arabism, 150–151, 152, 154
    pan-Slavism, 61, 64, 150
    role in war, 149–150
    Russian, 103, 119
    U.S., 189
    World War I and, 57–58, 63, 64, 65, 66f, 88
    World War II and, 88, 90, 103
Nationalists (China), 59, 80, 93, 125
Nationalization, 174
Natural resources, 51
Nazi Beer Hall Putsch, 97
Neoliberalism, 37–41
Nestlé Ltd., 7
Netherlands, 53
Neustadt, Richard E., 195
Neutrality, 55–56, 76, 91
New Guinea, 92f
New York Mercantile Exchange, 175
New York stock market, 165
New Zealand, 109f
Nicaragua, 54, 134, 136, 141, 148
Nicholas II, czar of Russia, 61, 64
Nigeria, 28, 138, 193
Nixon, Richard, 4, 115, 172
Nongovernmental organizations (NGOs), 6, 182, 185–186
Nonintervention. See Intervention
Noriega, Manuel, 23
North America, 190
North American Free Trade Agreement (NAFTA), 39, 168
North Atlantic Treaty Organization (NATO), 107, 125, 131, 132, 138, 187
North Korea, 100, 108, 109f, 128
North Vietnam, 123, 139
Northern Ireland, 68, 138
Norway, 85

Nuclear energy, 177
Nuclear Non-Proliferation
    Treaty (NPT), 115,
    128, 187
Nuclear Suppliers Group, 187
Nuclear war, 114, 122, 126,
    136, 154
Nuclear weapons, 1, 17, 131,
    132, 155, 163, 167, 181
    arms control, 21, 115, 116,
        187
    balance of power and, 9
    Cold War and, 100, 102,
        106, 107, 115, 116, 117,
        120–128
    destructive power of, 1, 8,
        31, 52
    deterrence and, 8, 71, 99,
        120–128, 188
    development of, 82, 86, 194
    ethical issues and, 122–123,
        125, 127–128
    proliferation of, 186–188
Nuclear winter, 120
Nye, Jr., Joseph S., 46, 178,
    179, 195

O
Obsolescing bargain, 172–173
Occam's razor, 30. *See also*
    Parsimony
Ogarkov, Marshall, 118
Oil, 155
Oil crisis of 1973, 161–162,
    164, 165, 171–173, 174,
    175, 177
Order
    in international politics, 3,
        19–23, 99, 100, 148, 181,
        188–189, 191–192, 193
    intervention and, 133–134,
        135–136
    new world, 181, 182,
        188–189, 191
Organization for Economic
    Cooperation and
    Development
    (OECD), 169
Organization of American
    States (OAS), 6, 39
Organization of Petroleum
    Exporting Countries
    (OPEC), 6, 154, 171,
    172, 173, 175, 177
Organski, A. F. K., 72

Orthodox approach. *See*
    Traditionalist approach
Ottoman Empire, 48, 58, 61,
    63, 141
Outer Mongolia, 92f
Overdetermination, 65, 126
Owens, William A., 195
Oxford Union, 18

P
Pakistan, 135, 149, 159, 171f,
    187, 190
Palestine, 151–152, 153,
    156–157, 159–160
Palestine Liberation
    Organization (PLO),
    154, 156, 159, 160
Palmerston, Lord, 54
Pan-Africanism, 29, 150
Pan-Arab Congress, 159
Pan-Arabism, 150–151, 152, 154
Pan-Slavism, 61, 64, 150
Panama, 22–23
Panama Canal, 56
Paris Commune, 48
Parsimony, rule of, 30, 33, 36, 60
Pascal, 44
Pax Americana, 189
Peace of Westphalia, 3, 5,
    47, 191
Pearson, Lester, 143, 147
Peel Commission, 159
Peloponnesian War, 1, 9–12,
    13–15, 16–17, 18, 21, 26,
    29, 31, 36, 54, 94, 113,
    123
Pendergast, Boss, 103
PepsiCo, 7
Perestroika, 117
Pericles, 12, 15, 16, 26, 29, 40
Perry, Commodore, 8
Persian Empire, 2, 9, 11, 26
Persian Gulf, 52, 160, 164,
    171–173, 174
Persian Gulf War, 20, 29, 42,
    128, 148, 155–156, 157,
    160, 164, 183, 188
Persians, 55
Peter the Great, czar of Russia,
    47, 111
Philip Morris, 7
Philippines, 91, 92f, 93, 109f,
    136
Phillips, Lucas, 92f
Phony war, 85

Plausibility, and counterfactuals,
    43–44, 45
Pluralism, 112
Pluralistic security communi-
    ties, 39
Podhoretz, Norman, 139, 158
Poland, 47, 48, 51, 78
    in Cold War era, 100, 104,
        112–113, 118, 132
    World War I and, 79f
    World War II and, 80, 87f,
        84, 86, 97, 105f, 144
Political culture, 17, 111–112
Population, 51, 52, 157
Portugal, 115, 141
Posen, 79f
Possession goals, 101, 112
Postrevisionist approach, to
    Cold War, 99, 101, 110
Potidaea, 11, 15, 26
Potsdam Conference, 100, 103,
    104, 106, 131
Power, 188, 191, 193. *See also*
    Balance of power
    resources, 51–54, 91, 174
    soft, 53, 118
Precipitating causes, 65, 89, 90,
    94, 117
Predictability, as reason for
    international law,
    142–143
Prisoner's Dilemma, 12–15, 16,
    39, 42, 154
Probability, 66
Process, in system level analy-
    sis, 31–33, 34–35,
    57–58, 61–64, 71, 88,
    110, 157
Propaganda, 16–17
Protectionism, 102, 186
Proximity
    in geopolitics, 28, 56
    in time, 43, 44, 65
Prussia, 32, 34, 35, 48, 51, 52,
    58, 79f, 150
Public opinion
    concerning nuclear weapons,
        125, 127
    in democracies, 107
    on European identity, 38
    in Germany, 40

Q
Quandt, William B., 158
Quebec, 192

R

Rabb, Theodore, 46, 72, 96
Rabin, Yitzhak, 156, 157, 160
Racism, 80, 86, 149–150
Radar, 82
Radio Martí, 134
Railway system, in World War
   I, 52, 66, 68–69, 71
Raw materials, 90, 91, 93, 161,
   162, 166, 173
Reagan Doctrine, 136
Reagan, Ronald, 116, 127,
   13116, 141
Realist view
   of balance of power, 41, 54,
      110, 135–136, 189, 192
   vs. complex interdependence,
      170–172, 174
   of ethics, 17, 19, 21, 23
   of international politics, 4–6,
      9, 24, 35, 36, 37, 38, 39,
      40f, 42, 148, 157, 161,
      188, 190, 191, 193, 194
   of intervention, 135–136
   of League of Nations, 77, 82
   of nuclear weapons, 128
Red Cross, 6
Red Sea, 153
Reformation, 99
Refugees, 135, 136, 153
Regime, oil, 171–174
Regional conflicts, 148–149,
   154, 156
Regional development banks, 169
Regional integration, 182
Reich, Robert, 179, 185, 194
Religion
   fundamentalism, 154
   nationalism and
   role in international politics,
      6, 148–149, 151, 157,
      184, 189, 191
Renaissance, 181
Renan, Ernest, 149, 157
Reparations, German, 78, 104
Resolution 242, 42, 144, 153, 159
Resources
   natural, 51
   scarcity of, 166, 183
   as source of power, 51–54,
      56, 138
   transfer of, 172
Revisionist approach, to Cold
   War, 99, 100–101,
   106, 110

Revolutionary politics, 42
Rhine River, 78
Rhineland, 82, 84, 97, 108, 144
Rice, Condoleezza, 47
Risse-Kappen, Thomas, 130
Ritter, Harry, 46
Robertson, Pat, 189
Rock, Stephen R., 72
Rohl, John, 72
Roman Empire, 2, 44
Romania, 67f, 73, 78, 97, 105f
Roosevelt, Franklin, 86, 88, 93,
   94, 100, 101, 102, 103,
   104, 105f, 106, 110,
   112–113, 131, 188, 192
Rosecrance, Richard N., 5, 25,
   37, 38, 45, 194
Rosenau, James N., 25
Ross, Graham, 95, 96
Rostow, Eugene, 40
Rotberg, Robert, 46, 72, 95
Rothschild, Lord, 151
Rousseau, Jean-Jacques, 162
Royal Dutch Shell, 6, 7
Ruhr, 78, 83, 97
Rusk, Dean, 123, 129
Russett, Bruce, 195
Russia, 17, 47, 48, 49
   economy, 7
   in eighteenth century,
      47–48, 51
   in international system, 28,
      33–34, 40, 78, 80,
      110, 119
   in nineteenth century, 48, 58
   post-Soviet, 128, 171f, 189
   power resources of, 52
   See also Soviet Union
   World War I and, 52, 56, 59,
      60, 61, 62f, 63, 64, 66,
      67f, 68–69, 73, 137
   World War II and. *See* Soviet
      Union
Russian Revolution, 59, 78,
   110. *See also* Bolsheviks
Russo-Japanese War, 49, 80
Rwanda, 135, 136, 137, 139

S

Sadat, Anwar, 153, 154, 160
Safran, Nadav, 158
Sagan, Scott, 72, 95
Salonika, 73
San Francisco Conference, 131
Sandinistas, 136

Sarajevo, 43, 64, 65, 66, 70, 73
Saudi Arabia, 144, 145f, 149,
   156, 159, 172, 174, 184
Schlafly, Phyllis, 17
Schlesinger, Jr., Arthur
Schlieffen Plan, 66, 67f, 68, 137
Schroeder, Paul, 33, 45, 46
Schumann Plan, 182
Schumpeter, Joseph, 118
Schuschnigg, Chancellor, 84
Scotland, 47
Secessionist movements,
   137–138
Second French Empire, 48
Security dilemma, 2, 12–14, 15,
   16, 24, 39, 40, 42, 101,
   113, 117, 123, 181
Security. *See* Military security
Self-determination, 74–75, 85,
   137–138, 192, 193
Senate, U.S., 77–78
Senegal, 28
Serbia
   conflict with Bosnia and
      Croatia, 138–139, 184
   post–World War II, 16, 41
   World War I and, 64, 65 67f,
      68, 70, 73, 127
Seven sisters, 171, 172, 173
Seven Years' War, 48
Shah of Iran, 148, 160, 165,
   171, 173
Shamir, Yitzhak, 156
Sharon, Ariel, 154
Shevardnadze, Eduard, 35
Shi'ites, 55, 148, 154
Siberia, 83, 164
Sicily, 11, 26
Siemens AG, 7
Sifry, Micah L., 158
Silesia, 32, 40
Simons, Anne Patricia, 158
Sinai, 143, 144, 145f, 153,
   154, 159
Sinai Agreement, 160
Singapore, 83, 92f, 93
Sino-Soviet pact, 131
Six-Day War, 153, 159
Skeptical view, of ethics,
   19–21, 24
Slovakia, 87f, 138
Slovenia, 138
Snyder, Jack L., 72
Social darwinism, 63, 71
Social issues, 6

Socialism, 61, 88, 136
Socialist Party (France), 135
Sohn, Louis, 195
Somalia, 136, 138
Sombart, Nicholas, 72
Somme, Battle of the, 59
South Africa, 60, 63, 109f, 136, 193
South America, 54
South Korea, 100, 108, 109f, 134, 187
South Vietnam, 114, 139
South Yemen, 134
Southeast Asia, 90–91, 92f, 93, 140
Sovereignty, 133–134, 140
   collective security and, 76, 77
   defined, 76
   intervention and, 22, 134, 136–23
   trade pacts and, 168
   world order and, 182, 185, 189, 190, 193
Soviet Union, 21, 30, 56, 192.
   See also Cold War;
   Cuban missile crisis;
   Russia
   in Afghanistan, 8, 22, 115, 116, 117, 122, 124–125, 127, 135, 137, 160
   in Arab-Israeli conflict, 143, 152, 153, 154
   balance of power and, 31, 35, 37–38, 167
   de-Stalinization, 114–115, 118, 132
   in Eastern Europe, 42–43, 51, 99, 100, 101, 102, 103, 104, 106, 107, 114–115, 117, 118, 119, 122, 136, 184, 187
   economy, 36, 118–119, 176
   end of, 99, 117–118, 138, 154, 186, 188
   interventions by, 137
   political culture of, 111–112
   post–World War II, 100, 101, 103
   See also Cold War; Russia
   World War II and, 51, 55, 56, 82, 83, 84, 85, 86, 87f, 88, 89, 91, 92f, 97, 100, 103, 112
Spain, 2, 8, 47, 53
Spanish Civil War, 84, 97

Spanish-American War, 40
Sparta, 1, 9–12, 13, 15, 16, 26, 31, 54, 56, 123
Spero, Joan E., 179
Sphere of influence, 55–56
   Soviet, 100, 101, 115, 122, 131, 136
   U.S., 122, 136
Sputnik, 132
Staab, General von, 68
Stability, 50–51, 71, 189
Staley, Eugene, 37
Stalin, Joseph, 17
   Cold War and, 99–100, 101, 102–103, 104, 105f, 106, 107, 108, 110, 111f, 112–113, 114, 131, 132, 140, 192
   de-Stalinization, 114–115, 118, 132
   pact with Hitler, 28, 51, 56–57, 85, 102, 112
   World War II and, 55, 86, 88
State Department, 176
State moralists
   view of ethics, 19, 21–23, 76
   view of intervention, 135, 136
State of nature, 3, 20
States. *See also* Anarchic system of states
   as actors, 4, 6, 170, 175, 178
   dynastic territorial, 3
   ethical concerns of, 17–24
   hegemonic, 8–9, 31, 38
   national interests of, 41–42
   nature of, 30
   relationships between. *See headings beginning with* International
   sovereign territorial, 3, 22–23, 181–183
Stein, Janice Gross, 96
Stobaugh, Robert, 178
Storry, Richard, 96
Straits of Tiran, 153
Strange Death of Liberal England, The (Dangerfield), 68
Strange, Susan, 179
Strangulation, 173–174
Structure, in system level analysis, 30–32, 33–34, 35, 55, 57, 60–61, 65, 71, 88, 108–111, 119, 165, 172, 188, 189, 193

Sudan, 63, 113, 145f, 147
Sudetenland, 84–85, 138
Suez Canal, 81, 143, 144, 153, 160
Suez crisis of 1956, 143–144, 145f, 152–153, 159
Sufficiency, 117
Sumatra, 92f
Sumerians, 2
Sunni Moslems, 148, 154
Sutterlin, James S., 195
Sweden, 47, 87f
Switzerland, 87f, 149
Sykes-Picot agreement, 159
Syria, 6, 7, 55, 144, 145f, 149, 150, 153, 154, 160, 171f
System level analysis, 29–30, 31–35, 36. *See also* International system
   of Cold War, 108–111
   of World War I, 57–58, 60–65, 71
   of World War II, 88–89, 93–94

T
Taiwan, 107, 125, 132, 187
Tangier, 73
Tanzania, 22, 135, 137
Taubman, William, 102, 129, 130
Taylor, A. J. P., 8, 47, 68, 83, 88, 95
Taylor, Maxwell, 126
Technology. *See also* Nuclear weapons
   changes in, 119, 166, 183, 185–186, 191
   as instrument of state, 32, 35
   transnational spread of, 173, 186–187, 190
   war and, 32, 35, 52, 82, 146
Territory, as resource, 51
Terrorism, 176
Tetlock, Philip E., 129, 157
Texas, 177
Thailand, 109f
Theory, 9, 30, 43, 44–45
Third French Republic, 48
Third Reich, 86
Thirty Years' War, 3, 47, 181
Thirty-Year Truce, 15, 26
This Endangered Planet (Falk), 182
Thrace, 73

Thucydides, 1, 9, 12, 14–15, 16, 17, 22, 24, 25, 54, 56, 181, 194
Tito, Josef, 105f, 113
Tocqueville, Alexis de, 110
Tojo, Hideki, 93
Toynbee, Arnold
Toyota Motor Corp., 7
Trachtenberg, Marc, 72
Trade
  agreements, 168, 169
  anarchic state system and, 4, 5, 41–42, 88
  boycotts, 80
  in Cold War era, 116, 118, 127
  economic interdependence and, 163, 167, 168, 169
  interference with, and war, 11, 15, 16. See also Economic sanctions
  liberal view of, 36, 37–38, 41, 102
  transnational actors and, 176, 185, 186
Traditionalist approach, to Cold War, 99–100, 101
Trainor, Bernard, 158
Transnational relations, 176–178, 182, 183, 185–186, 190, 193
Treasury Department, 176
Treaties, 141, 187
Treaties, environmental, 185
Treaty of Lausanne, 79f
Treaty of Locarno, 78, 82, 97
Treaty of London, 78
Treaty of Neuilly, 79f
Treaty of Rapallo, 28, 97
Treaty of Rome, 182
Treaty of Sèvres, 79f
Treaty of St. Germain, 79f
Treaty of Trianon, 79f
Treaty of Utrecht, 9, 32, 47
Treaty of Versailles, 78, 79f, 84, 85, 86, 88, 89
Treaty of Versailles, 78, 79f, 84, 85, 86, 88, 89, 93, 97
Triple Alliance, 48, 62f
Triple Entente, 49, 60, 62f, 68, 69
Trosky, Leon, 28
Truman Doctrine, 107, 114, 139, 172
Truman, Harry S., 100, 103–104, 105f, 106,

107–108, 110, 111f, 112, 113, 125, 131, 139
Trust, in international politics, 13, 14
Tsukuda, Vice Army Chief of Staff, 91
Tuchman, Barbara, 72, 127
Turkey, 6, 18, 47, 109f, 126, 149
  Cold War and, 105f, 106–107, 139, 172
  World War I and, 72f, 63–64, 65, 67f, 73, 79f, 159. See also Ottoman Empire
Turner, L. C. F., 72

U
U–2 incident, 132
Uganda, 22, 115, 135, 137
Ukraine, 86, 119
Unilever, 7
Unipolar hegemony, 189–190, 194
Unipolarity, 31, 33, 189–190, 194
United Arab Republic, 150
United Kingdom, 48. See also Britain
United Nations, 4, 6, 9, 101, 113, 187
  in Arab-Israeli conflict, 145f, 149, 151, 153, 159
  in Cold War era, 110
  collective security and, 100, 146–148, 154–155, 192
  environmental issues and, 183, 185
  formation of, 102, 131
  functionalism in, 182
  intervention and, 138, 145f, 190
  in Korean War, 108, 109f
  nuclear weapons and, 106, 121
  Palestine partition and, 152
  peacekeeping by, 138–139, 146–148, 153, 192
  powers of, 140–142
  Security Council, 143, 144, 146, 147, 148, 153, 160, 192, 193
  in Suez crisis, 143–144
United States, 7, 39, 176, 187. See also Cold War; Cuban missile crisis; Korean

War; Persian Gulf War; Vietnam War
  alliances of, 56, 59
  in Arab-Israeli conflict. See Arab-Israeli conflict
  balance of power and, 8, 54, 56, 88, 89, 106–107
  complex interdependence and, 170, 171f
  economic interdependence of, 163, 165, 167, 169, 186
  economy, 7, 88, 101, 167, 169
  in Europe, 35
  in Grenada, 17, 22, 135
  interventions by, 17, 22–23, 134–135, 136, 137, 139–140, 141, 143, 149, 159
  in Iran-Iraq War, 149
  isolationism in, 77, 88, 89f, 93, 102, 107, 111f
  League of Nations and, 75, 76–77, 80, 89–90
  military code, 21
  NAFTA, 168
  1973 oil crisis and, 165, 168, 172, 173, 174
  post–Cold War, 189
  power resources of, 52, 53
  in Suez crisis, 143–144
  trade relations with Japan, 165, 167, 185, 186
  United Nations and, 154
  in world economy, 168–169
  World War I and, 56, 69
  World War II and, 82, 83, 86, 88, 90, 91–94, 97
  after World War II, 100, 101, 102–103
United States Catholic Conference, 120, 128, 129
Uruguay, 141
Utilitarians, 17–18
Utley, Jonathan, 96

V
Values, 18, 188, 191–192, 194
Van Evera, Stephen, 72
Vandenberg, Arthur, 107, 139
Vernon, Raymond, 179
Victoria, queen of England, 48
Vienna, 32, 47
Vietnam, 7, 8, 22, 28, 30, 36, 56, 90, 135

Vietnam War, 21, 28, 42, 59, 114, 115, 122, 123, 127, 134, 137, 139–140, 172, 187
Vincent, R. J., 158

W

Wake Island, 92f
Wallace, Henry, 100
Wallace, William, 195
Walt, Stephen, 72
Walters, F. P., 95, 96
Waltz, Kenneth, 24, 25, 29, 30, 45, 46, 123, 124, 188
Walzer, Michael, 22, 136–137, 140, 157, 158
War
  balance of power and, 75
  causes of, 12, 29, 31, 36–37, 40–41, 50–51, 54, 182
  costs of, 5, 36
  ending, 146, 194
  in international politics, 8, 39
  inevitability of, 14–15, 65–69, 89–90, 108–110
  just, 20–21, 127–128, 136–137, 139
  League of Nations response to, 76, 80–81
  limited, 121–122
  neoliberal view of, 38
  policy choices and, 2, 15, 21
  preemptive/preventive, 71, 136–137, 155
  proxy, 122
  realist view of, 4
  rules of, 146
  technology and, 32, 35, 52, 82, 146
  in unipolar vs. bipolar systems
War guilt clause, 78, 79f
War of Attrition, 153, 159
War of the Austrian Succession, 47
War of the League of Augsburg, 47
War of the Spanish Succession, 47
Warsaw Pact, 132
Washington Treaty, 80
Washington, George, 77
Weimar Republic, 78, 79f, 89, 97
Weiss, Thomas George, 195
Welch, David A., 129
Welfare goals, 182, 194
West Bank, 152, 154, 154, 156, 159, 160
Western Europe, 40, 42, 44, 52, 125, 134, 144, 182, 184–185, 194. *See also* Europe
Wheeler, Burton, 93
Wilhelm II, kaiser of Germany, 29, 59, 61, 63, 64–65, 68, 70, 73, 115
William of Occam, 30
Williams, William A., 100–101, 130
Williamson, Samuel R., 82
Wilson, Woodrow, 4, 50, 74, 75, 77, 78, 110, 146, 188, 192
Wolfers, Arnold, 96
Working Peace System, A (Mitrany)
World Bank. *See* International Bank for Reconstruction and Development
World government, 2, 20, 76, 140–141
World Health Organization, 182
World imperial system, 2
World in Crisis, The (Churchill), 71
World order. *See* Order
World Peace Foundation, 37
World Peace Through World Law (Clark and Sohn)
World war, 9, 51, 121
World War I, 18, 28, 30, 32, 56, 80, 110, 128, 151, 175
  counterfactuals related to, 65–69
  effects of, 74–75, 76, 77–80, 88, 89, 120, 124, 169
  inevitability of, 65–69
  origins of, 29, 33–35, 36, 37, 43, 44, 50, 54–55, 57, 58, 59–65, 69–70, 73, 94, 95, 127, 146, 182
World War II, 5, 44, 115, 122, 131, 146, 151
  effects of, 56, 82, 101, 103, 110, 120, 124, 150, 152, 169, 192
  in Europe, 82–90
  inevitability of, 89–90
  origins of, 18, 29, 35, 82–89, 104, 182
  in Pacific, 83, 86, 90–95, 104, 131
World Watch Institute, 166
World Zionist Congress, 159

Y

Yalta conference, 100, 102, 104, 112–113, 131
Yemen, 134
Yemen, 145f, 159
Yergin, Daniel, 130, 178
Yom Kippur War, 153, 160, 174
Yugoslavia, 78, 105f, 113–114, 131, 138, 145f, 184

Z

Zacher, Mark, 157
Zaire, 6, 7, 136
Zelikow, Philip, 47
Zero sum situation, 163
Zimmerman telegram, 69
Zionism, 149, 151. *See also* Israel